Thomas Henry Tibbles

Hidden power

A secret History of the Indian Ring

Thomas Henry Tibbles

Hidden power
A secret History of the Indian Ring

ISBN/EAN: 9783337058227

Printed in Europe, USA, Canada, Australia, Japan

Cover: Foto ©ninafisch / pixelio.de

More available books at **www.hansebooks.com**

"LAW IS LIBERTY."—(*Inshta Theamba—Bright Eyes.*)

HIDDEN POWER.

A SECRET HISTORY

OF

THE INDIAN RING,

ITS OPERATIONS, INTRIGUES AND MACHINATIONS.

REVEALING

THE MANNER IN WHICH IT CONTROLS THREE IMPORTANT DEPARTMENTS OF THE UNITED STATES GOVERNMENT.

A DEFENSE OF THE U. S. ARMY,

AND

A SOLUTION OF THE INDIAN PROBLEM.

BY

T. H. TIBBLES

NEW YORK:
Copyright, 1881, by
G. W. Carleton & Co., Publishers.
LONDON: S. LOW, SON & CO.
MDCCCLXXXI.

Stereotyped by
SAMUEL STODDER,
ELECTROTYPER & STEREOTYPER,
90 ANN STREET, N. Y.

TROW
PRINTING AND BOOK-BINDING CO
N. Y.

DRAMATIS PERSONÆ.

Military Officers.

Colonel GREENE, Colonel COLDCRAFT,
Major HODSON, Captain HINKLE,
Captain BELFOR, Lieutenant BLAKE.

Washington Officials.

Secretary of the Interior.
Commissioner of Indian Affairs.
Senator L.
Congressman H. (or DAN).
Senator's Private Secretary.

Indians.

RED IRON, WAJAPA,
MEHA, LITTLE WOLF,
SWIFT WALKER, TWO CROW,
HAIRY BEAR, LITTLE WARRIOR,
BADGER, LEAN BEAR,
GRAY CLOUD.

Interpreters.

SHONNEE, PREEMO.

Scout.

CAPTAIN JACK.

DRAMATIS PERSONÆ.

Indian Commissioners.

H. O. Clark,
Mr. Smith,
Mr. Hilliard,
Mr. Hughs,
Mr. Borden,
Mr. Markam.

Indian Inspector.

J. Young Brown.

Missionaries.

Mr. Parkman,
Jennie Walker,
Mrs. Parkman,
Catholic Priest.

Lawyers.

Mr. Wilmot,
Bledsoe & Dosier,
Mr. Dawson,
District Attorney.
Attorney of Department of Justice.

Indian Agents.

H. L. Perkins,
John Hildreth.
Mr. Harkins,

Government Detectives.

C. C. Axell,
Mr. Loft.

Indian Traders.

A. S. Parker,
Mr. Cox.

Members of the Press.

Washington Correspondents.
Traveling Correspondent.
Editor of the *Pioneer*.

PREFACE.

If any reader of this book desires to make "invidious comparisons," between any of the characters portrayed in my story, and any senator, representative, secretary of the interior, commissioner, army officer, agent, trader, inspector, scout, lawyer, missionary, peace commissioner, or contractor, now living or dead, he will have to do so on his own responsibility, for I distinctly avow that no such incidents as are recorded herein ever occurred on the Little Blue or Missouri; that no such army officers' names were ever on the roster of the United States army, that I never knew any peace commissioner by the name of Clark, any army officer by the name of Colonel Greene, any contractor by the name of Perkins, or any Indian inspector by the name of Brown. I did know one Indian by the name of Red Iron, but he was hung by the whites a long time ago. He was a very bad Indian.

THE AUTHOR.

CONTENTS.

CHAPTER		PAGE
I.	The Scout's Wooing	11
II.	The Indians did it	26
III.	A West Pointer's First Service	36
IV.	A Secret Council	58
V.	Indians Discuss the White People's Religion	63
VI.	A Desperate Battle	68
VII.	Old Hairy Bear's Orgies and Meta's Heroism	81
VIII.	A Woman's Conquest	87
IX.	The Contractors' Harvest	95
X.	Meha Deceived	98
XI.	A Ride for Life	103
XII.	On the War-path	110
XIII.	Totally Depraved	112
XIV.	Twenty-five Thousand Dollars	122
XV.	Jack in Red Iron's Camp	124
XVI.	Treating with the Military	131
XVII.	Congressmen on a Spree	138
XVIII.	A Peace Commission	144
XIX.	A Guarded Approach	154
XX.	Military Meddlers	162
XXI.	A Government Linguist	169
XXII.	Secrets of the Indian Bureau	174

CONTENTS.

CHAPTER		PAGE
XXIII.	Official Information	181
XXIV.	What Could it Mean?	186
XXV.	Dividing the Spoils	193
XXVI.	Dying like Brave Men	204
XXVII.	Colonel Greene Disgraced	221
XXVIII.	An Agency School	228
XXIX.	The Mighty Monarch	233
XXX.	Wreaking Vengeance on a Woman	240
XXXI.	Jack's Stratagem	252
XXXII.	A Legal Tangle	256
XXXIII.	Indians Discussing the Whites	263
XXXIV.	The Exiles	270
XXXV.	Dawson's Discovery	277
XXXVI.	Dogged by Detectives	284
XXXVII.	Gone to the Arickoree	289
XXXVIII.	Defeated	293
XXXIX.	A Court-martial	299
XL.	A Secret Council	307
XLI.	A Reporter and a Priest	314
XLII.	A "Straight" Transaction	319
XLIII.	Meha's Fate	326
XLIV.	Jack's Opinion of Injuns	328
XLV.	Mrs. Parkman Translates a Cipher Letter	337
XLVI.	Beyond Control	340
XLVII.	Oh! for the Military	346
XLVIII.	Three Million Dollars	349

HIDDEN POWER.

CHAPTER I.

THE SCOUT'S WOOING.

WHEN Lewis and Clark made their voyage up the Missouri River in 1803, after toiling for many days against the rugged current of that turbid stream, they landed at a place on the eastern shore and held a council with the Indians. They named the place Council Bluffs, and it is so called to this day. Many years afterward, the outskirts of permanent settlements hesitated and stopped for a moment on the eastern bank of the Missouri, and was now just invading the verge of what was marked upon the atlas of those days as "The Great American Desert." A few houses, some more or less pretentious, made up all there was of the "city" of Council Bluffs.

In the bar-room of the hotel was assembled a crowd of men. Some were drinking at the bar, some were playing "poker," others looking on, or listlessly lounging about in different positions. Standing by a window and looking out over the wide, level bottom toward the river, with his hands clasped behind him, was a young military officer. He had calm blue eyes, light hair, was about five feet ten inches tall, a strong, muscular frame, a mild expression about the eyes and mouth, and a skin yet unbrowned by the Western sun and winds. His thoughts seemed to be in some far-off, distant land, and he paid no attention to what was going on around him.

In another part of the room a very different individual sat in a chair, with his feet elevated almost as high as his head. His eyes were said by some to be gray, by others to be black. Both were right. When his thoughts were pleasant, or when he smiled, the darkness faded out of them, but when excited or angry they gleamed with a terrible ferocity. He was six feet tall, yet he was so perfectly proportioned that he did not look so. His hands were small and finely shaped, his forehead high, his head large, and covered with a most luxuriant growth of black hair. At times his manner was perfectly fascinating. There was a sweetness in the tones of his voice, an indescribable tender look about the eyes, a sort of whole-souled way with him, that would impress the most stolid and indifferent.

Those who have conventional ideas, formed from the literature which has been current in the past, would not think this a good description of a frontiersman, scout and guide, but this is the way Captain Jack appeared to a quiet looker-on as he sat in the bar-room of the Causeland House on that day.

How did such a man adopt such a life? Well, I will tell you.

Jack's father moved to Illinois when it was a wilderness. As the country settled up "it got too thick for him," and he moved across the Mississippi into Iowa. When the land around him was all taken up, no "range" left for his cattle and horses, and no more game to hunt, he started to move on again. But his journey was short, for disease overtook him, and he died in his "prairie schooner," and was buried in a little grove of trees by the road-side. Jack's mother had died before, and a large family of children were left fatherless and motherless in a country where there were neither children's aid societies nor orphan asylums. Jack found a home in a frontier cabin, worked hard in the summer and went to school in the winter. He finally went to live with a western lawyer, and while there got a taste for reading, and devoured Blackstone, Kent and Puffendorf. Encouraged by his friend, he resolved on obtaining an education, went back East and worked his way through college.

Near the college, a cousin of Jack's resided, who was a Methodist preacher, and, like a good many of that denomination, was extremely fond of a good horse. He owned the wildest, most unmanageable and fastest horse in that part of the country. He had a junior preacher on the "circuit" with him who owned the famous trotting mare "Lilly Dale," but Lilly was as gentle as a lamb. Within the bounds of the "circuit" and in the suburbs of a large city there had settled an English family. The beauty of two of the daughters was the talk of the whole country round about. The family was very exclusive. It was known that the mother was a member of the English nobility, had married beneath her rank, and recently came to this country on account of some family unpleasantness which arose out of that circumstance. There was a great deal of talk about the beauty of the oldest of the two daughters. She did not go into society much, loved retirement and home, and had refused offers of marriage from the sons of some of the wealthiest families in the city. She had sometimes come to hear Jack's cousin preach, and he described her beauty, comparing it to what he imagined Rachel's to have been.

Jack had never been in society and was as rough and uncouth as any western barbarian could be, but he had heard so much of this English lady that he had a great curiosity to see her. One night Jack gave a lecture on "Life in the Far West," and she was in the audience. A few days after this she came to visit a family living in a neighboring village. It was the same house where the young preacher, the owner of "Lilly Dale," was residing. Without telling Jack that she was there, the young preacher one day invited Jack to go over home with him, and he mounted that unmanageable horse of his cousin's and went. Jack's arms were aching, and his hands were swollen with trying to hold the horse, when he arrived. They hitched the two horses and walked into the house. When Jack came into the parlor, he saw standing by the piano the most lovely woman he had ever beheld. She had that English complexion with rosy cheeks which is so seldom seen among American ladies, faultless form, rounded arms, white as snow, and dimpled hands. Jack had never seen such a sight before in all his life. He was astonished and overwhelmed. He stood like one petrified. But she addressed him in a manner so kind and self-possessed that his embarrassment soon passed away. She talked mostly about his lecture, the hardships he had endured, and denounced the treatment of the Indians by the American government in the most scathing terms, yet in the most ladylike way imaginable.

After a while they went out on the lawn, and he spoke of the English custom of ladies riding on horseback. She said she was very timid, and was afraid of almost every animal except a horse, but the horses were all her friends. Jack pointed to his cousin's horse, and told her there was an exception; that he was a regular villain, and would delight in nothing better than biting her head off.

"Oh, no!" she said. "You misrepresent the poor horse;" and she went up to him and patted him on the neck.

That villain of a horse actually put down his head and rubbed his nose against her shoulder. Jack was astonished. He had never seen him act that way before. She continued petting the horse, he became more and more docile, and finally said she would like to ride him.

"That would be madness," said Jack. "He is so hard-mouthed that the strongest man cannot hold him."

"Oh," said she, "that is because you are not kind to him. He is such a fine, strong horse, he could gallop over these hills without effort. I would like to ride him."

Jack looked at her in amazement. She smiled, and put on such a pretty, pleading look, he did not know what to say. It was the first time he had ever conversed with a cultured and refined young lady in his life. He did not know what was the proper thing to do. Finally he said:

"But there is no saddle; you cannot ride without a lady's saddle."

"Oh!" she replied, "if you will let me have the horse I will ask one of the servants if he will be kind enough to bring me a saddle."

That rebel of a horse was standing there as quietly as a pet lamb, and she stroked his head with her white, dimpled hand and looked up to Jack for an answer. Of course he said she could have the horse. A servant brought a saddle, and she went into the house and put on a riding habit. The saddles were exchanged, and Jack looked to the girths to see that they were all right and strong. She came down the pathway, and then he began to wonder how she was to mount that great horse. He said to her, as she went to the side of the horse:

"There is no saddle block here. How will you get on?"

She replied: "Oh, the servant will be kind enough to assist me."

The servant extended his hand, she put a dainty little foot in it, gave a light spring and landed in the saddle. As she gathered up the reins, the wind blew her long riding habit under the horse. He gave one plunge forward and reared upon his hind feet. Jack saw the old gleam come into his eyes. The next second the horse dashed away like an arrow shot from a bow. For a moment Jack was motionless with surprise and terror, the next, he was on the back of Lilly Dale. He had on a pair of Mexican spurs which he had brought from the West with him; he pressed them into the flanks of the mare, and she dashed away in pursuit, with the long, steady leap peculiar to her breed. But that mad, unmanageable, blooded bay, with the helpless lady on his back, was fully five hundred yards ahead of him. Down through the village he went, across the bridge, and up the rocky road along the mountain side. Jack urged the mare to her utmost speed, but the horse had a lighter load, and the ascent was steep. Jack pressed the spurs into her side until the blood ran out, and with nostrils extended and head stretched forward she plunged on. Jack saw it was no use, the horse was gaining on him. As the horse turned a point on the mountain side he saw her "sawing" on his mouth, but sitting firmly in the saddle. She had the reins wound around her hands. Nearly at the top, he passed an old farmer, carrying some sacks of grain on a horse. As Jack went by he cried out: "Hurry up, or that is a dead young woman sure." But the mare was doing all she could. She was breathing hard and fast, and the perspiration was running from her neck and shoulders in streams, while the greatest danger was going down the mountain on the other side. If the horse should miss his footing once, she would be dashed in pieces.

As Jack reached the summit he saw the horse, fully

a thousand yards ahead, going down the declivity in long and steady leaps, but *she was still sitting firmly in the saddle.* He saw no more until he reached the foot of the mountain, for the trees and turns in the road hid them from view; then, still further ahead, up a long, level lane, he saw the horse dashing forward, with those strong, measured leaps, while his mare was showing signs of exhaustion; but she *was still sitting straight in the saddle,* neither looking to the right nor the left. Presently the horse turned into a lane to the right, and ran straight against the wind. Jack could see her across the corner of the field, still with a firm hold on the reins. The wind blew her riding-hat off, but she did not turn her head. Just as he rounded into the lane, he looked up and saw the horse coming back. He either had turned himself, or she had turned him. Now was his opportunity. He checked up the mare, and, as the horse came back, turned in close to him, dropped the reins and caught him by the bits. The horse pulled Jack out of the saddle, but he held on with a grip like death. The blood flowed from the horse's mouth in a stream where the bits cut him, but was soon stopped. For the first time Jack looked up into her face. There was a little red stream trickling down over her cheek, where a branch of a tree struck her as she was dashing by, and all the color had fled from her face. As soon as the horse stopped, she bounded from the saddle to the ground. Jack was nearly exhausted himself, and he threw the reins over a fence post and came up to her. She was looking at her hands, from which she had taken her gloves. Around the center of each, where she had wrapped the reins, there was a bloodless white circle. Neither could ever remember what was the first words spoken, but after a moment or two Jack said :

"You are brave enough to be the wife of a frontiersman."

"Do you think so ?" she asked.

"Yes, indeed I do."

"That," she replied, "would be an honor for any true woman."

The earnestness and dignity with which she spoke these words went through Jack like an electric shock. He took her hand and kissed it, and she did not resist.

That was all the engagement they ever had.

Jack put the side-saddle on Lilly Dale and mounted that villainous bay himself. Upon inquiry he found that they were twelve miles from the village. Halfway back they met several parties coming in search of them, and the whole village turned out to meet them when they returned.

Two years after that the wedding-day was fixed. Jack had graduated with honors. Besides that, he had finished his legal studies, and read a full course of medicine. It was a bright morning in June when he took the cars for the home of his beautiful and loved one. At four o'clock in the afternoon she would be his own. On the way he read over her letters. How much he loved her no pen will ever write. It had been ten days since he had seen her. At that time all the arrangements for the wedding had been made. He could not wait for the train on which he had promised to come, but took one which arrived two hours earlier. He went to the door and rang the bell; a servant, whose eyes were red with weeping, opened it. As he stepped in he heard the sound of weeping.

"What has happened?" asked Jack.

"Oh, I cannot tell you," said the servant, and motioned him to come into the reception room. A few minutes later a clergyman of the Church of England came in.

"My dear sir," said he, "you must prepare yourself for sad news."

"Oh! what is it?" cried Jack, trembling from head to foot. "Is she dead?"

"I thought I would break it to you gently," said the clergyman.

The tremor in Jack's limbs ceased. He said not a word. No sound escaped his lips. A deathly paleness came over him, and he stood there like a marble statue.

Then the clergyman told him how she had gone down to the river, which skirted their grounds, to take her morning walk with her sister and her maid. She went out on the boat landing; a board slipped from beneath her feet, and she fell into the river. The body had only been recovered an hour before.

Jack took one look at the form, surprisingly beautiful, even in death. He shed not a tear nor uttered a sigh. He walked away. The next few months always seemed like a confused dream. Every hope and aspiration was in the grave of his loved and lost. He went West, loitered around in border towns for a while, and then undertook to shut civilization out of his sight by joining an Indian tribe. Sometimes he would come back to the towns, and seem to seek death in quarrels with the most desperate characters, but death never comes to those who seek it. Since that sad day, fifteen years had passed away. Jack had spent them among the Indians, in garrisons, on long and sometimes solitary journeys over the uninhabited country, in different Indian wars, in hunting and trapping. He had picked up the jargon of the frontier, and spoke in a dialect which would lead one to suppose that he could neither read nor write. Sometimes, however, when conversing with well educated people he would unconsciously drop it, and speak as good English as any one for a few sentences.

Such is a brief outline of the early history of the celebrated Captain Jack.

As he sat in the Causeland House that June afternoon, looking out of a window upon the street, an Indian woman passed by with a bright-eyed little pappoose on her back. Captain Jack smiled, Lieutenant Blake, the young officer, gave a look of mingled contempt and disgust. As the woman came opposite the wide-opened door, one of the other men called out:

"Hallo, there! you squaw! come in and take a smile. It will make you feel good all over. Hold on, I say! stop!" and, as the woman walked on, he called out again, "Stop, I say; stop!" and with that he rushed out, took hold of the woman, and pulled her inside the door.

Lieutenant Blake said not a word, but walked out of the room. The Indian woman stood before these men trembling in every limb. The rush of the hot blood to her cheeks could be seen through the brown skin. The bright-eyed little baby stared in wonder.

The man handed her a glass of whisky, but the woman shook her head.

"Oh, drink it," he said, and put his arm around her neck to force it down her throat. At this juncture Captain Jack came forward and said, in a low tone, which quivered with rage, while his eyes, now jet black, gleamed like balls of fire:

"Let go that squaw, er you will have more holes than a skimmer in ye, inside of a minute."

The man stepped back, and said:

"What business is it of yours?"

"Its anybody's business, I reckon," said Jack.

"Draw," said the man, putting his hand on the butt of his pistol.

"You are a cussed fool," said Jack, and he struck him a blow between the eyes which floored him instantly. Then he walked back to his seat, elevated his heels, and looked quietly out of the window. He saw the Indian woman fleeing toward the river, saw her throw away her blanket and skirt and disappear over the bank. She plunged into the muddy water with her baby on her back and struck out for the other shore, which she reached in safety.

When the man arose from the floor, he was ornamented with two black eyes.

"I don't want no more fighting here," said the barkeeper, "and I won't have it."

"P'raps you won't and p'raps you will," said the man.

"You want to git into business, do you?" said the man, addressing Jack, and he whipped out a small pocket revolver and commenced firing at him. He emptied his revolver, five shots, in quick succession. Jack did not move a muscle, but sat quietly looking out of the window. When the firing ceased, he looked up in the most unconcerned sort of a way, and said:

"Oh! you were firing at me, were you? Now let me give you a piece of advice. The next time you come out West, don't trust to a toy like that pistol of yours."

Jack pulled out an eight-inch Colt revolver, cocked it, and walked up to the man, who turned as pale as death. "Now, with this ere shooter of mine," said he, "I can hit any button on your coat at twenty yards." By this time the perspiration had started out of every pore of the man, his lips seemed glued to his teeth, and a glassy look came into his eyes. He did not say a word.

The bar-keeper was hiding behind the counter. Most of the men had fled from the room, and those who remained were crowding up against the wall, out of range of Jack and his man.

"You oughtn't to go away from here," said Jack, "without redeeming your reputation as a shot, 'cause you won't be safe nowhere with such a reputation as this. Every feller you meet will be picking a quarrel with you. Here, take this tool of mine and whack away a few times, and see if you can't do better."

Jack handed him his revolver, but it fell to the floor from his nerveless hand and discharged itself.

"I give it up," said Jack. "I don't believe I could ever learn you to shoot. Maybe ye ain't well, and sort of unnarved. Say, you bar-keeper;" and then, looking round, "Where in thunder is that bar-keeper?" and he walked up to the counter, looked over and said : "Bob, up here and give this feller a dose of your pizen. He's got out of order."

The bar-keeper's head instantly appeared above the counter. A glass and a big black bottle were set out. Jack poured out a tumbler two-thirds full, handed it to the man and said :

"I reckon this will waken ye up to a sense of your responsibilities, after which you'd better give that pistol to some baby for a plaything." Jack walked out and went off up the street.

A few minutes afterward, those who had fled when the firing commenced came back and pressed in at the door.

"Anybody killed?" asked one.

"No," said the bar-keeper, "but there's one feller about scared to death."

"Who is the feller who shot at Jack?" asked another.

"I know all about him," said one of the men. He is the son of a Congressman from Pennsylvania. He had a contract for one of the big agencies up the river, made a pile, then got to gambling, and lost it all, and now has a big claim for damages, caused by a raid from the Sioux, in which he claims he lost fifty thousand dollars' worth of supplies. My opinion is, we had better keep in with him, for he is likely to get the money."

An account of this affair appeared in the *Pioneer*, a weekly paper, published in the town. It was headed "A Disgraceful Row." The account read as follows:

"Just after we went to press with our last issue a most disgraceful row occurred at the Causeland House. A dirty squaw, belonging to the Missouri Indians, came to town with a pappoose on her back. She went into the Causeland House saloon, and begged a drink of whisky of a gentleman who happened to be in there at the moment. The gentleman at first refused, but she asked again and again, and said, 'Me heap sick. Git heap hot, then git cold.' The gentleman, thinking she had the ague, told the bar-keeper to give her a glass of whisky. Just then, a fellow who is pretty well known down the river, and who has since left town, snatched the glass of whisky from the squaw's hand and threw it on the floor. He then pulled out his revolver and fired several shots, some at the squaw and some at the gentleman first named. The firing naturally caused a good deal of excitement in the saloon and hotel, and it is pretty hard to get at all of the facts of the case. If we have not stated them correctly, we will take great pleasure in making any correction.

"The squaw, after leaving the Causeland House, hung around town for a while, at last got drunk, and threw her pappoose in the river and drowned it."

CHAPTER II.

THE INDIANS DID IT.

AS soon as Jack left the hotel, Perkins, his assailant, went to his room, where he held a long consultation with himself. It was evident he had "waked up the wrong passenger," and it would not do to remain where he was. He resolved to go down the river, and he took passage and stopped off at the first station, a little town on the bank of the river, which has since disappeared from the map; and not only from the map, but from the face of the earth, for it long ago tumbled into the Missouri river and went to increase the deltas at the mouth of the Mississippi. The place was called Hickman's. There was a "hotel," besides two or three other houses. It was a station on the regular stage-line, and a good many travelers stopped there. The five card-tables in the bar-room were generally occupied. There were a large number of Indians on the other side of the river, and Hickman drove a lively trade with them. The next day after Perkins's arrival a band of them came over and camped on the bank of the river, about a mile below. He soon found some who spoke the Sioux language, of which he knew enough to carry on considerable conversation. He was quickly on very good terms with them, and that night there was a blanket spread in a tent, on which a game of dice (Indian dice) was played. At first the Indians won. Then Perkins left, went to the hotel and returned with another man in a spring wagon, and the game was resumed. The Indians lost. Their money and their furs were soon all in Perkins's pocket or in the wagon. While the game was going on, a half-breed Indian had been sitting behind Perkins, and just as it closed, or rather what closed it was, this Indian went over to the others and said something to them. This Indian had discovered that Perkins had two sets of plum seeds (dice), and sometimes he played with one and sometimes with the other. This created a great uproar on the Indian side of the tent, and as Perkins did not understand a word of their language he was at a loss to know what it was about, for when Indians lose at gambling they always take it very calmly.

The noise in the tent attracted the attention of some Indian women outside. Two or three of them put their heads in at the door of the tent to see. One gave their greatest expression of surprise, " He-oo-oo," and all instantly withdrew. Immediately there was rapid talking and much confusion outside. All the Indians inside rushed out, and Perkins followed. There was evidently something wrong. A moment after an Indian came up with a woman. Perkins looked at her and saw the one whom he had dragged into the Causeland House. In one moment more he was in his wagon, and twenty young Indians after him yelling "like all possessed." Perkins put his horse to his highest speed, got to the "hotel," which was a big log-house, rushed in and cried, "The Indians are coming. They are all on the war path." In an instant the doors were closed, the shutters slammed shut, and every man in the house was looking to his arms. The women and children were crying and screaming, and general confusion and panic prevailed. Half the revolvers were empty just when they ought to have been loaded. There was a large amount of ammunition in the store, which was five hundred yards away, and the Indians howling around in every direction. Some of the gamblers got down on their knees and prayed, and some swore like pirates, to keep their courage up. In the Indian camp things were different. The chief, when the hubbub was at its height, came out of his tent, but before he could learn what was the matter, Perkins had fled and the young men had started after him without orders from anybody. The chief stood still for a few moments, during which time some of the older men gathered around him. To these he spoke about half a dozen words. A pony was brought to him; he dropped his blanket where he stood, leaped upon its back, and without arms of any kind, dashed after his young men. Within ten minutes every tent was down, ponies packed, and the Indian train was on the move through the heavy forest down the river bank. Before the chief had got to the hotel the young men had taken the contents of Perkins's wagon, cut the harness to pieces, and broken in the windows of the store. One word from the chief put a sudden stop to the doings of the young men. Five minutes later they were following the trail of the main body down the river. Before daylight they had crossed to the other side.

It was now as silent as the grave outside of Hickman's Hotel, but this only increased the horrors within. Some of the men had undertaken to steady their nerves and strengthen their courage by heavy potations of corn whisky. As the barkeeper had forsaken his post, any one could help himself. Some of the cooler-headed ones saw how that would end, and stationed a man at the bar with orders to shoot the first man who attempted to get at the whisky. Two men, already half crazed with fright and whisky, tried to overcome the guard, a fight ensued and one was stabbed, and his body thrown out doors.

Circumstances of great peril generally produce men who are equal to the occasion, and it so happened at Hickman's on that horrible night. It seemed essential that, to preserve their lives, there should be authority lodged somewhere to organize and conduct a defense. Five or six collected in a room and chose a quiet young man, who was stopping over there, because the stage driver had left his baggage at St. Joseph. He was a surveyor. The others swore solemnly to obey every order, and to exert themselves to the utmost to enforce obedience from the rest. The newly-made Captain stationed guards so as to view every approach to the house, inspected all the arms, and distributed them to the men in equal proportions. He tore up the floors and barricaded the doors and windows so as to be bulletproof, put the women and children in places of safety, and then sent for Perkins, to learn from him as nearly as possible the number of the Indians and the cause of the trouble.

Perkins said he was down at their camp just out of curiosity. The first thing he knew, a lot of Indians got around him and commenced a war-dance. He knocked two of them down and escaped.

The Captain then sent for the man who was with Perkins, and he told an entirely different story. He said that they had been running races and wrestling with the Indians, and he had thrown their best man three times, the last time very hard, at which the Indians got angry and tried to kill him.

The young Captain thought it was important to know the truth about the matter, so he sent for Perkins again, and looking him straight in the eyes, said:

"Perkins, you told me a lot of infernal lies when you were in here. Now tell me the truth, or as sure as there is a God in heaven I will throw you out of a window and leave you to the mercy of these savages. They would probably be satisfied if I should turn you over to them, and I have about made up my mind to do it."

Perkins immediately told the whole story correctly, so far as the gambling was concerned, and then he was dismissed.

All night long the sentries stood at their posts. Not a sound was heard, not a living thing was seen. It was the opinion of all, that the Indians would make an attack just before dawn, but at last the sunlight broke over the tops of the hills ten miles away, and then streamed over the Missouri bottom.

Shortly after the stage rolled up to the door. It was full of passengers, and carried a heavy mail. The passengers were greatly agitated when they heard the news.

The Captain of the night before made up his mind that the Indians had left. He took three men with him and rode out to reconnoiter. In a few minutes he struck the trail, and after following it for a mile or two returned. While he was gone, four or five of the men held a private council. They seemed to be old acquaintances.

"There is a big mail aboard of that coach," said one.

"Yes," said another, "and there is a treasure box and a lot express matter, too."

"How many men was there in it?" asked another.

"There are only three."

"But there is the driver and a lot of women and children."

"This is the best chance we will ever git," said one. "The Injuns did it. Don't you see? For that matter we could come right back here and be perfectly safe."

"If I ever git my fingers on that Wells, Fargo & Co.'s box, I think I'll see how much fun there is in St. Louis for a while. I'm in for going for it."

To this they all assented. They went into the hotel and waited for the Captain's return. Everybody agreed that the Indians had gone across the river. The four men then announced their intention of going down to St. Joseph, paid their bills, mounted their horses and rode away to the south. They all had a camping outfit with them. There was a roll of blankets and a pair of saddle-bags on each horse. They rode leisurely along for about a mile, and then spurred into a sharp trot for a while. At last they stopped, held a short consultation, and turned out of the road into the timber. After going eastward for a short time they changed their course to the north. The grass on the bottom was almost as high as a man on horseback, and made it very exhaustive work for the horses to press through it. They urged them forward as fast as they dared, and not break them down with their efforts, until they came into an old Indian trail which led in the right direction. They followed this trail until it intersected the stage road leading from Hickman's to Council Bluffs. A short distance ahead was a heavy body of timber. They rode into this, dismounted and hitched their horses. The men then stripped themselves to their skins; a paper of some kind of light brown dye was poured into a camp kettle, and it filled with water. In this they washed their hands, faces, arms and bodies down to their waists. With a sharp pair of scissors they had trimmed their beards close to their faces. Then they striped their faces and breasts with red and black paint. The change in their personal appearance was most marvelous. To all outward appearance they were Indians on the war path. They then stationed themselves by the roadside, but they had some time to wait, for to make sure that they would have time they had sent one of their number along the regular road to tear up a bridge which it would take some time to reconstruct to make it possible for the stage to pass over.

At last it came. With a regular Indian war-whoop

the men rushed out. Two caught the lead horses by the bits. A shot from another brought the driver to the ground. Several shots were fired from the coach by the passengers, one of which killed the robber holding the near lead horse, but the other one held on firmly. The freed horse plunged forward and this turned them nearly around. The other two robbers fired rapidly into the coach. One woman, one man and two children were killed and one man wounded. One of the robbers climbed on the boot and threw out the treasure-box. One passenger jumped out and fled into the woods. The terrified horses broke away from the robber who was holding them, and plunged head-long through the woods, over the bank, down into the river, and all who were in the coach disappeared beneath the muddy water. The three robbers carried their dead comrade out of the road and then scalped the dead driver in true Indian style. They were at a loss what to do with the body of their comrade. They finally concluded to wash the paint from the body, scalp it, and leave it by the driver. From the treasure-box they got thirteen thousand dollars. After they had mounted their horses and were ready to start, one of them suggested that the body of their comrade might betray them, for it might be recognized by somebody from Hickman's or the Causeland House. One of them said he would fix that; he rode back and so disfigured the face that it would be impossible for it to be recognized. The robbers then rode away.

No stage arrived at Council Bluffs that night, and the greatest anxiety prevailed. As the same coach was to go back, none could leave. About midnight the passenger who had escaped, arrived. The whole town was aroused and the entire population was panic-stricken. Two luckless Indians who came in early in the morning, entirely ignorant of what had happened, were shot dead at sight. The escaped passenger was the lion of the day. Every time he told the story of the attack on the stage-coach by the Indians, he put on a little more varnish.

About midday, Perkins arrived, on a horse white with foam, for, from the place where he saw the dead bodies to Council Bluffs, he had kept him at the top of his speed. He had come to tell the news of the attack on Hickman's. Thousands of Indians, he said, were to be seen on the west side of the river, all in their war paint. It was his opinion that every settler between the Bluffs and the Missouri line would be scalped before midnight. Messengers had been sent from Hickman's for troops.

All this added fuel to the flame, the wildest rumors were circulated, and everything was in confusion. A public meeting was called, and Perkins was the most prominent speaker. He urged the immediate formation of a military company. The company was forthwith organized, and he was elected Captain.

The *Pioneer* was a typographical curiosity when it appeared that week. Blood-thirsty head-lines, in displayed type, filled almost an entire column, indicating what was contained in the recital following. As the editor got his information from Perkins, and as Perkins had a vivid imagination, and was a master of descriptive eloquence, the horrible atrocities of those blood-thirsty savages, as recorded in the *Pioneer*, would throw any ordinary reader into a tremor. They had, without any cause whatever, assaulted Hickman's Hotel, and murdered one man, whose body was found just outside of the building. They made a raid on the store, which contained a large amount of ammunition, which they were about to seize, when they were driven away by a courageous sally from the Hickman House, led by Perkins. They then retreated and the next day assaulted the stage-coach, murdered all the men but one, disfigured the dead bodies, outraged the women, then murdered and scalped them, put their bodies into the stage coach, and drove them, with two children still alive, into the Missouri river. This was the substance of it, filled out with many horrible details, too disgusting to put into a permanent record, or be read by decent people.

Perkins ordered a thousand extra copies, some of the contractors two thousand more, and the editor had a lively time in his office for several days. The old hand press was worked day and night.

Perkins mailed a marked copy to each member of the House and Senate, to the Secretary of the Interior, Commissioner of Indian Affairs, and sent the remainder home to his noble father to be distributed in the East. This horrible outrage and massacre by the Indians was soon the subject of editorial comment in all the leading dalies all over the country. The conclusions generally arrived at was, "exterminate the whole tribe."

CHAPTER III.

A WEST POINTER'S FIRST SERVICE.

LIEUTENANT BLAKE was waiting at the Causeland House for orders. He had never seen any actual service, but his West Point training showed itself in the general panic. He took no part in the 'citizens' meeting, and when a committee waited upon him, he replied that he could do nothing, not even give advice, until he received orders from his commanding officer. The committee was disgusted with him. They unanimously voted him a snob. What did they pay taxes to educate him for, if when his services were needed and the whole State was in danger, he could not even lift his hand or open his mouth. They didn't believe that he knew enough of military tactics to drill a corporal's guard, etc., etc. Lieutenant Blake was exceedingly unpopular, and Captain Perkins was held in the highest estimation.

The news of the outbreak soon reached Fort Leavenworth, and three companies of cavalry were started up the river. Lieutenant Blake was temporarily assigned to duty with one of these companies. They came up the river on steamboats, and landed at Council Bluffs without any mishap. Six days had now elapsed and nothing more had been heard of the Indians. The commander of the battalion, Major Hodson, was at a loss just how to proceed. It was evident to him that the raid had been made by a small party who had immediately gone back to their tribe. There were some things about it he could not understand. No houses had been burned. No stock had been run off. Even the horses on the stage-coach had not been taken. That was not the way Indians generally carried on war. He resolved to send out a scouting party, and it was necessary to employ a guide who was acquainted with the country. He offered the place to Perkins, but that gentleman declined.

After making several unsuccessful attempts to get a competent scout and guide, he was surprised one morning to see, standing before his tent, Billy, the barkeeper of the Causeland House.

"Major," said Billy, "I think I know the man you want, and if you send him out you will git the bottom facts and no deceit. This Perkins, who is cavortin' around here, is a cussed coward, and the biggest liar on earth. If it wasn't for them scalped bodies down by the stage-coach, I'm hanged if I wouldn't say that no Injuns had been about at all, but that fact kind o' gits me. You see I meets a good many hard cases up at the saloon there, and I hears a good many things. That fellow who was killed down at Hickman's wasn't killed by the Injuns at all. When the row occurred Bill Shepherd and this feller Mike, who was killed, was drunk, and they two fit, and Mike was killed and thrown out doors. The feller who was stationed to guard the bar told me he seed it. If you want to know what is what about this business, send Captain Jack. He's over the river. He ain't afeerd of nothing."

Major Hodson sent for Jack, and the next morning he reported for duty. A detail of ten men was made, and Lieutenant Blake put in command. The orders Lieutenant Blake received were very minute. Besides the general instructions to scout the country to the east of the Missouri and along its banks, they directed him how he should approach a wood, cross a stream, and many other matters of the smallest detail, the commanding officer evidently recognizing that this was the Lieutenant's first actual service.

Lieutenant Blake was exceedingly anxious to meet the Indians. He marched directly down the river, and the first day made forty miles. No Indians or signs of Indians were seen. He went to Hickman's, but no new information was to be obtained there, and the second night, after thirty-five miles of hard marching, camped under the bluffs ten miles from the Missouri river. He was very much disappointed. Captain Jack had obeyed every order and answered every question, but made no suggestions. At Hickman's Jack met the whilom captain of a night, and got all the information possible from him.

After the guard was stationed, Lieutenant Blake seated himself by the fire. Jack walked past him and said:

"Lieutenant, don't you think it's a leetle risky setting there in the light of that fire, that is, providin' there's any red skins around?"

"I hadn't thought of it," replied Lieutenant Blake.

"I didn't think of it nuther, until I got a bullet through this shoulder, but since that time I generally think of it when I'm out on a scout. But I don't think there's any danger here. I don't believe there's an Injun on this side of the river; but then you know there's no use of running risks when you can't gain ary thing by it."

Lieutenant Blake walked away from the fire, spread out a blanket, half reclined on his saddle, and went into a fit of abstraction. Sometime afterward he called Jack to him, and addressing him, said:

"You said, awhile ago, you didn't believe there were any Indians this side of the river. What makes you think that?"

"Lieutenant," said Jack, "I'll obey any order you may give me. I'll show you the shortest and best way to any point in this part of the country, but when it comes to givin' opinions I ain't thar. That remark slipped out by accident."

"But there is no harm in giving an opinion when you are asked. Then I can adopt it or not, as I may choose."

"Well, I don't know anything for sartin' about this ere business. I have my suspicions; that's all. But if you want to know, I can find out. I know jest where to get sich information. Now, if you say so, I'll go and find out."

"Where will you get all this information? You surprise me."

"I'll git it of the Injuns themselves."

"You don't mean to say that you know where these Indians are?"

"Sartinly I do."

"Why didn't you guide me to them, then?" said Blake, in a curt tone.

"Now you see what comes of havin' opinions. A feller who is under orders never oughter have opinions, and it was only because you spoke in a friendly sort of way that I had any."

"I beg your pardon," said Lieutenant Blake. "I should have inquired of you before. Now, if you will tell me where these Indians are, I will instruct you to guide me to them."

"You can't do that, for our orders are to stay on the east side of the river, and every blasted one of 'em is on the other side. And now I am in the 'opinion' business I might as well let go another. I hadn't no idea you wanted to find Injuns, or rather, I thought the Major didn't want us to find any, for if he had, he'd have sent us where they are. He knowed mighty well there wasn't no Injuns on this side of the river. Do you suppose an old officer like him would have sent ten men out, all alone, where there was Injuns? I calkerlate not. No, I've heard all these stories, and to be honest, I don't believe a word of 'em. Leastwise, more'n half is lies. Now, Lieutenant, if you really want to know all about this ere business, I'll go and find out. I'll be back by three o'clock to-morrer, and we can git back to the Bluffs by sundown, and you can make your report."

"Tell me where these Indians are," said the Lieutenant.

"They're across the river."

"Do you propose to go over there alone?"

"Sartinly."

"They'll murder you."

"Don't you be anxious about that. I tell you I'll be back here by three o'clock to-morrer."

This was a new idea to Lieutenant Blake, and he sat and thought over it for some minutes. Then, without saying another word to Jack, he ordered the men to break camp and march immediately. When the men were in the saddle he said to Jack:

"You will guide us by the best route to the bank of the river opposite where these Indians are."

The command proceeded at a trot, with Jack in the lead. Three hours afterward, they came out on the bank of the river.

"There," said Jack, pointing to the dim outline of the hills on the other side, "camped under them hills is the band of Injuns who were at Hickman's the night the trouble commenced."

"I do not want to order you to go over there. I do not think I have authority to do so under my orders, but it is your own proposition. I give you *permission* to go if you desire to. I will camp here and await your return until three o'clock to-morrow. But how are you to get across the river?"

"If you'll leave yer men under command of the Sergeant and go with me about a mile up-stream I'll show you," said Jack.

The Lieutenant would not do that, but he took his whole command up to the point indicated. Arriving there, Jack took off his clothes, except his shirt and leggins. He then unsaddled his horse, and handing over his arms and accouterments to the Lieutenant, drove his horse into the river, taking hold of the horse's tail with one hand and swimming with the other. By this means he could keep the horse's head in any direction he desired. He was soon lost to sight in the dim starlight. Lieutenant Blake watched this performance with intense interest. He stood gazing over the water for some time in silence, then turned and gave the necessary orders for the disposition of his little force for the remainder of the night.

Jack's horse plunged forward through the muddy water, the rapid current bearing them down the stream one yard for every yard they advanced. On and on the horse swam, through the eddying, gurgling waters, to a sand-bar in the middle of the stream, then walking across the sand-bar and swimming the other arm of the river, they reached the shore. The bank was perpendicular, and Jack turned the horse's head down stream until he found a place where he could emerge in safety. Having fastened his horse in the willows near the shore, Jack started on foot for the camp, which was more than a mile away.

When some distance from the village he came upon a lot of ponies picketed out. He passed through these as quickly as possible, as they reared, plunged and neighed the moment he came near them. The tents of the village were in a semicircle at the foot of the hills. A hundred dogs, all, as at a given signal, set up a hideous yelping and barking, and numerous heads were thrust out from the tents to see what was the matter.

Without looking to the right or the left, Jack walked straight forward until he was in front of one of the tents. Any other course would have been death. If he had made the slightest motion, as if to conceal himself, a dozen arrows would have penetrated his body.

Standing in front of the tent, he said, in the Indian language, "I am a white man. I am a friend. I bring important news. I must tell it to the chief."

A brown hand was stretched out and clasped Jack's. Indians never shake hands with one another, but they all know that that is a sign of friendship among the whites. To an Indian, the sight of two men shaking hands is the most ridiculous thing in the world. The flap of the tent was thrown back, and the Indian led Jack in. An Indian woman raked over the few embers in the center of the tent, threw on some dry sticks, and a bright blaze sprung up.

Jack had been on the frontier nearly all his life. He had been in all kinds of trying circumstances, but the scene that met his eyes, on the opposite side of the tent, came nearer unnerving him than anything which had ever happened in all his life before. Lying on a buffalo robe was a fair-haired white girl. Her cheeks were flushed with fever. Her neck and arms were bare, and her eyes had a wild look in them. She did not seem to notice him. With every breath, a low, murmuring moan escaped her lips.

A thousand thoughts seemed to rush into Jack's head all at once.

"These Indians have done this devilish deed. There

is a captive white woman they have taken. She has lost her mind through fright and abuse, and here I am in the heart of this camp without arms."

But while these and ten thousand other thoughts were coursing through Jack's brain, not a muscle of his face moved. To all outward appearances he was perfectly calm.

It is strange how rapidly the mind works under such circumstances as these. In less than three minutes Jack thought over how these Indians had crossed the river, then, enraged at losing their money gambling with Perkins, and excited by whisky, had first assaulted him and then Hickman's. Perhaps some of their number had been killed by shots from the house, and their relations had in revenge attacked the stage-coach. In those same minutes he had planned at least half a dozen different modes of escape.

One by one the leading men of the tribe came in and seated themselves around the fire, until at least a dozen were present. Then they lighted a pipe, and after giving it a few puffs passed it to Jack. Jack smoked the pipe and passed it to the next one. Not a word was spoken until it had passed all around the circle. Then the chief arose, came across to Jack and shook hands, and retreated to his former position. It was a full minute after that before he said a word. Then he spoke as follows:

"My friend, we are glad you have come. We have known you in the past; we know that you are our friend. We seem to be wandering in the night, and there is a deep precipice every way we turn. We want a guide to show us the right way. We fear the white people are angry with us. We want to be friends of the whites. My young men are foolish. The fire-water of the white man took away their sense. They have done wrong. My friend, have pity on us. Tell the white people I will give them fifty ponies for the wrong my young men have done. We will give them part of our country here. We will be their friends. When the bad Indians from the north come to fight them, I will give them my young men to go on the war-path. But for us, we will live in peace together. We will be friends forever. I hear the Great Father has sent his soldiers to kill us. My friend, tell us if this is so."

"You lying, treacherous old hypocrite," thought Jack, but he did not say so by any means. He did not say anything. He pointed with a steady finger at the white girl lying on the buffalo robe. After some minutes, during which the pipe was passed around again, another Indian arose, shook hands with Jack, and spoke as follows:

"My friend, I shake hands with you, not only with my hand but with my heart. It was midnight when you came, but when you opened the door of my tent the sun shone in. Some of our young men did wrong. We are sorry. We are willing they should be punished. We ——" Then the Indian hesitated and Jack arose to his feet. He shook hands with all present, and said:

"I can only stay a few minutes. The night is now far spent, and you must talk quick. I can't wait. I don't understand what you mean. I want to know where you captured that white woman, and who it was that murdered the people in the stage-coach. I know about the trouble at Hickman's, you need not tell me about that. But this murder of the people in the stage-coach and having that white girl here, is very bad. What have you got to say about these things?"

The chief said, "I know nothing about anybody being killed. I never heard of it before. My young men——"

"Tell me the truth," said Jack. "To talk with a double tongue will do no good."

"It is night now," said the chief, "but the Great Holy One (Wa-Kan-tanka) sees in the night as in the day. He knows I tell the truth. I did not know that any one was killed. The next day after we came over the river, one of our young men walked by the river's side. He saw something in the river, and somebody holding to it. He swam out. It was this white woman. When she saw the Indian she was afraid and let go. She sank down in the water, and he dove down and took hold of her. Then he took hold of the thing she was floating on, and called for help. Some, who were fishing, heard him, and went in a canoe and brought them ashore. She has been sick ever since."

To prove that what he said was true, he sent out and had the thing on which the girl was floating brought in. It was the driver's seat and part of the top of the stage-coach.

The whole thing was plain to Jack now. The Indians had told him the truth. Instead of murdering anybody they had saved this girl's life. He spoke to them as follows:

"I believe you have told me the truth. I will do all I can to help you. You have asked me to help you. I do not say that I can, but I will try. But you must do what I tell you to do. If you promise me that, I will be your friend."

"We will do as our friend desires," said the chief.

The Indian woman threw another handful of sticks on the fire. The blaze flashed up and lighted everything in the tent. Jack went over to the side of the girl. The fever had gone down and she seemed to be asleep. The Indians departed one by one, and Jack went outside the tent. Great red streaks were shooting up from the eastern sky. A thousand birds in the branches of the trees burst forth into song. The open stretch of prairie in front was covered with flowers. Young rabbits were playing in and out of the edge of the tall grass. The ponies were feeding leisurely at the end of their lariats. Down near the mouth of the Platte were two or three tents, and a wreath of smoke was curling out at the top of one. To the west, up the Platte, was a small herd of buffalo. In a moment the sun touched the tops of the tall timber on the eastern side of the Missouri river, and then burst upon the circle of tents where Jack stood. All was stillness around him. Even the dogs were quiet. Then one by one the flaps of the tents were thrown back and the village began to stir. Camp-kettles were swung over the fires, which were made out of doors, and the women began to cook. Jack stood still for a long time meditating. He was awakened by hearing a low, sweet voice say, "How came I here?"

In a moment he was inside the tent. He knelt beside the young girl, who looked at him wonderingly He took hold of her hand and felt her pulse.

"I am a doctor," he said, "and I have come to see what I can do for you. You have been very, very sick, but you are better now. These people here are kind-hearted, and no one will harm you. You must have something to eat. I will have it sent to you right away."

Jack was about to rise when for the first time he thought of the scantiness of his costume. Instead of rising he gradually sank lower and lower. He glanced around him. At the other side of the tent was a blanket. An Indian girl was sitting at the head of the white girl, watching her. She took in the situation, arose and handed Jack the blanket; he wrapped it around him and walked out of the tent. He was about to request some one to prepare some food for the sick girl when he noticed an Indian girl coming toward him with something smoking hot in a wooden bowl. In a moment they recognized each other. It was the one he had rescued from Perkins. She hung her head in bashfulness, but he walked up to her, took her hand and said he was glad to see her, and for want of anything else to say asked her where her husband was.

"I am not married," she said.

"Not married! Then whose baby was that you had with you?"

"That was my little sister."

"What is it you have in your bowl?"

"It is stewed quail. I have made some every day for the white girl, but she will eat nothing. Sometimes I put the soup in her mouth and then she swallows. I made this last night and have just made it hot."

Meha passed into the tent, sat down beside the sick girl, took a spoon and offered her some of the food. When she had swallowed it, she reached out her small, thin, white hand for more. Meha smiled and said the only English words she knew, "Good, good."

"How long have I been here," asked the invalid.

"Good," answered Meha, offering her some more of the quail, and then she put her hand over her mouth in token that she must not talk.

A sharp shrill scream broke over the gentle murmur of the camp. Then another and another, and then all was still. Jack rushed into the tent. Meha was crying and holding the hand of the white girl, whose face was pallid as death, and her eyes glazed and still. She had fainted.

"Bring me water," said Jack.

Meha ran out and in a twinkling came back with a calabash full of water. Jack dashed handful after handful in her face, yet there was no sign of returning consciousness. He bound her arm and opened a vein, but the blood refused to flow. The tent was full of Indians, an old woman among them. She caught the girl by her feet, and by main force held her up, head down. The blood rushed back to the brain and she immediately revived. She attempted to speak, but Jack said:

"Don't try to talk now. I know all about it. You think all the people in the stage were murdered by Indians, and that you are here a captive. I am convinced that it was white men who did that bloody deed. These Indians are kind-hearted; they will not hurt you. Look at this one, little Meha, she is crying because you are so sick. You must be quiet and not afraid, until you get well enough for me to take you away to your friends."

"I don't know what made me scream that way," said the girl, "but it all flashed over me at once, and—"

"There, there," said Jack, "you know I said you mustn't talk yet awhile. I will come and see you again soon; in an hour or so. Meantime, Meha will take care of you."

Jack went out of the tent again. He intended to take the girl with him back to Council Bluffs. This terrible fainting spell had rather upset his calculations. He was afraid, in her present weak state, she would not be able to go. To leave her alone in that Indian camp seemed terrible. He must get back to Lieutenant Blake's camp by three o'clock or serious complications might arise. He could stay there until noon, and perhaps by that time she would be better. An Indian went down into the willows and took Jack's horse and picketed it out to feed. An Indian woman brought Jack his breakfast. She tried her best to make it just like the white people. From one of the packs, made of hard-tanned buffalo hide, she took out a plate and knife and fork. She took a piece of fine board (one of her treasures) about eighteen inches square, spread over it a piece of white cloth, placed the plate, knife and fork and tin cup on it, and then brought it and put it in front of Jack. Then she brought the food itself. It was soup made of dried buffalo meat. Before it is cooked this meat is black and hard as a stone. It is prepared by cutting the flesh into strips, three or four inches wide, ten or twelve long, and about half an inch thick. It is then dried in the sun. The soup made from it is delicious. What took the place of bread was corn, which had first been parched and then pounded fine. Jack was also treated to a whole cupful of "black medicine," *i. e.* coffee, which the woman had saved up for some extra occasion. She gave him the very best she had.

After breakfast Jack had another talk with the Indians. He told them that he would return and inform the military commander what they had said to him and lay before them all of the facts, and would come or send them word of what had happened.

About eleven o'clock they made a litter to carry the white girl on, of the kind on which the Indians carry their wounded. Two long tent-poles are fastened to a pony, reaching out far behind. Between these is stretched a buffalo hide, and on the hide is laid the person. The poles, being elastic, act as springs. It is rather a rough way to ride, but for one who could not sit on a horse it was their next best mode of conveyance. The girl was brought out and a start was made for the river. Fainting fits came on, and these were continued until

Jack had to give it up. He feared she would die before she got across the river. She was carried tenderly back to the tent, and Jack told her that he must go, but he would either come or send her help the next day, and bid her be of good cheer, for she was perfectly safe. He then returned to the river, a canoe was provided, Jack swam his horse beside it and an Indian paddled him over.

It was only one o'clock when Jack reported to Lieutenant Blake. A few minutes after the report was made the command was on the march for Council Bluffs, where they arrived a little before sundown. Lieutenant Blake made a verbal report to Major Hodson, who requested him to write it out in full that night and submit it to him in the morning. On going up into town Jack was surprised to find a very large number of strangers. There were eight or ten army and Indian supply contractors. A large train of empty wagons was corralled a little out of town, and the teamsters and train bosses were filling the saloons. Perkins had his company out on the streets drilling. There were two or three Indian commissioners and an inspector at the Causeland House. The town was crowded full, and business was "booming."

Jack had seen such things before. It was the hope of an Indian war which had drawn them together. After making the round of the saloons and seeing the sights, Jack started back to camp. As he walked down the street he passed a small frame house, containing two rooms. There was no inclosure around the house and the footpath went right by the door. A small woman stood in the doorway. She had a lithe figure, as perfect as was ever drawn by an artist, large brown eyes, delicately formed nose and mouth, and that indefinable look which denotes culture and refinement.

"Why! Captain Jack! is that you?" The voice was as soft as the tones of a Æolian harp.

Jack looked up in astonishment, first with a puzzled expression, and then a smile spread all over his face.

"How in the world," said he, "came you here?"

"We have just been transferred to this conference and stationed on this circuit. I am *so* glad to see you. We do not know a single person here."

This little woman, frail, delicate, refined and cultured, was the wife of the Methodist preacher. Jack had known her in other days. Jack went in and sat down. On the floor was a new rag carpet. There was a bed in one corner. The other furniture consisted of six new chairs, a small table and a book-shelf. There were not more than a dozen books in all. There was Watson's Institutes, Bledsoe's Theodacy, Upham's Mental Philosophy, two bound volumes of the Ladies' Repository, and Cruden's Concordance.

On the table was a large family Bible, and beside it was a well-worn copy of a French New Testament. The other room had no carpet. It contained a cooking-stove, table, cupboard and two or three chairs.

"You should never have come here," said Jack, "this is no country for a lady like you."

"Oh, Jack, you ought not to discourage me. I have been so brave. I think you ought to compliment me. When William concluded to enter the ministry, (he would not have done it, if it had not been for me), he said that he would go where preachers were needed, and not stay where there were two preachers for every pulpit. So we came first to the Illinois conference and then here. I am glad we have come, for this is a very wicked place, and we will have opportunities to do a great deal of good. He hasn't been able to get any place to preach in yet. Oh! there he comes now. He will be so glad to see you," and she ran to the door, every nerve quivering with delight, to meet her loved one.

Rev. Mr. Parkman walked in and shook hands with Jack. He did not look like the typical minister. He was tall and muscular, and had an intelligent countenance. By nature he was generous and tender-hearted. He was glad to meet Jack, not only "for old acquaintance' sake," but he was extremely anxious to get the news. Just as Jack had got to the point where he had found the white girl in the Indian camp, a neighbor woman came in and heard the remainder of it. When Jack described how sick the poor girl was, and how he was forced to leave her all alone in the Indian camp, a firm look came into the little woman's face, such as one might imagine the martyrs had when they walked up to the stake.

"William," she said, "I think it is our duty to go to this poor girl. She may be dying, with no one to pray for her, or to say a word of hope as she goes down into the cold river."

Tears stood in Mr. Parkman's eyes, but there were none in those of his little wife.

"Medie," he said, "I will go to her; I will start to-night."

"I will go too," she said.

"You go? Why, my little darling, it is impossible. Go into an Indian camp in time of war?"

"This sick girl needs the sympathy and care of a woman. It is my duty to go. God will take care of me."

It was no use to argue with her. There was something about her that could not be argued with. There are some women who never demand anything, who never command anybody, who seem utterly weak, and yet strong men bow before them, their wills are subservient to hers, and they seek to know her wishes that they may take delight in complying with them. Such women wield a power greater than the most determined purpose of the strongest minds. They make abject slaves of men, and men enjoy the slavery. When behind this indescribable power a woman has a holy purpose, the good she can accomplish cannot be estimated. Such a power had Mrs. Parkman.

It was decided that she should go, and they would start at twelve o'clock midnight. Jack first went to camp and got leave of absence from Major Hodson. He then went to town for some medical supplies, and at the appointed time rode up to Mr. Parkman's door. Two horses were standing there, one with a side-saddle on In a moment more Mr. Parkman and his wife came out. He reached out his hand, she placed a tiny foot in it and vaulted into the saddle. For some miles the bottom was prairie, and they followed an Indian trail in single file, much of the time in a slow gallop. Mrs. Parkman sat in that saddle apparently as easy as in a rocking-chair. On and on they rode, mile after mile, and just at dawn of day they came out on the bank of the river opposite the Indian camp.

Indians have what is called the sign language, which is common to a large number of tribes speaking different languages. This sign-talking is so far developed that common barter and trade can be carried on, and intelligence of startling events, such as war, or an intended visit by another tribe, can be expressed by means of it. They also have a code of signals. These signals are different among different tribes. They are made by swinging a blanket.

Jack climbed up in a tree which stood on the bank of the river, and commenced to make signals. He kept this up quite awhile before he attracted the attention of the Indians. At last he was rewarded by an answer. Soon after a canoe shot out from the shore and made straight across the river to where the party stood. An hour afterward they were all safe in the Indian camp. Mrs. Parkman sat down by the side of the sick girl. The sides of the tent were raised to let the cool wind pass through. Mr. Parkman walked around and looked into the tents. He had a great longing to preach to them, but not one word of his language could they understand. After awhile a few of them gathered together and he asked Jack to interpret for him.

"I can't interpret a sermon," said Jack. "I might make some miss, and send them all to hell by it. If your doctrine is true, and I suppose it is, it's too big a responsibility for me to undertake. I'll tell you what I'll do. I'll preach them a little sermon myself, and I can keep inside of safe lines;" and Jack held forth as follows:

"This man is a teacher about God. He wants to teach you the way to some happy hunting-grounds of which you never heard. He thinks you can't get there unless you do what is right. He knows all about it. It is a very hard thing to learn. I don't know much about it myself. I find out that the Great Holy One of the Indians is the same one that he believes in. That little woman is his wife. She came straight from the happy hunting-grounds, and some of these days she's going back. She knows all about it, because she has been there. I don't know when she is going back. Maybe to-morrow, maybe a year, maybe five years. But she is going back there, sure. When you leave your camp to go on the long journey, you will find her at the end of it. Now, you had better mind how you treat her."

"There," said Jack, "I've told them all about it. If they mind that sermon they'll all be saved, sure."

One of the Indians walked up to Mr. Parkman, shook hands, and fixed himself for a speech. Of all things, Jack hated to interpret. So he told the Indian he must say but few words now. He must wait until after the preacher spoke, or he would think it very bad. The preacher would speak to-morrow. So the Indian only said, "We are glad that you have come. We will listen to all the words you have to say, and we hope it will be many days before your wife goes back to the happy hunting-grounds."

Jack interpreted it as follows :

"He says he is glad you come. He will adopt your religion immediately, and he hopes you won't send your wife off to the happy hunting-grounds for some time yet."

"How dreadful is the lot of woman among the heathen!" thought Mr. Parkman. "That poor Indian thinks I am liable to kill my wife any time," and he made a note of it, to write home to the *Missionary Journal.* Soon after Jack left the camp and returned to Council Bluffs.

CHAPTER IV.

A SECRET COUNCIL.

THE population of Council Bluffs had greatly increased during the one day that Jack had been absent. The overland travel had been suspended. All sorts of stories were current of the atrocities committed by Indians on the main trail westward, and there was a general demand for a thorough campaign against the savages. Major Hodson had written a report which had been forwarded to the department commander, in which he stated his belief that the robbery of the stage-coach had been committed by white men, and that the affair at Hickman's was the result of a gambling row. He thought there was no use for any more troops. This was telegraphed to Washington, and the Commissioner and the Secretary of the Interior were furnished with copies of the report. A commission was made up of western men who resided near the scene, to investigate the trouble. Meantime the woman who had heard part of Jack's story had spread the news over the town that the Indians had in their possession a captive white woman.

When the commissioners arrived they were treated with the greatest consideration by Perkins and the contractors. They held their first session in the town. The first witness examined before them was the man who had escaped from the stage-coach. He testified that the coach had been attacked by a large band of Indians, and went into a great many details, most of which were drawn from his imagination. Then Perkins and two or three other persons, who were at Hickman's the night of the trouble, testified. From their testimony a very bad case was made out. Finally, Harkins, the young surveyor, who commanded on the night of the assault on Hickman's, asked to be heard. He told a straightforward story. How Perkins had acknowledged to him that the trouble was caused by gambling, that the man found dead was killed in the house, the only damage done by the Indians was cutting the harness and breaking in the windows of the store, from which they had taken nothing, and that they left immediately. He thought it was only a drunken fracas, which was liable to happen anywhere, and if they had all been white men nothing would have ever been heard of it.

Whoever committed the murder of the passengers in the stage-coach, he was certain that it was not this band of Indians, for he had followed their trail, and they had gone across the river. He further testified that he believed Perkins to be a gambler, and utterly unworthy of belief.

This testimony created a tremendous uproar. They said he was interested in surveying contracts, and was afraid a war would interfere with his business. The crowd hooted and yelled at him as he went out, and finally he had to flee to the military camp for protection.

A hot discussion arose between the members of the commission. Some were for immediate war and punishment of the Indians. One opposed it, and wanted further testimony taken. It was finally agreed to send for Major Hodson. The Major didn't believe there was any necessity for a war, thought that the people might go to their homes in safety, travel could be resumed, and as for the damage done at Hickman's, the chief of the party had offered to make full restitution. He spoke in such a calm and determined way, the four warriors of the commission were inclined to wait, and not press matters. Things took a decidedly peaceful turn.

Perkins, the contractors and speculators of all sorts, were at a loss what to do. That night the most desperate of them held a secret council in a private room in the Causeland House. In that council a plan was resolved upon to bring matters to a crisis. Just what conversation took place there will never be known, but during the next day some thirty men crossed the ferry to the western side of the river. They went over three or four at a time. They were all well armed and supplied. Ten miles west of where Omaha now stands, there is a beautiful grove, called Sahling's Grove. In this grove that night was camped a large train. The stock belonging to the train was picketed on the prairie near by. The thirty men congregated about a mile east of the grove, and one of the number crept up among the horses and cut all the lariat ropes. At a given signal the thirty men dashed down on the stock and they stampeded in one body over the prairie to the South. Before dawn they were thirty miles away. The wagons of the train had been corralled the night before, and behind them the men belonging to the train assembled and waited for daylight. Then a strong guard was sent on foot to Council Bluffs for help. The news that the Indians were murdering and scalping everybody on the main trail was carried through the town and it seemed that all went mad at once. The commissioners, in a body, called on Major Hodson and turned over all the Indians to the southwest to the care of the army.

Captain Jack was nonplussed. Even he was convinced that the Indians had gone to war. His first thought was of Mr. Parkman and the two women. He saw no possible way to save them. Major Hodson immediately moved his command across the river, and stationed them so as to protect the settlements and travel on the main trail, and awaited further orders from the department commander.

The commissioners held another session, and employed a lawyer to assist them in preparing their formal report. They laid the whole case before him, and asked his advice.

Lawyer Wilmot had recently arrived from the East. He had graduated at Yale, and studied law with one of the most celebrated lawyers of the time, one who was an authority on constitutional law. The advice he gave to the commissioners was something different from what they had ever heard before. Two or three of them had served on many Indian commissions; in fact, that is the way they had made their living for years. Wilmot stood before them with a huge law book in his hand, and said :

"Neither this commission, Major Hodson, the department commander, the General of the army, the Secretary of the Interior, nor the President, has any legal authority to declare war against these or any other Indians. The Constitution of the United States has placed the authority to declare war in another department of the Government. It has done this in terms so plain that no other meaning can be attached to them. Section 8 of article I. of the Constitution reads as follows: '*Congress shall have power to declare war*, grant letters of marque and reprisal, and make rules concerning captures on land and sea.'

"The power to declare war rests in Congress, and Congress alone. Expeditions carried on under any other authority are not war. They are wholly illegal, and every life taken under such circumstances is murder. If the Indian tribes are ~~mutinous~~ nations, Congress must give the authority to wage war upon them. If they are not ~~mutinous~~ *nations*, your only legal way to proceed is to issue warrants for the arrest of the supposed criminals. If the officer in whose hands they are placed is unable to make the arrest, he can call for a *posse comitatus*. If this is insufficient to execute the law, the Governor can call upon the President for troops. These troops, when so employed, are under the direction of the civil authority, and the force used must be for the purpose of executing the law. There is no other legal way to proceed."

The commissioners voted Wilmot a lunatic, and discharged him instanter.

CHAPTER V.

INDIANS DISCUSS THE WHITE PEOPLE'S RELIGION.

MR. PARKMAN found staying in an Indian camp, and not being able to speak a word of their language, to be anything but pleasant. He did not know that anything was going on more than the usual life of the Indians, but runners were coming and going between the different bands of the tribe all the time. His presence in the camp was thoroughly discussed. About listening to this new religion, two parties immediately arose. One was opposed to the whole thing. They did not want to hear anything about it at all. The other party wanted to hear, and then consider the matter afterward. These were composed mostly of the younger men. The old ones, and especially the old medicine men, were bitterly opposed. They said the young men were fools, and would bring some great harm upon the tribe. In one tent they got especially warm over it, and half a dozen of them were talking at once. Finally one man of about middle age, who was greatly respected by all, got their attention. He said:

"The white men and the Indians are all men. We have hands and feet and heads all alike. They are very powerful and we are very weak. I have heard that they have a book out of which they learned all these things which we do not know. The book, they say, was written by the Great Spirit. I would like to hear this man read something out of this book."

"I don't believe they have any such book," said another. "It is all a lie. The white men always lie. I don't believe this man is any different from the rest."

"Well, they have something which is different from us, or how could they make guns and a village which will float on the water and go up and down the river, as fast as a horse can run?"

Then half a dozen got to talking at once again. Finally, one, who had a stronger voice than the rest, called out so that all heard him:

"Hush, you are nothing but a pack of children. You don't know anything at all. You're all going to hear this man, for the chief sent after Shonnee to interpret, and he has come."

That settled it. No one said anything more, and

one appeared just as eager as another to hear the "talk."

Shonnee was a half-breed, who belonged to another band. His name was John, or Johnny, as he was commonly called, and that was as near as they could pronounce it. Besides, "Shonnee" was an Indian word, meaning, "sugar." Shonnee could talk Indian fluently, but his English was desperately bad. He went to Mr. Parkman and told him that he was an interpreter, and the Indians desired him to speak to them.

The whole camp assembled, the men sitting in a circle inside and the women and children on the outer edges, and Mr. Parkman undertook to preach his first sermon through an interpreter. He was very much puzzled what to say, where to commence or how to introduce a subject so vast and complicated as the Christian religion. This is what actually occurred.

Mr. Parkman—"I will first sing a hymn in praise of God."

Interpreter—"He says he will sing about God."

"Who ever heard of such a thing as that?" thought the Indians.

Mr. Parkman then commenced to sing a rattling, lively Methodist tune. The Indians were delighted and immensely amused.

Mr. Parkman—"Say to them I will pray to God."

Interpreter—"He says he's going to talk to God."

"That is good," thought the Indians, "we all do that," and they listened reverently. The prayer was not interpreted.

Then Mr. Parkman commenced to talk. The

substance of the sermon was that there was one God, who made all things. He sent his Son into the world to teach men, and they killed him. After he was dead he rose again, and went up to heaven. God had given to the white men a book which taught them all things which they ought to know. There were a great many nations of people on the earth, some of them on the other side of the great water. All the nations who read this book and followed its teachings were great and powerful. Those who did not have it, or did not obey what it said, were weak, and poor, and miserable. Now he would read some out of the book.

He then read the Ten Commandments, and part of the Sermon on the Mount. When he had finished, an old Indian arose. He was of the opposition party.

"My friend," said he, "we have heard what you said. The first part that you read from the book we have always known. Our law says there is a God, that we shall not steal, we shall not lie, that we shall not kill, except in war. I think that is the same as what you read, only you must have forgotten to read 'except in war.' That, I think, must be in your book, too.

"What you told us of God's son, we know nothing about. It is hard for us to understand that. Once before, a missionary came to us. He told us this same story. But he lied to us. He told us that one day in seven was God's day. That we must not do any work on that day. If we did, something bad would happen to us. He said we must not hoe our corn on that day. If we did, it would not grow good. Some of us thought we would try it, and every seventh day we hoed our corn, and on no other day, and the corn was better than that which was not hoed so much. So we know he told us a lie. The white people don't do themselves what is commanded in that book. There are white people just over the river. I know they do everything which you say the book says they must not do. My friend, you are in our camp, you eat with us. My heart feels good toward you and the two women. I have finished."

Mr. Parkman was not prepared to meet that argument. He was turning over in his mind what was best to say, when another Indian arose.

"My friend," said he, "it makes my heart feel good to hear what you say. What you have said is good. All of it is good. The man who has just spoken don't think so, but I do. He is old and he has forgotten some things. He remembers there are bad white people who tell lies and steal, and work on the holy day. He forgets about the bad Indians. He can't remember about Big Elk. He is too old."

The name of Big Elk had hardly been pronounced when a half dozen Indians sprang to their feet and a tremendous battle of words ensued. Big Elk was a relation of the old Indian who had first spoken, and of several others. He had become such a confirmed thief that he had been expelled from the tribe. It took the authority of the chief to restore quiet, after which, they dispersed. The new religion was the subject of conversation all over the camp, until late at night, and the two parties became more than ever set in their way of thinking.

CHAPTER VI.

A DESPERATE BATTLE.

THE night Major Hodson transferred his force across the river was dark and rainy. When they were in camp Jack went to the Major and told him the situation of Mr. Parkman, his wife and the young girl. Major Hodson was deeply interested and somewhat excited, and commenced to think over different plans to effect their rescue. Being convinced that the Indians had actually gone to war, he could think of no plan that seemed feasible. A sudden dash into the camp, if a complete surprise, might effect a rescue; but the Indians were, of course, on the alert, and there was no prospect of a surprise being effected. He asked Jack if he thought he could lead a band of men into that camp, and said if he could he would follow with the main force, and keep within supporting distance. It was an extremely hazardous undertaking. Jack thought if he had about twenty picked men, mounted on good horses, he could reach the camp before the break of day. The expedition was so extremely hazardous that Major Hodson resolved to ask some officer to volunteer to take command of this forlorn hope. Lieutenant Blake immediately offered his services, and was accepted, and in half an hour the whole command was on the march, the twenty men, led by

Jack and Lieutenant Blake, soon leaving the main body far in the rear.

Jack advised the lieutenant to march his men in "Injun file," as he called it. The night was very dark, but Jack knew the contour of every hill, and pressed forward with as much certainty as the needle points to the pole.

About an hour before day they reached the brow of the hill above the Indian camp. As silently as possible the men were formed and dashed down. But not a tent was there. The Indians had fled. To prevent a surprise, a retreat was made to the prairie back of the hills, to await the arrival of the main force. In the morning a trail was discovered leading across the Platte river, and then away to the southwest. From the size of the trail it was evident that the band did not number over sixty or seventy warriors, and Major Hodson resolved to send forty picked men in pursuit, under command of Captain Hinkle and Lieutenant Blake, and Jack as scout and guide. The men carried four days' rations and forty rounds of ammunition. It was ten o'clock when they were ready to start. Two horses were lost in the quicksand in fording the Platte, and the men were sent back on foot to the main command. By sundown they had marched forty miles, and the trail looked no fresher than it did in the morning. Coffee was made, a hasty meal eaten, and the command pushed on until the horses showed signs of exhaustion. A halt was made until daylight, and then the march commenced again. On through the hot sun they passed over the rolling prairie, covered with short buffalo grass, it always seeming that when the next swell was gained something different would meet the view; but it was ever the same never-ending billows of solid earth. The sun burned the untanned face of Lieutenant Blake to a blister. Men and officers suffered terribly for water and from fatigue.

It was two o'clock in the afternoon when a small stream was reached and a halt was called. Here the Indians had made the first halt since they had left their old village. All along the trail for the last few miles were found articles which the Indians had abandoned. Near the creek were the carcasses of four ponies which had evidently given out and then been killed. The horses were allowed to bait, and the men to rest for an hour and a half. Many of them had fallen to sleep the moment they had unsaddled their horses, and it was with much difficulty that they were awakened by the officers. Canteens were filled at the creek and the march was continued. Lieutenant Blake, unused to the saddle, was in a terrible condition. The great blisters on his face were perfect torture, and Jack began to fear that he would fall from his saddle, but not a word of complaint escaped him. The Indians had made a march of at least seventy-five miles without a halt. At about four o'clock in the afternoon, Jack, who was half a mile in front, discovered that another trail came into the one he was following, giving evidence that this band had been joined by another equally large. The fact was reported to Captain Hinkle, but the Captain resolved to press on. In another hour Jack called Captain Hinkle's attention to what appeared to be two bunches of grass on a swell of the prairie some distance in front and to the right.

Objects on or near the surface are very indistinctly seen on the prairie when at a little distance. There is always, on a clear day, a wavy, hazy look in the atmosphere at the point where the earth and sky seem to meet.

"There's no sich grass growing on the high prairie," said Jack.

"What is it?" asked the Captain.

"Injuns," said Jack.

They both kept their eyes on the objects for some time, but they did not move. The Captain ordered his men to close up and look to their arms. A detail of ten men was made to scour the prairie in that direction. When Jack reached the little hill where the objects had attracted attention, he saw beyond a wide valley, in the midst of which was flowing a beautiful river. Both to the right and left were heavy groves of timber. It was the valley of the Blue. No living object was in sight. Going back to the trail it led down to the river bank, and on the other side the Indians had made a halt much longer than at the previous place.

To a dweller in the Eastern States, it is a mystery how a scout can tell whether a trail is fresh or old, or how long a halt has been made at a camping-place. The amount of manure from the animals, the appearance of the camp fires, the condition of the grass, the well-trodden path down the bank of the river to get water, will easily tell any man with eyes such a thing as that,

In the boughs of some trees near the crossing were the dead bodies of an Indian woman and a very young baby. They had died from fatigue, and been buried there by their friends. One of the soldiers fired some shots into the bodies from his revolver. He was severely reprimanded and ordered on extra duty by Captain Hinkle.

It was absolutely necessary to halt here and rest the stock. A guard was stationed, and the other men were soon fast asleep. Before dark camp was broken and the march resumed. About midnight another halt was called, and camp was made on the open prairie, far from any timber, to prevent surprise. When daylight came the weary men were in their saddles and on the trail again. For two days they had all been on half rations. The day was intensely hot. It seemed as if the blazing sun would set fire to the crisp prairie grass. Indian cooking utensils, tent-poles, blankets, and other articles were found all along the trail during the day. Several broken-down ponies were also seen, showing that the Indians were fleeing as fast as it was possible. It was one o'clock in the afternoon. The water in the canteens was all gone. A hot wind was blowing from the southwest, so hot that it immediately dried up the perspiration on the horses and men. Jack knew that the first water they would reach was at the Little Blue, which must be many miles away. Captain Hinkle knew that to urge the horses under this hot wind would be certain death to them, and the command proceeded at a slow walk. As the afternoon wore away, the suffering from thirst, aggravated by the hot wind, made existence a perfect agony. Night came on and the Little Blue was not in sight. Wearily onward the command dragged itself. Many of the men were asleep in their saddles. Scarcely a word was spoken as mile after mile they crept over the prairie.

As Captain Hinkle rode at the head of his command he thought of his wife and children in the pleasant barracks at Fort Leavenworth. He thought of the happy time he had spent there during the last nine months, before he was ordered away on this expedition. He had seen a great deal of hard service in the ten years he had been in the army, and the few short weeks or months he had, at different times, spent with his family, were the only bright spots in his life. He cursed Perkins from the bottom of his heart, knowing that he was the cause of all this trouble, and the hardships he was forced to endure.

"If I were making such a forced march as this," thought the Captain, "in any civilized war, I might get some credit for it, perhaps promotion, but an officer never gets any credit for fighting Indians. If he is not successful against as brave a foe as ever carried arms, wily, alert and relentless as Satan himself, —and that, too, always fighting them with inferior numbers—he is denounced all over the West as an incompetent or a coward. If he is successful, he is denounced in the East as an inhuman butcher."

I don't suppose there was ever an officer on an expedition like this who did not think more or less of resigning his commission in the army; and Captain Hinkle thought of it too. But he did not know how to do anything on earth. In civil life he would be a pauper, he thought, and then what would become of his wife and children?

Suddenly, as they were plodding along, Jack's horse gave a snort, and would have given another if he had not given him an awful jerk in the mouth. He rode up to Captain Hinkle, and said:

"Captain, there's Injuns within five hundred yards of this place."

The command was halted, and with some difficulty formed in line. The officers had to ride up and down the column while they stood there, and slap the men with their swords to keep them awake, so utterly exhausted were they.

Skirmishers were thrown out, and every precaution was taken to prevent a surprise. Jack and Lieutenant Blake were sent to see what discoveries they could make. About half a mile to the front they came to the brow of a hill, and discovered by the dim starlight an Indian camp on the banks of the Little Blue. A few ponies were picketed out, and quite a number of tents could be seen.

When Jack saw the ponies he turned to Lieutenant and said:

"These Injuns are up to some deviltry. They've got more ponies than that. We'd better git back to the command or we'll be cut off. Where's the rest of them ponies?" The words were scarcely pronounced when a howl, as of a thousand demons, broke out over the still night. The Indians had attacked the main force.

The fierce war-whoops of the Indians seemed to put

new life into the jaded horses. In moments like those that followed it sometimes occurs that the commanding officer is changed without any formalities. Jack commenced to give orders to his superior officer, who did his best to obey them.

"Clap them spurs into that horse," said Jack to Lieutenant Blake.

"Lie down on the horse," was the next order.

"Be sure of your revolver, and have it ready."

Indian tactics are not according to Hardee, or any other standard military authority; nevertheless they have a system of their own. A warrior who should lead his men in a charge on the enemy, even if he was victorious, would gain no honor if he lost several of his men. Their system is based on the idea of killing without being killed. It is to lead the enemy into ambush, to surprise and slay him when he cannot resist. They adopt this mode from necessity. Their warriors are few in number, and a small loss seriously cripples them. Besides, it disturbs their family relations, and throws the support of the dead warrior's kindred upon those unable to bear it. They have no pension roll. If they seldom charge on batteries and lines of well-formed troops, it is not for the want of courage, as the United States troops have frequently learned from experience. In this case they were riding around Captain Hinkle's command at a safe distance, firing arrows from under their ponies' necks, and those who had rifles using them in the same way.

Through this line Jack and Lieutenant Blake had to make their way. When within about four hundred yards of the command the Lieutenant's horse was shot, and Jack's fell a moment afterward. They were not twenty feet apart. The horses were running at full speed, and the men fell heavily to the ground.

"Crawl up to your horse," said Jack. "Make a breastwork of him."

A band of twenty Indians rode down upon them.

"Keep still," said Jack. Not a movement was made until they were in revolver range.

"Now's yer time," said Jack. Three reports in quick succession came from Jack's revolver, and one from Lieutenant Blake's. A volley of shots and arrows was returned from the Indians. Two of them dropped from their ponies, and the others, stooping down, picked them up and retreated.

"Now's our time," said Jack.

"Save yourself," said Lieutenant Blake. "I cannot go. It is no use for you to stay. You will only be killed. Go on before they come back."

"Where are you hurt?"

"In my right leg. Go on. I'm as good as dead anyhow. Go on."

Jack stooped down, felt of the wound, and said, "I'll stay right here and fight it out."

Captain Hinkle heard the firing and could see something of what was going on, and he moved his whole command to where they were, the Indians circling around them and firing all the time. Besides Lieutenant Blake, he had already lost one man killed and two wounded. For the remainder of the night Captain Hinkle fought it out where he was. When the morning dawned upon those exhausted and thirsty men the clear water of the Little Blue was in plain sight through a break in the hills. His losses at daybreak were six men wounded, two killed and twelve horses shot. His command must have water. It was with the greatest difficulty that he prevented them rushing pell-mell down to the river, which he knew would be certain death to them all. He resolved to drive the Indians before him or perish, one and all, in the attempt. He formed his men and pressed forward, the Indians giving way before him, over the bluffs and down into the bottom. As they neared the river bank, it was plain that, concealed behind it, was a large body of Indians. One-third of his command was either killed or wounded by the heavy fire, and he was forced to retreat out of range. The Indians, encouraged by their success, swarmed around in overwhelming numbers, dashing down and firing, and then retreating. Every few minutes another man was wounded or killed. Captain Hinkle did not have more than twenty-five effective men and one officer left.

At last he ordered the horses brought into a circle and shot, and behind them the men lay down to fight it out to the bitter end. Jack said to the Captain, "If we dig down in this earth, I think in five or six feet we will come to water. I think if one man is kept at it all the time, we can reach it in three or four hours. Dig up the dirt with hunting knives and throw it out with the hands."

This suggestion was put into immediate execution.

Lieutenant Blake dragged himself up to the body of

a dead horse, took a carbine from a wounded soldier, and fought as bravely as if not half dead from thirst and suffering inexpressible agony with his wound. They found water, as Jack had predicted, but many of the men, when they drank, threw it up, and could keep none on their stomachs, until they followed the directions of the surgeon, to take a small swallow at intervals.

The Indians gave them no rest. They were constantly circling around them, rushing up, first on one side, and then on another, firing and retreating. As the day wore away, more and more men were wounded and killed.

About four o'clock in the afternoon a bullet pierced the brain of the brave Captain Hinkle. Never was there a more gallant officer, a better husband and father, a more generous and whole-souled companion. He was mercilessly sacrificed, as have been hundreds of others, in unnecessary Indian wars. Twenty minutes afterward, the only other officer was so desperately wounded that he was totally disabled, and Lieutenant Blake took command. Unused to such hardships, sorely wounded, almost exhausted from fatigue, during all that long night he never closed his eyes. He gave every necessary order, kept complete control of the few men who were yet able to fight, and every time an Indian came in the range of his carbine, its sharp report rang out on the still night air. Sometimes the Indians howled like so many devils. Sometimes it was as still as death, and then again there was a rain of arrows and bullets. When the sun arose the next morning, it never shone on a more horrible sight than that little circle. The dead had been thrown in the middle, and the wounded and those who were yet unhurt lay close up against the carcasses of the dead horses. Lieutenant Blake's leg was fearfully swollen, and he was suffering unspeakable agony, but he was not enduring more pain than some of the other wounded.

Some of the Indians brought water from the river and threw it up in the air. Lieutenant Blake could not imagine what they were doing that for, and he asked Jack.

"The infernal varmints," said Jack, "think that we haven't any water, and they want to tantalize us."

A few minutes afterward, Jack got a camp-kettle full of water and a tin cup, and commenced to throw it up in the air.

"Mebbe," said he, "when them red devils find out we have plenty of water, they will conclude they can't kill us for want of something to drink, and clear out."

It was certain that this performance of Jack's had had some effect on the Indians, for all their forces were drawn off. The spirits of the few half dead heroes, who were still able to handle their guns, arose. They thought the Indians were about to leave. A few minutes afterward the hope vanished, for over a hundred Indian warriors rode out of the woods, with the very evident intention of making a charge on the remnant who still lay inside of the circle of dead horses.

Lieutenant Blake spoke to his men :

"This," said he, "is the end of the struggle. If you repel this assault it will be their last. Load and be ready to fire at the word of command. Have your revolvers ready, and fight to the last. If taken prisoners you will be tortured to death. Let us die like brave men."

The Indians formed a line. The chief in gay dress and feathers rode along the line and took his station in the center. A chorus of war-whoops rent the air, and on they came. Across the dead horses was leveled every carbine. The Indians were about half a mile away. They put their ponies to the top of their speed. Their bodies were nearly naked, and their faces and breasts daubed with paint. They had made about half the distance, when a cry of surprise rent the air. The Indians turned, fled across the river, up the bluffs on the other side and out of view. Lieutenant Blake was struck dumb with surprise. As the Indians had fled, the men rose to their feet and watched them with eager eyes. The silence was broken by a soldier saying:

"Look! Look!"

They turned and looked. Down over the hills in their rear, at full gallop, came a company of United States cavalry, with Major Hodson at their head. Back on the hills they had come upon the mutilated and scalped bodies of the men who had been killed in the first onslaught. From there they had ridden at a full gallop.

CHAPTER VII.

OLD HAIRY BEAR'S ORGIES AND MEHA'S HEROISM.

WHAT occurred in the camp of the Indians after the preaching of the sermon by Mr. Parkman, will be hard for a civilized person to understand. Old Hairy Bear, who had made the speech against the white men's religion, went to his tent, and having gathered some of the familiar spirits of his own kind about him, wrought them into a rage by relating the attrocities which had been perpetrated upon them in by-gone days by the whites.

"Once," he said, "the Indians owned all this country. We were free and happy. Our young men were brave, our young women strong, healthy and good to look at. Game was everywhere. The Indian never went hungry then. Our lodges were made of the finest furs, and when a man laid down to sleep he wrapped himself in beaver and otter skins. There was no sickness in those days, but men died of old age. Then the white men came. They were poor. There were but very few of them. They came begging to our tent doors. We fed them, we gave them land. They said they would ever be our friends. But they were liars and thieves and murderers. They crept upon us by night and killed our warriors and women and children. My father was brave and kind. A white man killed him. My brother was a great hunter and warrior. They killed him. Our chief was a coward and did not revenge their death. The Great Spirit is angry with us."

Then the old heathen set up a howl, like a dying swan, pretending to lament for the dead, and the others joined in it. Another wrinkled old Indian, who knew he was too old to go on the war-path, told of the death of his relations and that God called upon them for vengeance. The tent was steaming hot and the excitement grew intense. A medicine man, with the sacred stick in his hand, which had the " big medicine " in it, got out in the center of the tent, and went through a series of most disgusting contortions, the others crooning a most melancholy tune, if tune it could be called. It was a jumble of words and sounds without meaning, lamenting the dead killed by the whites, who never would reach the happy hunting-grounds because they had not been avenged. After this had gone on for a while, and the naturally nervous temperaments of the Indians had been wrought up to a terrible pitch of excitement, by this sort of religious exercise, resembling very much the scenes which sometimes occur at camp meetings, the old medicine man began to prophesy, that all the woes which could be told would fall upon the tribe, if these wrongs were not avenged; and wound it up by the startling information that the whites at Council Bluffs had sent for the soldiers and they were then on the way to exterminate the whole band. This produced a yell of rage which startled the whole camp. The Indians rushed out of the tent, covered with perspiration, wild with excitement, arms in their hands, and ran for the tent where Mr. Parkman stopped, with the full intent of murdering them all. When they got inside they found the tent empty. Mr. Parkman and the two ladies were gone. In their rage they came near killing the owner of the tent.

Every tribe has its military organization; from the want of a better term, it is known among the whites as the "Soldier Lodge." The man in command is called the "Head Soldier." When on a hunt or on the war-path, the penalties for disobedience of orders are very severe, sometimes even death. Besides the Head Soldier, there are other officers, which are usually called "policemen." The Head Soldier gets his orders from the head chief. The chief knew of the orgies which had been going on in Hairy Bear's lodge, but as they indulged in that sort of thing more or less frequently he had no thought of anything serious coming of it. Now he walked up to the raving Indians, proclaimed a state of war, and ordered the old Crier to spread the news and call a council. The first cry of the old man brought the Head Soldier to the chief's side. Only a few words were spoken, but there was instant obedience on all sides.

Badger, the head chief, had kept himself pretty well informed of the movements on the other side of the river. He knew of the arrival of the troops and the uproar among the whites, and had made up his mind, to avoid war, it was better to leave that part of the country and go far into the interior. He had intended to break camp and march in the morning. He told the head men when in council that he had received the news from a runner that the soldiers were coming. It was, therefore, necessary for them to go immediately, to get out of their way, until he could be joined by other bands and be able to fight them. Before midnight the whole camp was on the march.

Little Meha lived with her uncle in her uncle's tent, for her father was dead. Her mother lived in the same tent also. Her uncle had no children, and but one wife. He had lost all of his children and one of his wives in the great small-pox epidemic. When the orgies commenced in Hairy Bear's tent she listened. As they increased she began to fear for the white women, whose kind treatment of her had completely won her heart. As the orgies increased in fervor, she was certain that they would end in the death of the whites. She went and told her uncle, and he went down near the tent and listened. He was also convinced that Hairy Bear's orgie had been gotten up on purpose, with that end in view. But what could he do? He could do nothing. He told Meha they had all better go out of the tent and leave them alone. He felt sorry for the white people, but he could not help them. Hairy Bear and his relations would kill him if he interfered. So Meha's uncle, mother and aunt went off to another tent. Meha looked into the tent and saw the sick girl sleeping, and the lovely and kind Mrs. Parkman sitting by her side watching her. She sat down and cried. Then she made a resolve to save them.

She went into the tent, her eyes full of tears, and put her arms around the neck of Mrs. Parkman and sobbed as if her heart would break. Then she commenced to make signs. She got a knife, drew it across her own throat, and made a motion as if to scalp herself. She put her hand on her lips to indicate silence, and started toward the tent door, and motioned to follow her.

The whole truth flashed over Mrs. Parkman in a moment. She did not faint; she did not scream. She walked across to the other side of the tent and awoke her husband. She told him that the Indians intended to murder them, and Meha had come to warn them. The girl, who had greatly recuperated, was awakened, and told that they must leave immediately. The calm courage of Mrs. Parkman imparted itself in some degree to her. When they were ready to leave the tent, Meha took a knife from her belt and cut some of the tent fastenings on the back side, raised it up, and motioned for them to go out that way. There was a heavy growth of black jack and hazel brush coming up to the tent. A narrow path led through this brush, over the point and down into the Missouri river bottoms. Along this path the Indian girl led the little party. One Indian only saw their departure. He was a relative of Hairy Bear. He was as savage-looking a human being as could be found on all the plains. His face was always daubed with paint. His tent was as dirty as a pig-sty, and his wife was just like him. As Mr. Parkman walked along in the rear there was a moccasined foot which kept time with his own, coming stealthily after him. Meha caught a glimpse of the dark figure, stopped, allowed them to pass her, and just as the hand was raised, threw herself between the Indian and his intended victim. The knife cut a heavy gash across the top of her shoulder, and the villain turned and fled.

Meha's uncle was one of the police. He saw this Indian emerge from the brush and suspected what his object had been. Hairy Bear's party were just making the raid on his own tent, and it was through this villain that Meha's uncle came near losing his life. The sudden order issued by the chief gave Meha's uncle command over this Indian, and he sent him to the mouth of the Platte with a message to the three lodges camped there.

After this incident, the little party were led on as fast as possible by Meha. There was another Indian village up the river, inhabited by a kindred tribe, who spoke the same language, had intermarried with this one, but were entirely separate as a tribe. To this village Meha intended to take the white women. She did not know where else to go. She was afraid to go to the whites. They arrived at the village just at daylight, and found it in an uproar. The head men were all in council. Major Hodson's command had marched by in the night, not very far to the west of them. At first, it was thought they were coming to attack them, but after the command had passed on, they could not decide what it meant. The council concluded they would send a delegation to overtake the command and inform the officer that they had had nothing to do with the troubles which had occurred, and were anxious for peace. In accordance with this conclusion, the chief and head men started immediately. This tribe was rich in horses and cattle, had never been at war with the whites, and earnestly desired to live in peace.

Mr. Parkman, his wife, the young lady and Meha, were given a tent to themselves, and every honor paid to them that the Indians could devise. Their best blankets and robes were given to them, and much food brought and placed before them.

Meha came into the tent, pulled her blanket up over her head, placed her face in her hands and remained perfectly motionless for a long time. At last Mrs. Parkman went to her, and, to attract her attention, raised her blanket, and saw the wound on Meha's shoulder. Then she realized the heroism of the brave girl, who had received the stab intended for her husband, and, though sorely wounded, had led them to a place of safety.

CHAPTER VIII.

A WOMAN'S CONQUEST.

RED IRON and his men, delegated to interview Major Hodson, started out, struck the trail and followed on. After a few miles they saw the Major's command returning. They halted on a hill-top in plain view, and waved a piece of white cloth. Then Red Iron went forward with his interpreter. He told Major Hodson that he was a friend of the whites and wanted to have a talk with him. After some friendly words from Major Hodson, he signaled for the rest of the delegation to come forward.

A long council followed, during which Red Iron made several set speeches. One was as follows:

"I have always been a friend of the whites. When others counseled war, I would not agree to it. I cannot fight the whites if I desired to. I have but few warriors. The Great Father has so many no man can count them. I will do anything the Great Father says. This country is mine. I will give part of it to the whites, if I can keep the remainder. My tribe has many horses and cattle. We can watch them, and live happy, and at peace. We are ignorant, and the whites know, it seems to me, almost everything. I am old and cannot learn, but my children can learn, and I want them to know the ways of the whites. These other Indians have gone to war. They did not consult me about it. They knew I would not agree to it. Other tribes will join with them, and there will be a long war. The war will be right in this country where I live, and I am afraid that the soldiers will not know my people from them and kill them. Tell me what to do to have peace, and I will do it. I have some warriors. I will give you some to fight these bad Indians. I do not say that the Indians are all wrong and the whites all right, but I am very angry at them that they have gone to war. There is a better way. The Great Father sent his commissioners to me, and they said they wanted peace, and I made a treaty with them. I said I would always live in peace with the whites, and I will keep my treaty. The commissioners said the Great Father would send us presents twice each year, if I would give him the part of my country which was on the other side of the river. The presents have not come. But the Great Father has many things to attend to. He has forgotten it, but some day he will remember it and then he will send them. My heart does not feel bad about it. If my tribe can be at peace, I will do whatever you say. One white man and two women were in Badger's camp, and they tried to kill them. This has made me very angry. An Indian woman brought them to my village and I have given them a tent and food. They can live with us as long as they want to. If they want to go back I will take them.

" My little children play around our tents. My young women have glad hearts. The older women look at them and laugh. My young men count their ponies and find there is a great number. We are happy, and I want to live in peace. When I die, let it be said that Red Iron never raised his hand against a white man. If I knew of anything I could do to make the whites know I am their friend, I would do it. It is true that some of my people have bad hearts, because the presents have not come which the Great Father promised. But none dare disobey me. After awhile the presents will come and then they will know that I was right. I have come to ask you what I shall do to keep out of this war."

Red Iron was tall, graceful and courtly in his bearing. He had a mild expression, and a personal magnetism about him which won the confidence of all with whom he came in contact. Major Hodson was greatly impressed by his speech. He *felt* that every word of it was the true sentiment of the old Indian's heart. He shook him by the hand, and said:

"I believe you have spoken to me with no double tongue. Your tribe shall not be molested if I can prevent it. But this country here will be the theater of the war, and many troops will be marching over it. I think you had better move your tribe up on the Elkhorn. You can live there, and be out of danger. I am glad to hear that those white people are in your camp. I thought they had either been killed or carried off by Badger. I wish you would send them across the river to Council Bluffs. You had better move up on the Elkhorn river right away."

Red Iron made particular inquiries about just the place on the Elkhorn that the Major desired him to go, and the council broke up. The next morning he had his whole tribe on the march for the spot designated, and after they were located sent down and asked that an officer be sent to see if he was in the right place.

Shortly after Red Iron left Major Hodson a courier came with orders. A large body of troops had arrived, the general commanding the department having forwarded all the troops he could spare from other points. They were in command of Colonel Greene. Colonel Greene was called upon immediately by Perkins and several other " prominent citizens " (all contractors), and all the information he had was their version of the story. Perkins offered him the assistance of his company of volunteers, which was declined. This set the Governor, who had come in person, and all the newspapers, to denouncing Colonel Greene. They were unanimously of the opinion that one company of western frontiersmen was worth more than a whole regiment of regular cavalry in fighting Indians. The orders which Major Hodson received instructed him to press the fighting, and strike a decisive blow, if possible, against Badger's band. So Major Hodson started to reinforce Lieutenant Hinkle.

When Red Iron returned to his camp, he first set himself about performing his promise to send the white people over the river. He owned a spring wagon, which among the Indians was a possession of which the whole tribe was proud. He sent his interpreter to tell them, and the interpreter brought back the astounding information that they refused to go. Red Iron could not understand it, and it caused him the greatest anxiety. If they were not returned to their friends it might get him into trouble, so he went to them himself. He said:

"My friends: It makes my heart feel good that you like my people, and desire to live with us. If it were not for this war I would make a big feast, and we would all rejoice. But if you do not go the officer will say I did not keep my word. I will give you five ponies to take back, and when the war is over you can come again and live with us always."

"We would be glad to go," said Mr. Parkman, "but I cannot persuade my wife to leave this poor wounded girl, who risked her own life to save mine."

Although this was correctly interpreted, Red Iron was as much in the dark as ever. He replied:

"Why don't you tell her to go? If I want my wife to do anything, I tell her to do it, and she does it."

Mr. Parkman thought of the note he had written in his memorandum-book about the degradation of women among the heathen. But Red Iron was much more astonished when Mrs. Parkman came up to him and said, in her sweet and quiet way:

"Brother Red Iron" (the Methodists call everybody brother or sister, and it becomes such a habit with them they are not conscious half of the time that they do it), "Brother Red Iron, God teaches us in his holy book that we must do good to all men, and his Son, when he was in the world, told a parable about a wounded man who lay by the roadside, and many men passed by on the other side of the way and did not help him. God is angry with every one who does that way. Here is this poor wounded girl. If I should go away and leave her, God would be very angry with me. Please let me stay and take care of her until she is well, and then we will go. I won't make you any trouble at all."

This was something that Red Iron was not prepared for. He replied:

"But I have received orders to move away from here. We are to go two days' journey further away from the whites."

"Where she goes I will go," said Mrs. Parkman, "and her—" She was unconsciously repeating Scripture, but when she was about to say "her God shall be my God" she hesitated, and thought, "is the God of the

Indian girl my God?" "Yes, he is," said she mentally, and then she went on:

"Where she goes will I go, her God shall be my God, and her people shall be my people. Do you know, Red Iron, that one God made us all, and he loves us all? He wants us to live in peace, to do good to one another, to love one another, and do you know that he is preparing a place for us, and by and by, he will take us all there. We shall live on the banks of a beautiful river. No wicked men can ever come there. There will nevermore be any sickness or death or hunger or thirst. Our hearts will never be sad, for God will wipe all the tears from our eyes. Won't you promise to go to that beautiful place with me, Red Iron?"

The beauty of her countenance, the earnestness of her manner, the heavenly sweetness which came over her face, sent a thrill through the old Indian's heart which he had never felt before, although he had to wait to hear it all interpreted sentence by sentence. He replied:

"I would go, but I do not know the way there."

"Then let us stay and we will teach you the way," she said.

"I will do anything you say," said Red Iron.

The weakness and gentleness of a delicate woman had conquered. Nothing would give Red Iron greater pleasure than to obey her. She wielded a power stronger than the dictates of councils, or officers, or commissioners. He went to his tent and sat in silence for a long time. He named her "Sunshine," and thought over and over all that she had said. After a while he went back again, and stood hesitating at the door of the tent. Mr. Parkman asked him to come in. When he had seated himself and waited a due length of time, according to Indian etiquette, he asked Mr. Parkman if his women and girls should learn this way, "would they be like Sunshine?" "How long would it take them to learn?" "Was it very hard to learn it?" and many other questions, to which it was very hard for Mr. Parkman to find answers. Red Iron finally concluded that Mr. Parkman did not know as much as his wife did.

Mrs. Parkman was writing on some of the blank leaves of Mr. Parkman's memorandum book. When she had finished she folded them up and gave them to Red Iron, and asked him if he would not send them over to the town, saying it was a letter to tell the white people where they were, and why they did not come back. The chief then asked Mr. Parkman to write a letter to the military officer there, and tell him why he did not bring them back, which Mr. Parkman did. The next morning they were placed in Red Iron's spring wagon, and went with the tribe to the new location.

CHAPTER IX.

THE CONTRACTORS' HARVEST.

THE first thing Major Hodson did after his arrival on the field which had been so bitterly contested by brave Captain Hinkle and his heroic handful of men, was to care for the wounded and then bury the dead. The loss was nineteen killed and mortally wounded and twelve wounded, with a total loss of all the horses of the first command. A scouting party of fifteen men were sent on after the fleeing Indians. They followed the trail for about twelve miles, when it broke in every direction. The Indians had separated into small parties, with the intention of meeting at some appointed rendezvous. Major Hodson's horses were worn out, he had but a day and one-half full rations left, and he was nearly two hundred miles from his base of supplies. It was absolutely necessary for him to return. When he got back and the news of the battle and its results became known, the military were furiously assaulted by the Governor. The battle was called a cold-blooded massacre, and a general cry was raised for the extermination of all the Indians in the south-west. Colonel Greene was denounced as an incompetent, and a military martinet, and his refusal to accept the services of Perkins's company was set down as proof positive that he was unfit for the position he occupied. Colonel

Greene forwarded his formal official reports to his commanding officer, but made no defense of his conduct. He was an old officer, grown gray in the service of his country, and he knew there was a long and costly war on hand, and that it was not to be fought out with newspaper articles or one company of militia. He recommended the erection of a fortified fort on the Little Blue, to be well provisioned and garrisoned. From this as a base, expeditions could be made into the heart of the Indian country, their villages destroyed, and the bands so harassed and punished as to bring them into subjection. His recommendations were adopted, and a fort was commenced and pushed with all vigor, so as to be completed, provisioned and garrisoned before winter. The site of the fort was two hundred miles from the river, and all supplies had to be hauled in wagons.

Now commenced the harvest the contractors had been waiting for. Freight was let out by contract to the lowest bidder. The contractors held a council and an arrangement was made, so that, in fact, there was no competition. The first bids were all rejected by the quartermaster as too high. Then a howl went up from the newspapers, the Governor, the friends of the contractors, the hundreds of men who were waiting for jobs, such as teamsters, wagon-masters, etc., as was never heard before. The fort would not be built in time, the whole country would be over-run by Indians, thousands of lives would be lost, and the settlement of the country set back for a generation. A delegation started for Washington immediately, to impress upon the President the importance of removing Colonel Greene from the command. Bids were advertised for, a second time. They were a shade less extortionate than before, and as time was pressing they were accepted. Then another delegation was started to Washington to overhaul the first, and change the programme. The contracts were let, and things were all right. Cavalry company after company kept arriving. Corn, which at the commencement of the trouble was worth only ten cents a bushel, went up to a dollar. The Missouri river was lower than ever before (so the contractors said), and it was almost impossible for the boats to get up it at all, and contracts could not be made for transportation for less than five times the amount asked two months before. Business in Council Bluffs was "booming." Everybody discussed Indians. They were red devils. They were blood-thirsty beasts. They cut out the hearts of their victims and ate them. They ate the entrails of animals without cleaning them. The "bucks," as they called them, did nothing but roam over the country and hunt for scalps during the day, and return home at night and beat their "squaws" with war-clubs. They were so dirty that you could smell one of their villages five miles. In fact, they were not human, but a sort of wild beast, and there was no more harm in killing one of them than in killing a wolf—and in all the cityfull of people there was not one to dissent to any of these statements.

It was four weeks before the expedition was ready to start. It was composed of three regiments of cavalry and one of infantry. A block-house had been built at the mouth of the Elkhorn on some earthworks thrown up. Two companies were stationed there. A hospital, stables for the horses, barracks for the men, and quarters for the officers, were built in a very short time. The work was mostly done by the soldiers themselves. In this hospital Lieutenant Blake and the others wounded from the battle of the Little Blue were left. No one not acquainted with such expeditions can imagine what an enormous amount of freight must be transported. The trains stretched out for miles over the prairie. The progress must be extremely slow even in a prairie country. Streams must be bridged, banks in the deep "draws" must be cut down, and in some places wells must be dug, from seventy-five to a hundred feet deep, to furnish water at the end of each day's march. The stopping places for other trains, which are to come afterward, are all located as the command proceeds. It was nearly a month after the command started before the site for the fort was located and work was commenced.

CHAPTER X.

MEHA DECEIVED.

ON the banks of the Elkhorn, with the endless rolling prairie stretching to the west, and the ever-advancing white settlements to the east, Red Iron made his new location, in accordance with the directions received from the officers.

His tribe was rich, as riches are accounted among Indians. They were at peace with the whites, and with other Indian tribes. There was plenty of water and grass and timber near at hand. Not far to the northwest were elk and deer and endless herds of buffalo. It was time for the beginning of the fall hunt. Nearly all of the active men and many of the women and children went on a hunt. The old and infirm, and enough well and active to take care of the stock, remained behind. It was a gala day, and had been preceded with games of all sorts and a big feast. There had been horse races, foot races, wrestling matches, "shinny," and all sorts of fun. The whole tribe was happy, and the families parted, doing all sorts of foolish things for "good luck," some to go on the hunt and some to stay at home.

Meha's wound had healed, and she was bright and happy. Mrs. Parkman had won her heart. When it was proposed that the three white people should go back to Council Bluffs, not only Meha, but many others, shed bitter tears. They were given many presents, and the thought of parting with them cast a gloom over all the village. Meha refused to be comforted. At last Mrs. Parkman, moved by Meha's deep grief, proposed that she go with them and stay until spring. Mr. Parkman was very anxious to devote his life to work among the Indians, but he must wait for the church authorities to sanction it. He thought, if Meha would go with them, he could learn the language from her. She had already learned a great many English words from Mrs. Parkman, and pronounced them all perfectly correctly. So Meha went with them. They went down the Elkhorn to the blockhouse and stopped there over night.

Lieutenant Blake was still suffering from his wound, and was not able to walk. Besides him there were many others wounded, and some sick in the hospital. A great pressure was brought to bear upon Mr. Parkman to remain there, and he finally got permission of his presiding elder to do so.

Lieutenant Blake's long confinement had made him morose and melancholy, and to keep up his spirits he had drank, pretty regularly, more than the Government ration of whisky. He was not the man he was six months before. He needed an attendant, and when he saw Meha he thought it would be a good thing to secure her services for himself and another officer who was just recovering from a long siege of typhoid fever. Meha came; she watched with them by day, and stayed with Mrs. Parkman at night. Lieutenant Blake amused himself with her a great deal. At first she was too bashful to talk, but little by little it wore off. He pretended to learn the Indian language from her, and she really tried to learn English from him. Then he taught her to play games, backgammon, checkers and cards. Sometimes when her hand lay carelessly upon the board he would take hold of it. He was amused to see the hot blood rush to her cheeks, and show even through her brown skin.

There is a wondrous mystery in a woman's heart, which no science has fathomed. And this is as true of the Indian girl on the plains as of the educated and refined daughter of the eastern merchant prince. Little

Meha stood in awe of Lieutenant Blake at first. He was the wondrous white chief, the bold and gallant warrior, so far away and above her that she could only look on him and admire. Then, as in every-day life she came in closer contact with him, learned to speak his language, and he grew to take more and more notice of her, strange thoughts came into her mind. She tried harder than ever to be like the white women. She put up her hair; she took off the large brass rings which she had worn, and dressed as near as she could like Mrs. Parkman. The metamorphosis in her personal appearance was wonderful. She was now a shy, bashful, very dark brunette, with the natural dignity and grace of her people.

One day Lieutenant Blake received orders to join his company. He sent for Meha and told her he was going away, and said to her, "I have no wife, would you like to go with me and be my wife?"

She said, in broken English, she would go and tell Mrs. Parkman. Her father was dead and her mother was with Badger's band, she had no brother or sister, and she had no one else to tell. That was her home, and he must come there and get her. Then she would go with him.

The Lieutenant replied, that the ambulance in which he was to go was ready. He had said good-bye to Mr. and Mrs. Parkman and all the officers. If she was to be his wife, she must get in the ambulance and go then. He was going through a big town, and he would buy her a great many nice dresses and everything she wanted. He would always be good to her.

By and by, after the war was over, he would try to find her mother and she should come and live with them. He put his arm around her and kissed her. They walked toward the door, and—and Meha got in the ambulance with him and rode away.

After they had started Meha looked up to Lieutenant Blake and said:

"Is this the way the white people do? Is this the way they marry?"

"They have a great many different forms," said Lieutenant Blake, "and I suppose this is as good as any."

CHAPTER XI.

A RIDE FOR LIFE.

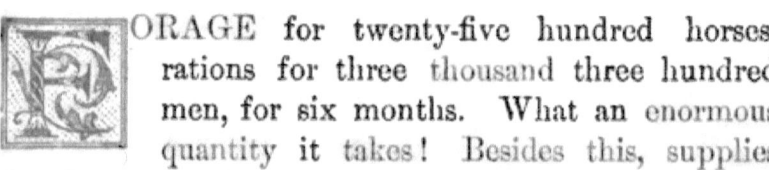ORAGE for twenty-five hundred horses, rations for three thousand three hundred men, for six months. What an enormous quantity it takes! Besides this, supplies for fifteen hundred civilians, wagon-masters, teamsters and hangers-on. It soon took all the products of the farmers in that sparsely-settled country, for a hundred miles around. Corn and pork and beef, for which there was before no market at all, brought prices far above what the produce could have been sold for, after transportation to New York. There was not a human being in a radius of one hundred and fifty miles who was not directly interested in that Indian war. On

this self-interest the hatred of the Indian race was fed, until it became second nature. It was instilled into the children, and fair young girls gave utterance to sentiments concerning them that, under other circumstances, would be thought a disgrace to Feejee islanders.

All the horse thieves and robbers in that section of the country congregated in proximity to the scene of war. Around Council Bluffs, to the south and east and north of it, a great many horses were stolen. It was all accounted to be done by the Indians. Red Iron's tribe were the ones who were doing it, without doubt, was the accepted theory, and they must be punished. The matter was laid before the military officers; they made a thorough investigation, and ascertained beyond the possibility of a mistake that the old chief and his men were sacredly keeping their compact of peace. Then the military were denounced again. They were harboring savages almost in the very midst of the innocent and unprotected settlers, who might at any moment, scalp, burn, and murder without let or hinderance. It was not in human nature to endure it, and it would not be endured, was the substance of the whole discussion of the subject.

Red Iron's band of women and children, the old and infirm, were quietly sleeping in their tents beneath the still star-light. The old men dreamed of the happy days that were gone, and the young of the happy days to come. Mothers unconsciously hugged their babes to their bosoms. Not a breath of air was moving. The bright stars twinkled above the silent camp. A hundred armed white men crept up through the timber. There were no sentinels to give warning, for they slept in perfect confidence in the white man's word. There was a sudden volley and leaden missiles pierced every tent. Then into the tents they rushed. Mother and babe, young men and maidens, old men and little children, alike were soon writhing in the agony of death, before the smoking revolvers. No resistance was made and not one was spared. Many of them were scalped and their scalps tied to the horses' bridle bits. All their little store of wealth was taken and all their ponies. The bodies were left where they were slain, to be food for the wolves. Perkins led his gallant band of brave men back, after his "glorious victory," and received the plaudits of the whole country round about. It is true that the people believed these Indians to be guilty, and the men who won the "victory" never gave the details. They said they had "surprised an Indian village and destroyed it."

There was one man who was not satisfied with the account given by Perkins, and that was the lawyer, Wilmot. A keen and sharp thinker, a close reasoner and a good judge of men, he was not to be deceived by such an improbable tale, that a whole Indian village could be attacked, captured and sacked without the loss of a man. It would not have been safe for him to say so in public, and Wilmot, being a prudent man, did not express any opinion on the subject. He resolved to ride over to the block-house, and see what the officer in command there thought about Perkins's "victory."

Arriving there, he found that the military had heard nothing about the matter, but the officer said instantly:

"I know what he has done. Red Iron and his able men are all on a hunt, and Perkins has crept up on a band of helpless old men, women and children, and murdered them in cold blood. It is nothing but murder, sir, cold-blooded murder; a crime which would be a disgrace to savages, and which will bring retribution upon us all. Red Iron had offered to help me defend this post, and the Colonel had relied on his aid in case we were attacked. I haven't a dozen fighting men here, having sent a heavy guard with the last train. If I had the power I would court-martial Perkins and his band of assassins, take them out and send for Red Iron to come and shoot them dead in their tracks. That is what justice demands, and that is what I would do if I could. I ought to have the power to do it. In any other country an officer set to guard a frontier would have some authority; but this infernal Indian system of ours is a mass of contradictions. It isn't war we are engaged in at all. It is a sort of murdering, marauding, banditti affair, in which every man can take a hand to suit himself." Here the officer used some adjectives concerning Perkins which were more emphatic than polite.

"Excuse my 'French,'" he said, "but Perkins has not only murdered a band of Indian women and children, but he has murdered all at this post, in all likelihood. As soon as this massacre spreads abroad, all these Indians to the north-west will be down upon us. Red Iron and his warriors will be turned from friends to fiends, thirsting for vengeance, to lead them on."

Here some more "French" was resorted to in giving a second opinion of Perkins, which, however, did not differ much from the one before expressed, and the officer walked away and commenced to prepare immediately for a vigorous defense.

Captain Belfor got an ambulance, put four of the best horses to it, told Mr. and Mrs. Parkman, Lawyer Wilmot and the young lady to get in, and get across the river to Council Bluffs as soon as possible, for there was no telling what minute the post might be attacked by the Indians, and in that case it was no place for women or civilians. On going to the ambulance, Mr. Wilmot was introduced to Miss Jennie Walker. The driver was told to get the best time out of those horses there was in them. They dashed out of the post and over the prairie on a keen run. Half the distance had been made when, on looking back, they saw riding after them a hundred savages, naked, except breech-cloth and moccasins, daubed with paint and furious with rage. The driver plied his whip, the foam-covered horses sped onward, the wheels spun around like tops. In crossing a draw the right front wheel struck a bank, and was knocked into splinters. The front of the box dragged on the ground. Wilmot sprang out, and called out, "Cut loose the horses." In less than a minute they were free from the ambulance, and the driver mounted one and ran away. Wilmot held two of the horses by the bits, and Mr. Parkman the other.

"Put your wife on this horse," said Wilmot to Mr. Parkman, and in a moment she was on its back. The two men then mounted the other two horses. Miss Walker was running down the road, wild with fright. As Wilmot came along by her side he checked his horse, and, stooping, took her by the arms, close to the shoulders, and said "jump," and she was seated in front of him on his horse. This accident had allowed the Indians to come almost within rifle range. Indeed, a few shots were fired. The American horses on which the party was mounted out-ran the Indians' ponies, and gradually the gap between them was widened. Two or three miles from the river they came upon the first settlements. They could only cry out to them "The Indians are coming," and press onward. They reached the ferry in safety. Mrs. Parkman alighted from her horse and stood on the deck erect, calm and dignified. Poor Miss Walker had long lain limp in Wilmot's arms, perfectly unconscious. A blanket was spread out on the deck of the boat, and she was laid upon it.

Mrs. Parkman approached Wilmot, and said:

"Cannot something be done to aid the settlers on the west side of the river?"

"I am afraid it is too late," he said, sadly.

Great excitement was occasioned in town upon their arrival. Wilmot sought out Perkins and plead with him to take his company of volunteers, and cross the river for the protection of settlers and succor of Captain Belfor. Perkins was suddenly taken sick, and not a man of all his heroes could be mustered, now that there was actual fighting to be done. It was proved afterwards that Perkins took nearly a teaspoonful of ipecacuanha and half a box of pills.

Wilmot could not drive away from his mind the wild and terrified look of the women and little children he saw by the road as he was dashing along. He sometimes cursed himself for a coward, that he did not stop, although he knew it would have only been certain death to do so, not only to himself but to them also.

That night there was a public meeting held, and Wilmot addressed them as follows:

"Fellow-citizens: Affairs have arrived at a crisis, which requires the wisest and most prudent action on the part of the citizens of this part of the country. I cannot now discuss, or I may at some future time, the causes which have brought this state of affairs about. The question for us to decide to-night is: What will we do to save the lives of hundreds of innocent settlers, men, women and little children, to whose homes is to-night laid the torch, and over whose heads is circling the scalping-knife of the savage. The men who have brought this calamity upon us have fled like cowards. Now you, who have wives and children, who have had no part in what has passed, must take the direction of affairs and meet the Indians upon the field and drive them back. This will be no raid, under the cover of night, upon helpless women and children, but it is war, war to the knife and the knife to the hilt. The sky to the west is red. You know what that means. It is from the flames of burning cabins of settlers. The men and children have been murdered and scalped, and the women carried off prisoners to a fate worse than death, and that will be our fate and the fate of our wives and children, unless we prepare to fight. There is no other recourse now. I——"

A grave old gentleman interrupted him.

"I have," said he, "just received a note from the Governor, in which he says that as soon as the official papers can be made out, a call will be made for the formation of several companies of militia, and if this meeting can take any action to-night about organizing, it will be so much time gained."

Wilmot took from his pocket a sheet of legal cap paper, at the head of which was written a few lines.

"This is not a resolution," said he, "it is an agreement of enlistment in the militia for one year. I enlist as a private," and put down his name.

One could not help noticing the difference in this meeting and the first one that was held in regard to the Indian troubles. There were no drunken men there, and no bummers. It was composed of the best citizens of the place and neighborhood. The men who put their names down on that paper were men with families, men who had some property, and men who belonged to churches, owned stores, supported schools, and formed the solid framework of society. The next morning, when they went to the rendezvous appointed, to elect officers, the most of them left weeping wives and children behind.

CHAPTER XII.

ON THE WAR-PATH.

WITHIN twenty-four hours after Red Iron's women and children had been slaughtered by Perkins's tribe of white savages, the hunting party returned, rejoicing at the successful result. They came down the Elkhorn, through the timber, and saw nothing of the awful tragedy until they stood on the very spot. There the bodies, mangled by the wolves, laid before them. Red Iron was speechless. He had always been the friend of the whites, and there had always been a large party in his tribe who had derided and opposed him. He sat down, drew his blanket over his head, and moved not a muscle nor uttered a single sound. He was wifeless and childless. Perfect, absolute despair seized him. The others burst out in the wildest howls and groans, the nature of which it is perfectly impossible to describe. This soon gave way to rage and ferocity. The Head Soldier proclaimed war, and orders were soon issued which secured perfect quiet. Still Red Iron said not a word. The chiefs and head men gathered around him. The leader of the opposition upbraided him, and applied every vile epithet which the language contained to him. He was called a dog and a coward. He had better put on a woman's dress, and a hundred other things of like nature. The Indian who spoke trembled with rage.

Red Iron's particular friends were silent. They could not say a word in his defense.

At last Red Iron spoke:

"Why do you denounce me? Have I not suffered as much as all of you? Are not *my* wives and *my* children all dead? Do I not see their mangled bodies before me? What tribe was happier than mine up to the present time? Have you not been rich while others were poor? Has not my advice always been good? Am I to blame for this? Is there one of you who advised me not to come here? Did you not all rejoice when I made peace with the white officer? Stand back and obey my orders, or I will kill every one of you. When the time comes to fight we will see who will be brave. There has been some mistake. I don't believe the white officers have done this, knowing it to be Red Iron's tribe. I will send first and see. Then, if they have, I will hunt the whites and kill them as I would kill snakes."

The proposition to send a delegation before going to war raised an instant rebellion. Most of Red Iron's friends walked away from his side and joined the other party, and after consulting together they delegated the Head Soldier to speak their sentiments. He said, "Red Iron, you are our chief. The white people have come and murdered our wives and children without cause. You are not our friend if you refuse to avenge this wrong. If you will lead us to war it is well, we will follow you. If not, we will have a chief who is not a friend to murderers and who will avenge our wrongs."

Red Iron knew what this meant. If he did not lead them to war they would kill him. Why should he die for those who had killed his wives and children?

He was too dignified to make any reply, but he commenced giving orders to the Head Soldier as if nothing of the kind had been spoken. An hour afterward Red Iron and his whole tribe were on the warpath. He made terrible work of it on the west side of the river. Men, women and children were mercilessly slaughtered and scalped. Twenty families, together numbering more than one hundred persons, were bleeding and mangled corpses before the sun went down that night. About the dawn of day the next morning they assaulted the block-house, but Captain Belfor held them at bay for over two hours, when they beat a retreat, and started with their bloody trophies toward the northwest, taking with them the few women and children who went on the hunt with them and thus escaped the Perkins massacre.

CHAPTER XIII.

TOTALLY DEPRAVED.

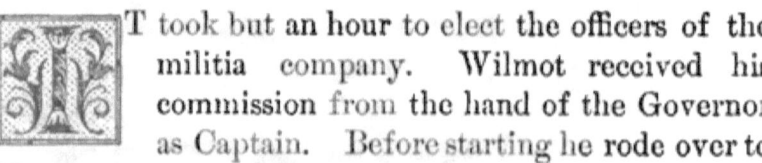

IT took but an hour to elect the officers of the militia company. Wilmot received his commission from the hand of the Governor as Captain. Before starting he rode over to Mr. Parkman's to bid them good-bye.

"I am glad you are going," said Miss Walker. "I hope you will kill every one of them."

"Do you want me to kill the women and children?" asked Wilmot.

"What is the use of their living?" she replied. "They will only raise more warriors to scalp white people. The sooner they are all dead the better."

"Those are very harsh sentiments for a young lady," said Wilmot, with considerable bitterness in his tone.

"If you had seen poor little children shot, who had never done them any harm, as I did in the stage-coach, you would not like Indians any better than I do."

"Did not an Indian save your life?"

"Suppose he did?"

"Do you want to see that Indian killed?"

"Yes, I do. I have no doubt that he was the one who tried to stab Mr. Parkman because he was taking me away."

"Do you want me to kill Meha?"

"She had better be dead than leading the life she is."

Mr. Wilmot was getting angry. He had no idea that the fair-haired girl whom he had held in his arms during that long and fearful ride would entertain, much less express, such sentiments. He replied:

"I don't think there is much difference in human nature, whether it be red or white. I suppose that is about the way the young Indian women talk to the warriors as they start on the war-path."

"Do you mean to compare me to a squaw?" she said, and her eyes flashed with indignation and rage.

Mr. Wilmot smiled. He was just as angry as she

was, but he was a trained lawyer, and did not allow his feelings to be reflected in his face.

"You should not apply a general remark to a particular case. I did not intend to speak offensively," he said. "You know it is natural for a man to philosophize."

"Well, if you aren't going to kill Indians what are you starting out on this expedition for?" she asked.

"I expect to engage in honorable war, not in slaughtering women and children. If you admire men who engage in that sort of thing, I advise you to make the acquaintance of that heroic gentleman, Captain Perkins."

Mr. Wilmot had risen to his feet, as he finished speaking he bowed and walked out of the room. He was, as he afterward expressed it, "mad all over." He had expected a very pleasant interview with Miss Walker. He thought that because of the timidity she had manifested in danger, that when she knew that he was going forth to fight the Indians, she would express fears for his safety, and in all probability would endeavor to persuade him not to go, and he had found her the very opposite of what he expected. He was interested in her. To tell the truth, he thought it was much more like what a woman ought to do, to faint away in his arms perfectly helpless, than to sit on a horse in perfect steadiness, and ride ten miles at a breakneck speed, like Mrs. Parkman, when a band of howling savages were after their scalps.

After Mr. Wilmot left, Miss Walker went to a window and sat looking out on the prairie for a long time. She thought she had been very ungrateful to Mr. Wilmot. He had saved her life, and yet the first time he had called on her afterward she had quarreled with him. She said to herself, "I am a coward. Every time I am in danger I faint away; and, like all cowards, when I am out of danger I am talking about killing people as if it amounted to nothing. Now Mrs. Parkman never talks that way, and when she is in danger she don't faint away. She is as brave and cool as a man. I am very, very sorry that I talked to Mr. Wilmot that way. He must think I am a dreadful creature." Then the tears began to trickle down her cheeks, and she resolved she would write a letter to him, and apologize. But how would he get it? He was going off into the Indian country, where there were no stage-coaches or post-offices. She would put it in the post-office at Council Bluffs, and write on the envelope, "Please forward." This was the letter:

"Dear Mr. Wilmot:

"I am afraid you will think I am worse than a savage. I am very sorry for the way I talked to you. I don't know what made me do it. I know I am very, very grateful to you for saving my life, and that you expressed only such sentiments as a brave man would. I don't know how to write to you about it, but when you come back I hope to see you, and then I will tell you. I do hope that you will not get hurt, and soon come back, so that I can apologize.

"Very truly,
"Jennie Walker."

Mr. Wilmot got his company across the river as soon as possible. He gave orders in a stern and severe tone. There was a clouded look on his face, and an irritable manner, which was entirely foreign to his usual habits. The officers and men thought how the elevation to office had affected him. No one would have believed—he would have denied it himself—that all this change had come over him because of words spoken to him by a young lady. Yet such was the case. He could not drive her out of his mind. As he rode up over the hills on the west side of the river he thought less of the Indians than he did of Jennie Walker.

Coming upon the ruins of burned cabins and the bodies of the dead soon drove all thoughts of her out of his mind. A hasty glance was all he gave to these, and pressed on to the relief of Captain Belfor. But the Indians had fled before he arrived there.

Soon after this Perkins called upon Miss Walker. He brought word from her father, who was a trader among the Indians far to the north. He had written to Jennie to come to Council Bluffs, and expected to meet her there in June; but he had got into a new speculation, and would not come down the river until the next year, when he would bring an immense quantity of furs. He sent a large check on a bank in New York to pay her expenses until he should come. Perkins offered to get the check cashed for her. She was about to employ him to do the business when she thought that Mr. Wilmot was a lawyer, and when he returned she could go to him with perfect propriety on business, and then would have an opportunity to speak to him. So she declined Mr. Perkins's offer, saying she had no need of money just at present, and would rather have the check.

"I am surprised," said Perkins, "to see you looking so fresh and rosy after the terrible sufferings you have endured among the Indians."

"Oh! I was treated in a splendid way by them. They were just as kind as they could be, and gave me the best they had."

"I suppose that the chief had promised you to some of his young men for a wife is the reason they treated you so well."

"No, I don't think so, for they seemed to think even more of Mrs. Parkman, and treated her just as kindly as they did me. Many of the women cried when we came away, and the chief offered us presents of horses. I think they are very nice, kind people when they are at peace."

"But they *will* go to war," said Perkins. "Every one of them lives in hopes of that all the time, and when they are making the greatest pretensions of friendship is the very time they are plotting murder. There was never an Indian who was not treacherous. What cause had they to assault the stage-coach?"

"I was told," replied Jennie, "that some white man was down there and cheated them gambling. I think that gambler was more responsible for the murder of the people in the stage-coach than the Indians were."

"That is one of their lies," said Perkins. "Nothing is more true than what one of our United States

Senators recently said, that they can outlie a minister plenipotentiary."

"If that is so, why do you blame Indians for doing the same thing that the minister of the great civilized states are proud of?"

"Yes, but when civilized nations make a treaty of peace, they don't go to plotting murder under cover of it."

"I heard Mr. Parkman say that General Harney swore before a committee at Washington that he never knew an Indian tribe to be the first to break a treaty," said Jennie, "and thought the wars were caused by bad white men."

"The officers at the post have been filling your head with nonsense," said Perkins. "They are a hard lot. The only titled aristocracy we have in this country. They have done more to demoralize and degrade the Indians than all other things put together. About half of them have Indian wives. Look at Lieutenant Blake."

Mrs. Parkman replied to this. "I know," said she, "that Captain Belfor and many other of the officers denounced Lieutenant Blake. They said that he would be denied social recognition by other officers wherever he went. They looked upon it as a disgrace to the army, and were greatly mortified."

"Well, the Indians are a dirty, degraded, treacherous, fiendish set of blood-thirsty savages, and no one who knows anything about them will say anything else," said Perkins.

"And the gamblers who cheat them, the agents

who rob them, and the cowards who kill their women and children are worse," said Jennie.

Both of them were getting somewhat warm over the subject, and Mrs. Parkman changed the conversation to a discussion of the weather. After Perkins had gone, Jennie said to herself, "Why couldn't I have talked that way to Mr. Wilmot? I suppose it is because I am totally depraved. Mr. Parkman says that everybody is totally depraved until they are converted, and I am sure I am, or I should never have acted so. I do hope he will come back soon. I'm sure I want him to think well of me."

Miss Walker had two admirers, and she had quarreled with both of them during their first call upon her.

However, it was only a day or two before Perkins called again. He drove up in a buggy, to which were attached a magnificent pair of bays, and asked her to take a ride. The day was beautiful, and Jennie went with him. Prairie roads are as smooth as a floor, and a carriage rolls along without a jar. As the horses sped away the bracing, pure air acted like a stimulant and soon put Jennie in the best of spirits. Perkins did his best to be entertaining and pleasant. He told her of his intimacy with her father, of their hunts and perils together, and dilated upon what a fine man he was. Then he talked of her mother, who had died when Jennie was a little girl. It was because of her mother's death that her father had come West. He could not remain where the old scenes constantly reminded him of her, and how for the last two years he had been longing to see his daughter. He knew, he said, that it was something far out of the common run of business that had kept him for another year in the fur regions of the north. But when he came he would be independently rich. Not a word was said about Indians, and when they returned after a two hours' drive, Perkins was satisfied he had made a very favorable impression upon her. From that time, Perkins was a frequent visitor at Mr. Parkman's, and the buggy rides in the afternoon were almost a daily occurrence. It became the common talk of the town that Perkins and Miss Walker were engaged.

One day Perkins informed Jennie that he was going away for a short time. He had got a contract to cut hay out at the new fort, on the Little Blue. He would be gone about two weeks. He tried in every way to get some expression of regret from her, concerning his proposed absence, but did not succeed.

The next day after Perkins left, Mr. Parkman was astonished to see Captain Jack walk in. "I've come," said he, "to bid you good-bye. I don't suppose you will ever see me agin. I've resigned my place as scout. I reckon a good many hard things will be said agin me when I am gone, but I wanted you and Mrs. Parkman to think well of me. I don't care about the rest. I can't stand this fighting old Red Iron. I've lived in his tent many a month, and he allers give me the best he had. There's no better man on earth than old Red Iron. I knowed his wife and children. When I heard that they had all been murdered, I just give up. Think of it! That old man hasn't a child nor a wife left, and he thought as much of them as any white man ever did. How much he used to play with Minnie-chuck. She was about twelve year old, and as good a girl as ever lived. I won't fight old Red Iron. I am going out to find him and I will stand by him to the end. The time is coming, of course, when he will have to give in, 'cause a few Injuns can't fight this Government more'n a year or two, and then he will need somebody who knows the ways of those white devils to help him."

"Did you see Mr. Wilmot?" asked Jennie.

"Yes, I seed him, and he looked sort of down-cast and heart-broken, not like himself at all. He was guarding a train through. He didn't say so, but I know he hain't got no heart in this war at all."

"You did not come all the way here to say good-bye to us," said Mrs. Parkman. "Now tell us, Jack, what else brought you here?"

"Well, I kind a thought it would be pleasant to have an interview with Perkins," said Jack, "so I could tell Red Iron that I had seen him, you know."

"Oh! Jack!" said Mrs. Parkman, who fully understood the meaning of Jack's significant sentence, but Jennie did not understand it at all.

"I am sorry," she said, "but Mr. Perkins went away yesterday. I know he would have been delighted to have met you, for I have heard him speak of you, and you both have been great Indian fighters."

"When did he fight Injuns?" asked Jack.

"Oh! up north, and he led the men who captured and destroyed a hostile Indian camp not long ago. He told me all about what a terrible fight they had. He was very sorry about Red Iron's band, but he had nothing to do with that, although some of the men in his company did."

"He told ye that, did he?" said Jack.

"Yes."

"And you believed it?"

"Certainly."

"He is the very man who murdered, in cold blood, Red Iron's helpless women and children."

"Oh, the monster!" said Jennie. "I will never speak to him again."

There were tears in Jack's eyes when he shook hands with them.

"I ain't going to fight agin my own color and flesh and blood," he said, "but I'm going to find Red Iron, and help him all I can," and he went away.

CHAPTER XIV.

TWENTY-FIVE THOUSAND DOLLARS.

RED IRON'S successful raid on the settlements brought about another great outcry against the military. Colonel Greene was denounced in the papers as utterly incompetent to manage the campaign, and a great pressure was brought to bear upon the President to remove him. Colonel Greene made no defense (regular army officers never do), against such assaults. He forwarded his regular official reports, which gave a truthful and minute account of what was transpiring. He was pushing forward the construction of the fort with all the force he had at hand, and making ready for a vigorous winter campaign, when Perkins arrived on the spot with his contract to cut several thousand tons of hay. The contract specified that the Government would reimburse him for all losses from the Indians. Perkins carried with him three or four old mowing-machines, all but one being totally worn-out and unfit for use. He had, perhaps, a dozen broken-down old horses, so poor, that it was a hard matter to get them through to the fort alive. With this outfit, he went about five miles from the fort and camped, where the tall grass was of the kind from which prairie hay is made. A few swaths were cut before sundown, and the men retired to their tents for the night. About midnight, Perkins arose, went out, fired several shots from his revolver, and cried at the top of his voice, "Injuns, Injuns." The men all ran away.

Perkins put in a claim for twenty-five thousand dollars for losses incurred by a raid from the Indians. It was rejected by the quartermaster, for it was positively proved—first, that he did not have over five hundred dollars' worth of property on the ground, and second, that no Indians had disturbed him, for not a sign of a trail could be found, except what the men had made themselves in going out and coming back. However, Perkins got a pile of affidavits, proving the raid and his heavy losses, and had a bill introduced in Congress for his relief. It was not many months before he had his money in his pocket, except what he had to divide with his associates in Washington and the affidavit-makers. He kept his promise to Miss Walker, and was back to Council Bluffs within two weeks.

CHAPTER XV.

JACK IN RED IRON'S CAMP.

JACK never had a sadder heart but once in his life than when he started on his chase after Red Iron. There was a firm friendship between these two men, cemented by many acts of kindness on both sides. Once, when Red Iron and a few men who were with him were assaulted by an overwhelming number of a tribe hostile to them, Jack had, by his unerring rifle, saved the party, and the old chief had tried to repay him by every means in his power. Jack started out prepared for a long journey. He had two pack-horses and one which he rode. The pack-horses were ladened with blankets, provisions and ammunition. He knew that Red Iron would try to unite his force with Badger's band, and he thought they must be somewhere on the Arickoree river. There the winters were mild and game was plenty. Twenty-one days after he left he came across signs of Indians, and the next day he rode into Red

Iron's camp. The meeting of these two men can scarcely be described. When he rode up to Red Iron's tent, the old chief came out and took his hand in silence. Then he motioned to Jack to come in. They sat down on a robe and smoked in silence for a long time. There were no women or children about the tent. At last Jack said:

"I have come to live with you always. I think I can help you if you will let me. You know that there is no man on these plains who is better with the rifle or revolver than I am. I want to be a member of your tribe. There may be a long war, but after a while it will come to a close somehow, and then you will need some one who will be able to help you with the whites. You and I have been friends in days which have passed, let us always be friends."

"You shall be my son," said Red Iron.

To become a member of a tribe the person must first be adopted into some family. All tribal government is founded on kinship.

Nothing more was said that day, but the next they talked for hours together. Red Iron told the story of the massacre, and then said:

"I wanted to live in peace with the whites. I know I cannot fight them. They out-number me a hundred to one. They have plenty of arms and ammunition. They have gold and silver. Of these I have none. They have driven us back from the great water to these plains, and thousands of them are going on by us to the great waters beyond. After a while they will take all this country, and there will be no place for us to go. I know we will soon have to change our mode of life. We will have to plow instead of hunt. I know that, but I can't make my people understand it. I would go in and make peace to-morrow if I could have a piece of land which was my own, and on which the white men would let us live in peace. I can carry on this war for a while; but if we kill the soldiers who are sent to fight, they will only send more. If we are killed, there are no more to take our places. I went once to Washington. I passed through a great many cities. I saw the white people. No man can number them. The men of my tribe cannot believe what I tell them. They seem to know nothing at all, and sometimes I think that I do not."

"Things are very bad," said Jack. "If we retreat much further, we will come into the country belonging to the Indians who have always been at war with you. As soon as the fort on the Little Blue is completed, and they have plenty of rations there, the soldiers will march against us. Then we must fight or surrender. The cavalry will scour all over this country. There will not be a stream on which you can camp that they will not march up and down. If the cavalry are not strong enough, they will halt and wait for the infantry and the field battery to come up. We can't fight infantry and artillery."

"I know all that," said Red Iron. "I knew it before I went into this war. I was forced into it. There seems to be no spot on all the earth where I can go and live in peace. There is no place anywhere in all this big earth for me and my people. We are all to be killed. There is but one thing we can do. We can die fighting, and not die like cowards. Then in the future, when they see our graves, they will at least say, 'these were brave men.'"

"Do you think that Badger and the others would make peace?" asked Jack.

"I don't know," said Red Iron; "they talk of nothing but war. We have about fifty men out, under a young chief, and he has been very successful in assaulting trains, and has captured a great many horses. He is young, and made very proud by his success. He has more influence than Badger. His name is Little Wolf. His head is turned. He thinks he can whip the whole white race. If he lives to be as old as I am, he will then see how foolish such thoughts are. I don't believe we could do anything with him. He will be for war until he gets badly defeated in some fight, and then he will be for peace. Two or three times he has come back with a herd of horses and a large amount of plunder. It is about time he was back again. I think as soon as he comes we had better call a general council, and talk over what we will do."

During the next four or five days Jack and Red Iron had several more long conversations, and it was their conclusion that the best thing to be done was to make a treaty of peace, if such terms could be got as the preservation of their lives, a piece of land which was to be theirs forever, and an agreement to learn the ways of the whites. This was a conclusion which was a secret between the two. Red Iron knew that it would meet with small favor, if openly advocated, in the present state of feeling in the tribe.

The days wore away one after another, and not one of Little Wolf's band returned. Nearly three weeks afterward, a haggard and foot-sore Indian came into camp. He said they had all been killed, and that he was the only one who had escaped. Then the relations of the dead sat down in their tents and commenced to wail.

An Indian's relations are much more to him than a white man's, for he has nothing else on which to set his affections. The white man has the world of art and literature, his business, a thousand things, to draw off his thoughts and assuage his grief. The Indian has nothing; so, male and female, they sit down and wail until they are perfectly exhausted. It is enough to drive a white man crazy to listen to them.

But the escaped Indian was mistaken, they were not all killed, for one by one they came into camp until more than half of them had returned, and among the number was Little Wolf himself. The story they told was as follows:

They were watching a large train, with which there were no soldiers. At a camping-place they undertook to stampede the stock, and partially succeeded in doing so. A great number of men, who were not soldiers, mounted other horses and made chase. They overtook them in the hills and timber of the Big Blue, and a terrible battle ensued, with victory on neither side. Then a large body of soldiers came upon them in the rear and surrounded them. They fought until night, and stole out as best they could and fled, every man for himself.

This disaster to Little Wolf greatly reduced his influence in the tribe. The relations of the dead warriors were very bitter against him.

Red Iron thought it a good time to hold a general council, and all the chiefs and head men, to the number of about twenty-five, assembled. After the usual formalities were gone through with, Red Iron spoke. He talked very fast, in a high key, and gesticulated with great energy.

His speech was full of the most bitter invective against the whites. He called them dogs, wolves, thieves, murderers, cowards and liars; related instances to illustrate each charge he made against them, and gave a picture of his camp when he came back from the hunt. He told how they were now building a fort in the heart of their country, in which they would harbor thousands of soldiers, to raid upon them and kill them. The country back to the great water was full of soldiers. They were heartless, and had no pity in them. This was the wily old chief's opening. It was made simply for effect, and it accomplished the purpose intended.

He knew there was a large party who would oppose anything he would suggest, and he wanted to get them to talking peace first, and then he would come over to their views. The stratagem succeeded better than he had hoped. Old Two Strike arose and addressed the chiefs. He thought they had whipped the whites already. He descanted upon the great victory of Badger over the soldiers who had followed them. They had killed nearly every one of them, and they had given up the chase. He thought they had gained a grand victory.

This stirred up the Head Soldier of Red Iron's band. He told how many scalps he had taken in one day, and had driven the whites clear out of the conntry. Every one who was not killed had fled across the river. He was certain the whites were eager for peace, and the only question was for them to decide whether they would grant them peace or not.

Little Wolf hadn't anything to say. He had done more fighting than any of them, but he was in disgrace on account of the loss of half of his warriors.

The council lasted for several hours and adjourned without any decision, to come together the next day. Meantime Red Iron had his emissaries to work, arguing that the whites were so anxious for peace that they might expect great concessions, perhaps big annuities, for many years to come. In this way a sentiment was worked up in favor of making peace, but they held councils for three days before it was finally decided that a delegation should be sent to ask for peace. Then there was a great contest about who should go on the delegation, and it took a good deal of sharp managing on the part of Red Iron to get it arranged so as to promise any hope of success. It was finally agreed that it should be composed of Red Iron, Badger, Two Strike, Little Wolf, and Red Iron's Head Soldier, White Hawk.

Jack agreed to go in first and arrange for a meeting with Colonel Greene, and then come back and take the delegation.

CHAPTER XVI.

TREATING WITH THE MILITARY.

THE nights were cold and frosty when the delegation started for the fort on the Little Blue. The greatest precautions were used to prevent surprise, as they might at any time meet with the cavalry, and be killed before any explanation could be made.

Jack left the delegation twenty miles from the fort, securely concealed in a thick growth of underbrush on a little stream, and went on alone. Arriving at the fort, he went directly to Colonel Greene's head-quarters and made a full report. It was slightly colored in favor of the Indians, but he could not well help that, for not only did he sympathize with them, but he was acting for them, and he was determined to get the best terms he could. He represented that there were a very large number of Indians well armed and supplied, and if the war went on could make a very vigorous resistance, which would cost the government many millions of dollars and thousands of lives, but now a peace could be made on very favorable terms.

Colonel Greene and the senior officers at the fort

were delighted with the result of their plans. A winter campaign in the fierce cold and storms of the plains was a prospect which was anything but pleasant. It had been Colonel Greene's idea that the establishment of this fort, heavily garrisoned, in the heart of the Indian country, would awe them into subjection, and now he saw it realized. He knew of the efforts which had been made to remove him from his command, and he smiled as he thought how utterly ridiculous those speculators and politicians would appear when they heard that all the hostile Indians had surrendered to him.

The fact was that Jack's expedition to Red Iron's camp was planned by Colonel Greene himself, and Jack resigned his position as scout and undertook the difficult task almost as much out of regard for Colonel Greene as for his friendship for Red Iron, knowing very well that if these two men could be brought together, a peace, honorable to both, would be the result. Yet he doubted very much whether the Indians would make peace so soon after the great outrages had been committed upon them, and it was understood by Colonel Greene, that if they would not, Jack would remain with his friend Red Iron.

Jack returned to the delegation with a safe conduct and brought them into the fort. Colonel Greene assigned them as pleasant quarters as was in the fort, and treated them as well as if they had been a delegation from a civilized power with which he had been at war. A day was given for them to rest, and then they assembled in council. There were present Colonel

Greene and his staff, Major Hodson, Captain Belfor, Mr. Wilmot and several other officers. Jack acted as interpreter. The chiefs were dressed in their most gorgeous Indian costumes, and the officers in full-dress uniform. An adjutant made a *verbatim* report of every word that was said, a thing that any expert long-hand writer can do, where everything has to be interpreted from one language into another.

Red Iron made a set speech. He told of his continued friendship for the whites; of his agreement with Major Hodson; the massacre of his women and children. "That man," said he, pointing to Major Hodson, "knows that I have spoken the truth." (Indians never speak of a person by name if they can possibly avoid it. They consider it very impolite to do so. The United States Senate has adopted this custom, and never address a senator by name.) He then claimed a large sum for damages for the outrages committed upon his people, and for the presents the Great Father had promised him, but which he had never received. When he sat down he asked Captain Belfor and Major Hodson to state if he had not told the truth. They both said he had given a correct account of the whole matter.

Colonel Greene then undertook to explain to him that he was a military officer. He had only authority in time of war. He could not negotiate about annuities or damages, that must be done by commissioners sent by the Great Father. He could only talk about war, and conditions of surrender.

Jack interpreted the speech with care, and then tried to explain to Red Iron our form of government.

He told him about the great council (Congress), the different departments at Washington, the Indian Bureau and the Secretary of Interior, and the Indians were more in the dark when he finished than before he began to talk. Red Iron replied:

"I can't understand this. I come here to make peace, if we can agree upon the terms. If you have no authority to make peace, I had better go back and wait until some one comes who has."

"I have authority," said Colonel Greene, "to make the conditions of surrender; and whatever conditions I make, the authorities at Washington are bound in honor to maintain. I have command of all the soldiers in this part of the country, and all the officers. They must obey every order I give. Whatever I agree to do will be done. Now, if you want to make peace and come in I will talk about that. I have no doubt that if you surrender Congress will give you a reservation and annuities. You can have schools, and learn to be like the white people, and become rich and powerful."

Red Iron took that as a positive promise that he should have a reservation and annuities, as every Indian would, and always has. They know nothing about hypothetical propositions. There seems to be no "ifs" in an Indian's thoughts. Then the other chiefs talked. One of them demanded a hundred boxes of gold ($100,000) as damages, another that the murderers of Red Iron's women and children should be turned over to them for punishment, another that the whites should vacate all the country west of the Missouri river, and the tone of the whole council was to the effect that they were the aggrieved parties, and had come to demand satisfaction. While they were respectful in their language, their bearing and tone was haughty and imperious.

Red Iron saw that it was time for an adjournment, and asked permission to retire and talk over the matter, and come back the next day.

During the interval he sought a private interview with Colonel Greene.

When he and Jack were alone together he spoke without any reserve whatever.

He said, "I know that I cannot fight the white people long, there are too many of them. I want to surrender and make peace if I can do so, and thereby save my people. I know we must learn to farm. What I want is some land I can call my own, which shall be mine forever, and annuities to live on for a few years until we can learn to farm. I want a pledge that none of the Indians who have been in this war shall be harmed if they surrender. If I can have these things I will submit. But if my men are to be killed for going to war, and I can have no place I can call my own, I will go back and fight until I die. I had better do that than die like a coward, or all of us become beggars among the whites."

Colonel Greene thought over the matter for some moments. He was in a very perplexing situation, as many other officers had been before him under the same circumstances. He knew he had no authority to make a promise of annuities or a reservation. That was not in the province of the War Department. If the authority was vested anywhere it was in the Interior Department. He certainly had authority, if this was war in which he was engaged, to make conditions of surrender. He could pledge them that they should be protected in their lives and he could hold them as prisoners of war until peace was declared. His pledge the Government was bound to keep. He finally said to Red Iron:

"If you will come in and surrender, I will promise that none of you shall be harmed. I have no doubt the Government will give you a reservation and annuities. This country is yours, and the Government can't take it away from you, without your consent, if you are at peace; but if you are at war it can take it by conquest. Therefore it is better for you to made peace as soon as you can. I will issue rations to all of your people who will come in, until the Great Father sends a commission to fix the details of the settlement. They will say how much annuities you shall have and where your reservation shall be. You had better come in and surrender. It is the best thing you can do."

The following was said to Jack in the Indian language, and of course Colonel Greene could not understand it.

"Is this man my friend?"

"Yes, I think he is," said Jack.

"Tell him that it is very hard for me to surrender, without knowing what is to become of me afterward, but I am helpless and cannot do otherwise. I want to save the few who remain of my people. I put all our lives into his hands, Badger's band and all the others who are with me on the Arickoree. He has pledged me that their lives shall be saved. I have nothing but his word. To him I give the lives of the men, the women and the little children. He will see that they are not killed by the bad white men. Ask him if he will do this?"

This was interpreted to Colonel Greene. He replied:

"Tell him, I pledge him my word, upon the honor of a man and a soldier, that not even a hair of their heads shall be harmed."

This ended the private council, and the next day, at the formal one, it was agreed that the Indians would come in, surrender their arms and their horses, and receive rations until they should be provided for by a commission from Washington.

In accordance with this agreement the Indians came to the fort and surrendered their arms and their ponies. An Indian without arms or a pony is perfectly helpless. He cannot hunt or go to war, and is absolutely at the mercy of the Government.

It was with many misgivings that Red Iron did it. He had risked all on the word of one white man, Colonel Greene. He would not have done it if there had been any other course open to him. War would only result in extermination, and this was a chance, if only a chance, for life.

CHAPTER XVII.

CONGRESSMEN ON A SPREE.

IT was mid-winter when Mr. Wilmot returned to Council Bluffs and took his seat in his office. He never received Jennie Walker's letter, for Perkins had been intrusted with the mail that was forwarded to the fort on the Little Blue, when he went out to cut hay. He noticed it among the dozen others which were committed to his charge, and opened it. Then he tore it in a thousand fragments, and scattered them to the winds. Jennie had kept her check as long as she could, so as to have an excuse to call upon Mr. Wilmot when he returned, but his long absence made it necessary for her to have it cashed before his return. Mr. Wilmot did not call upon her. He heard the current stories of her engagement to Perkins, and in every way avoided meeting her. Although residing in the same little town together they never met. She saw him once at church but he did not seem to see her. She went to several parties, against the wishes of Mr. Parkman, in hope that she might meet him, but Mr. Wilmot was not there. Mr. Wilmot stayed in his office. He was never seen in the saloons or hotels, and seemed to have no acquaintances, except in the way of business. Perkins called upon her frequently; she felt bound to treat him with politeness on account of his relations with her father. She declined his invitations to ride, and to parties and balls. The parties and balls were interdicted by Mr. Parkman, the Methodists holding them to be exceedingly sinful. She gave her time to religious work, attending all the meetings held by Mr. Parkman, and as she had a beautiful soprano voice, aided much in the singing.

Life in a frontier town is exceedingly monotonous. There are no theaters, no lectures, no libraries, no newspapers, except the weekly local paper, which can be read through in fifteen minutes.

Only once was there any stir in the town during the long winter. It was when a committee of Senators and Congressmen arrived, during the holiday recess, to investigate the recent troubles. Their arrival was announced two or three days in advance, and the Causeland House was put in the best order possible. They sent an order for dinner for fifteen, and the proprietor, who was a poor man, went to a great expense to prepare for their reception and entertainment. When that august body came, they went directly across the river, and did not stop at the Causeland House at all, nor in any way offer to reimburse him for his loss. An escort was waiting for them, and they went directly to the fort on the Little Blue.

They arrived there late at night, and the next morning walked around and looked at the defenses. About ten o'clock they went into the council room. Only two chiefs were there, Two Strike and Little Wolf. The other chiefs had not been notified in time to get there.

The following conversation took place:

Senator.—You have recently been on the war-path, haven't you?

Two Strike.—There was trouble between the Indians and the whites last fall, but it has all been settled, and we have made peace.

Senator.—Do the military officers treat you well?

Two Strike.—Yes. We have no complaints to make.

Senator.—Have you anything you desire to say to us?

Two Strike.—We have a great deal we want to say, but the other chiefs are not here, and we wish to wait until they come.

Senator.—We are in a great hurry. We leave to return to Washington at one o'clock. If you have anything to say you must say it now.

Two Strike.—I cannot speak for the other bands. Their chiefs must speak for them. It seems to me that it will take a long time to settle all these matters. It cannot be done in an hour.

Senator (to interpreter).—Ask the other Indian if he has anything to say.

Interpreter.—He says he has nothing to say before the other chiefs come.

Senator (to interpreter).—Say to them that we will excuse them for the present. We want to consult together about what is best to be done for them.

The interpreter and the chiefs walked out and the committee was left alone.

"It is very evident," said Senator L., "that they

have no idea about what they want. They are like little children, and we must do the best we can."

"It is a waste of time," said Representative H., "to talk with them. We must exercise our own judgment about what is good for them. There is a gentleman here who is perfectly familiar with the whole matter, and I think we would save time by asking him to come in and give us his opinion."

No objection was made, and soon after Representative H. walked in with Perkins. "This gentleman," said he, "has been here during all the war, knows all about it, and knows Indians thoroughly. Besides, he is a lifelong friend of the Indians, and his opinion should have great weight."

"We would be glad to hear anything you have to suggest," said Senator L.

"I am glad," replied Perkins, "to have an opportunity to say something in behalf of these poor people. If they were treated with kindness we would never have the least trouble with them. An Indian is naturally very independent and desires freedom of action. The strictness of military rule is very irritating to them, and the consequence is, that every once in awhile they break out into open war, hoping thereby to better their condition. There are as fine men among them as can be found among any race. Some of them I have known for years, and there is a cordial friendship between us. They have been hunted by the military like wolves, and no mercy has been shown them. Those who are here are very poor, and every consecration of justice and humanity demands that they should have a liberal provision made for them by Congress. I should suggest that they be divided into two tribes of about equal numbers, and each given a reservation, one on the Arickaree and the other on the Baha Taya. They should have annuities granted them of not less than a hundred thousand dollars a year for five years, and gradually reduced after that. The annuities should run for at least thirty years, until a new generation grows up who can be made capable of taking care of themselves. My heart aches for these Indians. When I first knew them they were rich and prosperous. Now they have been robbed of everything they had by the military and are in a desperate condition. A liberal provision for these Indians, I am sure, would meet with the approval of the whole country. I have written several letters to different religious papers in the East, describing their terrible condition, and I am sure that all the great religious bodies will greet such action by Congress with their hearty approval. I have thought of going East and speaking in their behalf, in order to excite some public interest and thus influence Congress to grant large appropriations. I am sorry you have not time to go with me into their camp, so I could show you the utter destitution existing there. It is a disgrace to the nation, which has taken from them their lands and deprived them of their natural means of living. Whatever Congress may do, it will not be a gratuity, for if we should pay them for the lands we have taken from them, it would amount to a great deal more than what I have asked in their behalf. I hope you will not recommend less than a hundred thousand dollars to each of the bands. That is simple justice. Anything less would be robbing them of what is actually due them."

After hearing this plea for the Indians the committee adjourned to hold their next session in Council Bluffs.

Arriving at Council Bluffs, they went to the Empire House, upon the invitation of Perkins and his associates, where he desired them to consider themselves his guests. Their entertainment there cost the contractors two thousand dollars, but they counted the money well invested. The most costly wines and cigars had been brought up from St. Louis. Toasts were proposed, speeches were made, and they held high carnival until long after midnight. The arrangements were perfect, and nothing occurred, in the least, to mar the enjoyment of the occasion. But Perkins made one mistake. He forgot the editor of the *Weekly Pioneer*, until ten o'clock in the evening, and when he sent for him, he was so angry, he would not come. The consequence was, that the next paper contained a minute account of this drunken carousal. It gave samples of speeches made by the honorable gentlemen after the wine had driven all sense of the fitness of things out of their heads, and a comical account of how one representative was carried to bed up a very narrow pair of stairs. They did not seem to be in nearly as great a hurry to get back to Washington as when they were at the fort, for they stayed two days in Council Bluffs.

CHAPTER XVIII.

A PEACE COMMISSION.

PERKINS'S letters to the religious press had the desired effect, and soon after a "peace commission" came out, composed of men "eminent for their philanthropy." These gentlemen, for the most part, were honest, upright and benevolent. They came at the request of charitably disposed associations and churches, and had no other desire than to defend the Indians against the oppressions of the whites, introduce schools and spread the Christian religion among them. They were without experience, and knew nothing practically of either Indians or contractors. This was true of five of the seven commissioners. The other two were in good standing in the churches to which they belonged, but one was a contractor for Indian supplies, the said contracts having been taken under a fictitious name, and the other one had come, not for any love for the Indian, or any benevolent purpose whatever, but because he owned a large amount of wild lands, and he would have an opportunity to see the country and look out for his own private interests. Mr. Wilmot had paid his taxes and done his business for him, so he called to talk over matters with him. Commissioner Hughs, having no real interest in the Indian question, one way or the other, listened to what Mr. Wilmot had to say on that subject, and replied that he would introduce him to Commissioner Clark, who was president of the board, and had the civilization and christianizing of the Indians greatly at heart. This led to an invitation to explain his views to the full board, and a meeting was called for that purpose. When they were assembled, Mr. Wilmot said:

"Your object, I understand to be, to protect the Indians from the encroachments of the whites, to establish schools and propagate the Christian religion. Upon the subjects of school teaching and preaching the gospel, I would be a poor counselor. I would refer those matters to men who have had experience in educational affairs, and to the clergy. It seems very evident to me that not much can be accomplished in either direction until some form of government is established among them, with sufficient power to enforce its decrees. As far as I have been able to look into history, I do not find a single instance where any advancement from the primitive condition of man has been made until some form of government has been established.

"When Moses undertook to lead the children of Israel from a state of bondage, to a condition in advance of that, the first thing he did was to give them a code of law suited to the conditions which surrounded them.

"These Indians could live far separated from the whites, under laws of their own, regulating matters concerning only themselves. That is no longer possible. Laws must now affect both them and their relations to the whites who surround them. There is constant intercourse, and it must increase year by year. There should be laws under which all disputes or disagreements between them and the white settlers could be adjudicated."

"I have often said," remarked Mr. Clark, "that there should be a simple code of laws applicable to their present condition."

"I do not know," said Mr. Wilmot, "what you mean by 'a simple code of laws, applicable to their condition.' All law is enacted and enforced for the purpose of protecting the life, liberty and property of the individual. Law is for the benefit and protection of the weak against the strong. The weaker and more ignorant the person is, the more careful have the enactments been in his favor. The minor and the imbecile are more carefully protected by law than those of full age and strong mind. The law will annul and set aside a contract made by a minor, in which he has been cheated, but will not do it with one of full age and strong mind, unless fraud is proved."

"I don't see what all that has to do with Indians," said Commissioner Smith.

"It has this to do with it," replied Wilmot. "You want to civilize and christianize the Indians. You cannot build that superstructure upon any other foundation than written law. The law preceded the Gospel, not, I fancy, by accident, but by infinite wisdom. Without the law of the Old Testament there would have never been the Christianity of the New Testament. I read a story somewhere about a man who built a house upon the quicksand, and the first rain that came washed away the sand, and down went the house. You go out here and build a school-house and a church among the Indians. Soon there is a dispute between some of the Indians and the whites. There is no tribunal before which it can be tried. Both sides resort to force. Then we have war, and that is the last of teacher or school-house, and of the preacher and the church. I I wish I could remember where I read that story about the house built on the sand. It is a perfect illustration of this whole business."

There was a broad smile on the faces of the commissioners, and Wilmot wondered what amused them.

"I may not make myself understood," said Wilmot, "but the whole subject seems very plain to me. For many thousand years the best minds of every race and every generation have been thinking out a system of law for the government of men. We have divided it into civil and criminal, statutory and common law. Underlying it all are the great principles of equity, first recorded by Moses. It is scarcely possible for a crime to be committed or a dispute to arise, but that we shall find in this law, either enacted in form, or applied by some learned and just judge, a true principle for its just punishment or adjudication. It is applicable to every possible phase of human existence. Its enforcement among any people will render life and property safe, punish crime, make regular and orderly habits, stimulate thought, promote industry, make sacred the family relation, and this, if it is not civilization, is the beginning of civilization. On such a foundation you can build your superstructure of schools, colleges, churches, eleemosynary institutions, and from it springs the arts and sciences. Without law you have chaos. The weak are trampled down by the strong, and might alone makes right."

Mr. Parkman was a deeply-interested listener. To some of these ideas he fully subscribed, but after all it did seem as though there was something not quite right about it. He said:

"I agree with some things which Mr. Wilmot said, but I cannot agree to others. He seems to argue that law must precede Christianity. I think that Christianity must precede law. No race of men have ever been civilized until the Gospel has been preached among them. A thousand years ago our ancestors were wilder and more savage than the Indian of to-day. Paul first preached the gospel to them, and as Christianity spread among them they adopted just laws."

"The Romans were there with their laws first," said Wilmot.

"I must ask again," said Commissioner Smith, "what all this has to do with the Indians?"

"I think that the whole problem could be solved," said Wilmot, "by extending over them the jurisdiction of our courts."

"I know one band, at least," said Mr. Parkman, "who are very anxious to have missionaries and teachers sent to them. I think, if their wishes in that regard were complied with, in a few years you would find them a self-supporting and Christian community."

"I think you would still have a band of paupers.

That thing has been tried now for a hundred years, and the mass of Indians to-day are just where they were then. Give them legal security for life and property, and thus stimulate enterprise and industry, if you want them ever to become self-supporting."

"I think," said Mr. Clark, the *sub rosa* contractor and president of the board, "that our business is with things as they exist. These Indians, at present, if put on a reservation, cannot be self-supporting. The government should take a paternal charge of them, and supply them until such time as they may be able to take care of themselves. For these reasons, large appropriations should be made for them."

"That will be the ruination of them," said Wilmot. "There can be no development without exertion, and there will be no exertion as long as they are supported by appropriations made by the general Government. If you want to ruin any set of men, just place them by themselves, clothe and feed them, and give them nothing to do."

"There is nothing to hinder them from working if they want to," said Mr. Clark.

"I never heard of any set of men 'wanting' to work," said Wilmot. "Men work because necessity drives them to it, and when the necessity ceases the work always stops. Look at the sons of our millionaires. Do they work?"

"I don't see at all what this has to do with Indians," said Mr. Smith.

"And how soon do the sons of the rich become profligate," continued Wilmot, without noticing the remark of the commissioner, "and waste the accumulations of their fathers. Necessity forces men to labor, and labor develops them. When you provide for existence without work, you plan for the lowest possible grade of existence."

"Mr. Wilmot," said Mr. Smith, "if you have any suggestions to make I would be pleased to listen, but I cannot see what this kind of talk has to do with Indians."

"I have nothing further to say," replied Mr. Wilmot, and he immediately left the room.

That night, as the commission were holding a private session in a room of the Causeland House, a knock was heard on the door.

"Come in," said Commissioner Clark.

The door opened and Perkins walked in.

Mr. Clark, who seemed to be an old acquaintance, introduced him to the other commissioners.

"This gentleman," said he, "is the author of the letters making such eloquent pleas in behalf of these poor Indians. If it had not been for the unselfish interest which he has manifested, they would have been allowed to perish of cold and hunger."

Then, addressing Perkins, he said:

"I am delighted to meet you. I am sure my associates will give great weight to any suggestions you make."

"I hope," said Mr. Smith, "that this gentleman may have something to say about Indians. The last one introduced by you wanted to talk about everything else except Indians."

"I fancy you will find Mr. Perkins a different sort of man from that lawyer," said Mr. Clark.

"What lawyer?" asked Perkins.

"Mr. Wilmot."

A look of utter disgust came over Perkins's face.

"Do you know him? What kind of a man is he?" asked Mr. Hughs.

"Oh, he is a shrewd, sharp lawyer," said Perkins, "and is trying to work up a case, and pocket a fee."

"Just what I thought," said Mr. Smith.

"The war," said Perkins, "was perhaps necessary to teach the Indians the power of the government, but the extreme cruelty practiced by the military was wholly unnecessary. Now that they are subjected and docile, it is eminently proper that mild influences be used. The military have robbed them of everything. If they are not fed they will die of starvation. It is inhuman cruelty to leave them to take care of themselves, as has been suggested by some who think the whole race should be exterminated. If that is the object, let them form them in line and shoot them dead, but not sentence them to the slow torture of starvation. There is a very large number of Indians at the fort on the Little Blue. Congress should appropriate not less than two hundred thousand dollars a year for them. With such an amount churches and schools could be erected, agricultural implements purchased, and the industries of civilized life introduced among them."

"There, that is something practical, something

humane," said **Mr.** Smith. "I am very glad you have come in."

"But two hundred thousand dollars a year is a very large **sum**," said **Mr.** Hughs.

"It **is** much cheaper than **war**," said Perkins. "This campaign has already cost over seven hundred thousand dollars."

"That is very true," said Mr. Clark. "It is much cheaper to feed, clothe, educate and christianize **the Indians** than to fight them. I—"

Here another knock on the door interrupted them. A servant entered and handed Mr. Clark a hugh envelope. He opened it, and after glancing at the contents, said :

"This is from the President, authorizing this commission to proceed to the Little Blue and make treaties with all the bands of **Indians** now there, or who may assemble there before we return."

Some of the commissioners **did** not seem pleased **with** this announcement, but it was very evident that Perkins and Mr. Clark were delighted. Shortly after, the commission adjourned until the next day. Perkins remained with **Mr.** Clark after the others had **retired**.

"Things are working splendid," said Perkins.

"Yes, better than I expected. I did not look **for** this for four or five days yet," said Mr. Clark.

"If you can get out there, make the treaties and **have** them confirmed before Congress adjourns, two years from now **we** will all be well heeled. But are you certain about this commission? Hughs, Smith and yourself **are all** right. You have got to have one more on whom you can rely. It takes four to make a majority."

"I have been troubled about it, but I could not get it made up any other way. There is Borden. He is very conscientious, religious and tender-hearted. You struck the right theme in what you said to-night. I saw the tears come into his eyes when you were talking about the Indians starving. You keep that up and he will be all right for big appropriations. Wilmot made sure of Smith. Smith is an old blue-stocking, and when he was talking about giving the administration of the law precedence over preaching, Smith set him down for a regular heretic. He's down on Wilmot, and when he once gets set, he's there while time lasts."

"I am more afraid of Wilmot than any man in this country," said Perkins, "and I have been thinking that we had better take him in. There is not much paying law business in this part of the country, and I think a moderate-sized slice would satisfy him. He's as sharp as lightning, and I don't want him to be fighting us. I'll tell you why I think he would accept. When the trouble first commenced he was terribly opposed to the war, but when he was commissioned as captain of a company, he accepted and fought like a tiger. It was him who gave Little Wolf such an awful thrashing. The military were all afraid of Little Wolf, but when Wilmot got after him, he made short work of it. If that Injun hadn't got whipped they would have been fighting yet."

"I don't know about that," said Mr. Clark. "Are

7*

you sure he would come in if we gave him something pretty nice?"

"Of course he would. Every man has his price."

"He would have to be approached very carefully," replied Mr. Clark. "I'll feel of him a little, to-morrow, and see how he takes it."

"Hadn't you better get out to the Little Blue as soon as possible?" asked Perkins.

"No, that would be the worst thing in the world. You see we don't want too much time out there, for complications might arise. Now, there are two or three men on the commission who have very large business interests on their hands, and must necessarily soon return East. If we can manage to keep them here for a week, they can't possibly stay there more than a day or two, and that is as long as it is safe."

"I'll give in to you for management every time," said Perkins with a laugh, and the two men separated.

CHAPTER XIX.

A GUARDED APPROACH.

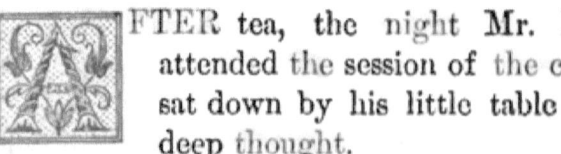AFTER tea, the night Mr. Parkman had attended the session of the commission, he sat down by his little table and fell into deep thought.

"A penny for your thoughts," said Mrs. Parkman.

"I was thinking of what Mr. Wilmot said to-day," and then he told her of the discussion, and how he did not seem able to answer the argument which Mr. Wilmot made. "I know," said Mr. Parkman, "that men are only regenerated, saved and elevated by the Gospel. I know that in towns where the Gospel is not preached and no public worship is held, that in a short time the whole population becomes depraved. Now, there is the town of Riverton. Last week some of the greatest sinners in the place came to me and asked that regular preaching be established there, for, they said, that the place was becoming so desperately wicked that some of the best citizens threatened to leave. There is no murdering or stealing there, or anything the law can take hold of, but the men are drunken, the little children on the streets are shockingly profane, the young of both sexes are losing all virtue and sense of modesty. Now, the law won't save a place like that, and I know it. Yet Mr. Wilmot insists that all there is good in the world grows out of the enactment and enforcement of good laws. There is something wrong about his argument."

"I think," said Mrs. Parkman, "that you forgot that your professions lead you into entirely different spheres of thought, and that both of you may be right. Law protects life and property and preserves liberty. This brings material welfare to men, and makes it possible to densely populate the world. It pertains entirely to creature comforts. It does not of necessity bring peace and happiness. A man may be eminent in science and art, and of the profoundest scholarship, have all of what we call civilization, and yet be more miserable than the untutored savage. You may take the savage, build him a palace, give him gold and silver, the finest raiment, and surround him with all the luxuries of civilization, and yet he is a savage still. If he is blood-thirsty and cruel, you may add to that a finished education, and you have simply made him more powerful to do wrong. There is something to be done *in* the man, which cannot be effected by outward circumstances—something that law cannot do. His desires and aspirations must be changed. Revenge and cruelty must give place to love and peace. Law cannot accomplish this. Your field of labor lies in this direction. Mr. Wilmot's in securing to them life, liberty and property."

"I will tell him that the next time I meet him," said Mr. Parkman.

"Why not invite him over here to tea some evening?" asked Mrs. Parkman.

"I wish you would," said Jennie Walker, "I do so like to hear such discussions."

The next day Mr. Parkman went into Wilmot's office to extend the invitation to him, and found Commissioner Clark there, and it was arranged that they should both spend the evening with Mr. Parkman. He stayed only a moment, for Wilmot was just starting to the court-room to argue a case, and could not wait.

Jennie's quick ears heard Mr. Parkman's announcement to his wife of the coming of Mr. Clark and Wilmot, and her heart bounded up in her throat.

To a woman who has a musical taste, it is as natural

to sing when she is happy as for a bird, and all that afternoon, every few moments she sang scraps of songs or hymns, as she made preparation for the expected guests.

After tea was over, Mr. Clark said:

"I called upon Mr. Wilmot to-day to have a talk with him privately, for I was very much impressed with what he said to the commission."

"So was I," said Mr. Parkman, "although I did not entirely agree with him. I have since thought over the matter, and I want to explain my views to him."

Then Mr. Parkman repeated what his wife had said.

"I guess you are entirely right," replied Wilmot. "I said in the beginning I would be a poor counselor in regard to those matters, and referred them to the clergy."

There was evidently to be no discussion of those points, and Mr. Clark thought it a very favorable time to sound him on the point in which he was interested. This is the way he "approached" him.

"I understand," said he, "that you rather outfought the regular soldiers during the late war."

"That is a mistake," said Wilmot; "I don't see who could have been so foolish as to have so informed you."

"Why, I was informed that you were the officer who finally defeated Little Wolf."

"My company had a skirmish with that chief, but we would have accomplished nothing had not Major Hodson come upon them in the rear with two companies of cavalry. My part was a very small one in the late war, and I am glad that it was. There is nothing to be proud of on our side."

Mr. Clark saw he was on the wrong track. Wilmot did not seem to appreciate compliments, so he "approached" from another direction, and said:

"If these Indians make a treaty with the Government, and agree to go upon reservations, the control of them must be put into the hands of agents. My experience has taught me that it is very hard to find men having the necessary qualifications, who are willing to accept of such positions. To be a successful agent, a man must possess great executive ability, have a good knowledge of commercial affairs—for large amounts of goods of various kinds must be handled and inspected by him. He must understand farming, superintendence of schools, have mechanical knowledge sufficient to direct their rude efforts at building themselves permanent habitations; he must oversee the building and running of saw-mills, flouring mills, blacksmith shops, carpenter shops, and the introduction of various other industries among them. He must be a man of the purest morals, and have the power to command men; establish laws and regulations for the formation of society; and be a mild and firm judge, for to him must be referred all the disputes which may occur among a large number of people. Of course any man who may be selected will fail in some of these departments; but if he is honest, energetic and intelligent he will succeed in most. The country will soon settle up around them, and a new state will be formed in a few years. The man who can take these Indians, and make of them a prosperous and self-supporting community, will do a great service to his country and to humanity."

"I don't know where you could find a man who possesses the qualifications you have enumerated," said Wilmot.

"I do not expect to find one possessing them all, but I hope to find one possessing most of them."

"It would take a George Washington, Alexander Hamilton and Judge Marshall combined," said Wilmot.

Mr. Clark laughed, and Mrs. Parkman said:

"There is one other qualification, and the most important of all, which you have not enumerated. He should be a thoroughly religious man."

"And there is another," said Jennie. "He should understand the Indian language."

"A man who would undertake to perform such duties, with any expectation of succeeding, would have to possess an unlimited amount of self-confidence," said Wilmot.

"Some one *must* undertake it," replied Mr. Clark, "and he who does so, is engaged in a noble work. It is not for himself he labors. It is to help others who cannot help themselves."

A sudden seriousness came into the face of Mr. Wilmot. Mr. Clark had found the right line of "approach" to his man. I do not know that there has been another man in these modern times like Wilmot. Through all his life there were never more than one or two persons who understood him. Unselfishness is a good trait, but an abnormal development of it produces a character, which, to the world at large, is an enigma. Mr. Wilmot was not a minister, but a lawyer, and yet, the only real enjoyment he ever had in life, was when he was helping others. He never could lay plans to help himself. He never could become interested in anything which pertained to himself. He would work for a client with untiring energy, and while the contest went on he was happy. When he did not have some one to help, he sunk into chronic melancholy, and only came out of it when some new opportunity to aid somebody else presented itself. Another trait of his character was abnormally developed, and that was sensitiveness. But this was only in one direction. He would go into an election and work for a candidate whom he took a fancy to help, with an energy that never ceased, until the last vote was counted. If harsh things were said about him, if he was charged with all manner of crimes, it did not affect him in the least. In fact, he rather enjoyed it. But let some one whom he considered his friend say one harsh word, and Wilmot was wounded to his very heart's core, and he would suffer the most intense agony for days. Most of those whom he had aided turned against him. While this caused him the most intense suffering, he was just as anxious the next day to help somebody else, or if one of them should come to him again, he was just as ready to assist as he was the first time. If one did seem to appreciate his kindness, the slightest expression of it put him into a state of perfect bliss. He always denied, and honestly too, that he deserved any credit for the assistance he rendered others. He said he did it because he would feel bad if he didn't, whereas the man whom it made to feel bad to do it, and, notwithstanding that fact, did help others who needed aid, ought to have great credit for doing so. He deserved no praise for saving Jennie Walker, for if he had not, he would have abandoned himself to a fate a hundred times worse than death, for existence would have been a continued agony ever afterward. Of course, everything a man like this did was misrepresented. If he devoted his time, money and energies to building a church, for the purpose of helping some poor preacher, or feeble congregation, it was said he was trying to get political influence with that denomination. If he supported a man for office, it was agreed that the spoils should be divided. The consequence was, that although it was conceded he was a talented man, he was about as unpopular with the general public as a man could be. He went away from Mr. Parkman's absorbed with the subject of helping these Indians. He thought over all the men he knew, in the endeavor to select some one competent to undertake the charge of them.

The next day Mr. Clark called at his office and proposed that he should accept the appointment. The offer was a perfect surprise to Wilmot. At first he absolutely refused, then agreed to take the matter into consideration, and finally, before the commission left, consented to take it if it was offered to him.

In conveying the information to Perkins, Mr. Clark said: "I am not entirely satisfied about Wilmot. It is one of three things with him. He is either entirely unsophisticated in these matters, or he intends to get on the inside and beat us, or he wants more than we can give him. That fellow is shrewd and deep, now, I tell you."

"He'll want something pretty nice, I expect," said Perkins, "but if we get these appropriations through we can afford to give it to him. Whatever happens, I don't want to fight him. It is a good deal cheaper to give him something."

CHAPTER XX.

MILITARY MEDDLERS.

THE commission remained in Council Bluffs six days before they could get away. Great delay was caused in securing transportation, and when they were finally ready to go and drove to the river, they found that the ferry-boat was disabled, and could not be used for a whole day. At last they arrived at the fort, were assigned quarters, and the Indians were informed of their presence and the chiefs invited to come in.

The council opened with a statement from Mr. Clark, and a letter of the President, appointing the commission and defining its powers, was read and interpreted to them by Jack. Just as Jack finished, a messenger handed Mr. Clark a letter. He seemed to be somewhat disturbed by it, and spoke to Mr. Smith and Mr. Hughes. Then Mr. Clark arose and said that the commission, before further proceedings were had, desired to consult together, and they retired to another room. All were anxious to know the contents, and crowded around Mr. Clark, who held the letter in his hands.

"I will read it," said Mr. Clark.

"My Dear Mr. Clark:

"I understand that parties who are opposed to granting annuities to these Indians, have had several interviews with Captain Jack, and made arrangements through the military to have him act as interpreter. He has considerable influence with the Indians and would be very unreliable in that capacity. I would recommend for that place Shonnee, an Indian, and not a white man. He belongs to Two Strike's band. They should certainly be allowed to have one of their own race to act for them in a matter which is of so much importance to them. Yours truly,

"H. L. Perkins."

"That seems only just," said Mr. Borden. "White men who live with the Indians are never to be trusted. I am in favor of sending for this Indian to act as interpreter."

"I hope he is near at hand," said Mr. Hilliard. "For positively I can't stay here after to-morrow. I must be back to attend the directors' meeting of my company."

The commission returned to the room, and inquiry

was made for Shonnee. In a few minutes he came in.

"Do you speak English?" asked Mr. Clark.

"Yes," he replied.

"Are you a full-blooded Indian?"

"Yes."

"What tribe do you belong to?"

"Two Strike's tribe."

"Are you willing to act as interpreter to this commission?"

"How much pay?" asked Shonnee.

"We will give you three dollars a day."

"I will talk English a heap," said Shonnee.

There was an animated conversation going on between Jack and Red Iron in the Indian language, and presently Red Iron arose to address the commission and Jack stood up by his side to interpret.

"We have dispensed with your services," said Mr. Clark to Jack. "If the chief desires to speak Shonnee will interpret."

Jack's eyes began to flash fire. He unconsciously shifted his revolver belt around. Red Iron spoke a few words.

"He says," said Jack, "that I am his friend and he wants me to interpret for him."

"Did he say that?" asked Mr. Clark of Shonnee.

"He say Jack heap bad," said Shonnee.

"You're a liar!" said Jack, and he jerked out his revolver, but Red Iron struck his hand up and the ball went into the ceiling. In a second more the strong arms of Red Iron were clasped around Jack and his pinioned to his side. The two guards who were on duty took away his pistols and he was led off to the guard-house, and Mr. Clark's interpreter had the floor.

"What a desperado that fellow is," said Mr. Borden. "It is lucky you got that letter from Mr. Perkins, or we might have been led into another war through him."

No more counciling was done that day.

Jack had not been in the guard-house half an hour when Colonel Greene called in person. Jack sat on a bench in moody silence.

"Why, Jack," said the Colonel, "I am surprised. What have you been doing?"

"Making a fool of myself," said Jack. "Red Iron has got more sense now than I have."

"I know all about it," said Colonel Greene. "You did act foolishly, but you mustn't stay in here. This will never do."

"How am I to get out, I would like to know?"

"I'll issue an order for your discharge, providing you will give me your word to keep the peace toward Shonnee, Perkins and the commissioners."

"Good Heavens! is Perkins here?"

"Yes, he came last night."

"That accounts for the whole business."

"Well, will you keep the peace?"

"I reckon I'll have to. They took my shooting-irons away."

"That is rather indefinite. Will you keep the peace?"

"Now see here, Colonel, that's being pretty hard on

a feller. I'd swore to shoot Perkins on sight. He's the worst devil on earth," and Jack scratched his head and shifted himself around.

"You don't want to stay here, do you?" asked the Colonel.

"Can't say that I do."

"Well, if you will give me your word that you won't do any shooting at Perkins, Shonnee or the commissioners, you may go out."

"Every cussed one of 'em ought to be killed, and you know it; but I reckon I'll have to promise, providing they don't shoot first."

The door was opened and Jack walked out.

Both Perkins and Mr. Clark were very much enraged when they learned that Jack was at liberty; but when Perkins found out the conditions of his release he was somewhat easier in his mind.

Jack went straight to Badger's camp, and there he found out that Perkins had had Shonnee with him all night at the fort, where he had given him a rifle, four or five blankets, some money and a lot of trinkets of various kinds. Two or three of Badger's band could understand some English, and through them the band had learned that it was proposed to make Perkins their agent, they having overheard something that one of the commissioners had said. The whole band was in an uproar about it, Meha's uncle taking a very active part in the discussion. Perkins was known among them by a name which signified "The-man-who-cheats." They declared they would not submit to have him their agent, and appointed a delegation to go to Colonel Greene and protest against it.

About sundown the delegation came to Colonel Greene's head-quarters, with Jack for their interpreter. Meha's uncle was the first to speak. He said:

"We have heard that The man-who-cheats is to be appointed our agent. He is a very bad man. We do not want him. Since we surrendered you have been very kind to us and we think you are our friend. We need somebody to help us and we come to you for help. We want you to prevent this man from being appointed our agent. We want some good man."

"Tell them," said Colonel Greene, "that I cannot help them in this matter at all. I have nothing to do with appointing agents."

After the Indians had consulted together over this answer, Jack said:

"They want to know if you won't write a letter to the President and tell him what kind of a man this Perkins is."

The Colonel said he would write the letter, if they desired him to do so, but that it would do no good.

(That night Colonel Greene sat down, and wrote, giving Perkins's history, and the Indians' objections to him. The letter was opened by the President's private secretary, who seeing that it referred to Indian affairs, sent it to the Secretary of the Interior. By his private secretary it was sent to the Commissioner of Indian Affairs. The Commissioner glanced at it, and seeing that it concerned the Indians at the fort on the Little Blue, filed it away with other papers, to be turned over to the Peace Commission when it returned. The appeal went back to the very persons appealed from, for final decision, and that is the result of all such efforts.)

That evening the commission had a session to discuss matters among themselves.

"I do not like the looks of that Indian, Shonnee," said Mr. Borden.

"Nor I either," said Mr. Hillard. "I don't think he is truthful. He said he was a full-blooded Indian, and he is evidently a half-breed."

"You can't tell whether an Indian is a half-breed or not by his color," said Mr. Clark. "Many of the full-bloods are lighter than some of the half-breeds."

"Well, it won't do to trust to that ruffian Jack," said Mr. Smith.

"It was a direct insult to this commission," said Mr. Clark, "for the military authorities to release him. In every effort to civilize and christianize the Indians we have to meet the opposition of the regular army.

"Who is this Captain Jack, as they call him," asked Mr. Hilliard.

"Oh! he is one of the low whites who live with the Indians; one of those ruffians, who, to escape the punishment of crime, has fled from the vengeance of society to live among the Indians," said Mr. Clark.

"But this Indian Shonnee does not speak English well at all," said Mr. Hilliard, "and I am afraid he will not be able to interpret correctly. I don't like the shape affairs have assumed. I had a talk with Colonel Greene, and he seems to be a perfect gentleman. He says he has always found Captain Jack to be honest and reliable, and that Red Iron and he have long been friends, and he thinks that Jack interpreted correctly what Red Iron said."

"Colonel Greene has the outward appearance of a gentleman," said Mr. Clark, "but he wants to get up another Indian war, thereby hoping to get promotion and glory. I never take the word of these military men unless it is confirmed from other sources. Their influence upon the Indians has been of the most degrading character. Not long since one of them, Lieutenant Blake, enticed away an Indian girl who was living in the family of a missionary. If we are ever to teach them correct morals we must manage to keep them from contact with the soldiers. Army officers are always meddling and interfering with the work of properly-constituted commissions."

CHAPTER XXI.

A GOVERNMENT LINGUIST.

THE next morning the council assembled again. The chiefs were all there and Shonnee was ready to interpret. Mr. Clark addressed them: "We," said he, "are sent here by the Great Father himself. What we say is the same as if the Great Father was here and said it himself. We have come to help you, to hear what you have to say and to make a treaty with you. Now we will hear you."

This is the way Shonnee interpreted it:

"He says the Great Father has sent them to make a treaty. The Great Father wants to give you a great many presents. He will make you rich, if you will do what he wants you to do. He wants to help you."

A long silence followed. Not an Indian moved or spoke.

"Tell them," said Mr. Clark, "that we are ready to hear what they have to say."

"They want you to make some speeches," interpreted Shonnee.

Then there was another long silence.

"Why don't you talk?" said Shonnee to Red Iron.

"We want Jack to interpret for us," said Red Iron.

"What did he say?" asked Mr. Clark.

"He want to know Captain Jack where is?" said Shonnee.

The commissioners consulted together, and Mr. Clark replied:

"We do not know anything about Captain Jack since he was taken away by the soldiers. We can have nothing further to do with him."

"He says," said Shonnee, "that Captain Jack is a very bad man, that he knows nothing about him, and will have nothing to do with him, and that I am a good interpreter."

At this point Badger arose and shook hands with the commissioners. He folded his blanket around him, leaving his right arm free, and standing perfectly erect, said:

"We are willing to make a treaty with the Great Father, but there are some things we want to know first. We have heard that The-man-who-cheats is to be made agent for us. We know this man. He is a very bad man. If he is to be made our agent we would rather not make a treaty. We want two or three interpreters present, so we will be sure to understand and not make a mistake."

"He say," interpreted Shonnee, "he heard Captain Jack be made their agent. It make him heap mad. He no make treaty. He want five, six interpreters here. He 'fraid you make mistake, not give him presents enough, unless five, six interpreters here to count them."

"Tell him," said Mr. Clark, "that we can't waste our time staying here, there are no more interpreters to be got. Tell him we come here to make a treaty. If he won't make a treaty that shows he is still at war, and the Great Father will order the soldiers to kill them."

"He says," interpreted Shonnee, "that the Great Father is angry with you, and will send the soldiers to kill every one of you, unless you make a treaty of peace, and he says you can't have any other interpreter than me."

The Indians made no reply to this whatever, but sat still in stolid silence.

"Why don't they talk?" asked Mr. Clark.

"He says if you don't talk he will order you sent to the guard-house," said Shonnee.

"I don't believe he has got the power to do it," said Red Iron.

"He say he dare you to do anything," interpreted Shonnee.

This brought consternation to the commission. None of them had thought of affairs taking such a turn as this. A hurried consultation was held, and it was resolved to adjourn until afternoon. The Indians departed, and Colonel Greene was sent for. A request was made for a stronger guard to be stationed in the council-room in the afternoon, and he was informed of the impertinent language of the Indians.

Colonel Greene was somewhat surprised at the statements made to him, but complied with the request for a stronger guard, making a detail of twenty men, under the command of a lieutenant, to be stationed in the council-room.

In the afternoon the council assembled again. The chiefs were astonished to see so many armed soldiers present, and they began to think that the threat to kill them was to be carried out immediately. Red Iron was the first to speak, but he did not speak until he had said a few words in private to Shonnee. Whatever he said, it seemed to have a powerful effect on Shonnee, who was so agitated that he could hardly talk at all at first. Colonel Greene and some of the officers of the fort were also present. Red Iron said:

"I shake hands with you because I desire to be friendly with you. I desire to make peace with the Great Father, to go upon a reservation, and to learn to farm, to have teachers sent to instruct the children, and men to teach us the ways of the whites. But I made a treaty once before with some men the Great Father sent, and the presents promised were never sent. I do not know whether the Great Father ever sent those men or not. Now, before I make a treaty, I want to go to Washington and see the Great Father myself. I think that is the best way to do. If you are willing to let us go to Washington, I promise to make a treaty when I get there, if he will give us a piece of land, teachers for the children, men to show us how to farm, and pay us for the damages done by the whites, and for the land which has been taken away from us."

Shonnee did his best to interpret this correctly, and this is how he succeeded:

"He say shake hands. He be a friend. He want to make peace a heap, and live on reservation. He want heap schools. He make treaty one time, and Great Father no keep it. He no send presents. He not know whether Great Father send you or not. He go to Washington; make treaty there. No make treaty here. Treaty here no good. He want heap pay for land. Great big heap, 'cause whites kill 'em."

This speech caused another adjournment of the commission for consultation.

Mr. Smith, who did not feel at all safe in the country where there were Captain Jacks and Indians, and Mr. Hilliard and Mr. Borden, who had business interests which imperatively demanded their immediate attention, were earnest in their advocacy of granting the request of Red Iron. Other members of the commission honestly thought that no treaty, which would be beneficial to the Indians, could be made while they were under the influence of the military and such men as Captain Jack.

The commission stood five to seven for taking the Indians to Washington, Mr. Hughs and Mr. Clark opposing it; and so it was resolved that the chiefs should go. It is true, the commission had no authority for taking such action; but Indian commissions are sometimes not particular on that point.

The next day eleven chiefs, or what they called chiefs, started. In fact there were but four chiefs, the other seven being selected by Perkins from among the men whom he thought it would be easy to manage. Badger was not allowed to go. Captain Jack found out that he was not able to help Red Iron as much as he had imagined he could. Shonnee was taken along as interpreter for one part of them, and for the others, who spoke a different language, another half-breed called Pree-mo.

CHAPTER XXII.

SECRETS OF THE INDIAN BUREAU.

ARRIVING at Washington a council was held with the Commissioner of Indian Affairs, and speeches were made by the four chiefs. The others said nothing, because they did not know enough to say anything. Not one of them had ever made a speech, not even in their own councils at home, and when invited to talk they simply said that the other chiefs had expressed their views.

Red Iron gave a detailed account of the war, but it was so badly interpreted that it was almost impossible to understand any of it. Now and then a sentence seemed to have some point to it and that was all. To Little Wolf had been assigned by the Indians the stating of what they desired put in the treaty, but here again the interpretation was so bad that little could be got out of it. That night, at the Indian commissioner's house, the whole matter was talked over between him, Mr. Clark, Perkins and a Member of Congress, and a treaty was drawn up in the stately and formal language such as is used in these documents. It provided for the creation of two reservations, and the following officers on each:

1 Agent, at	$1,500
2 Clerks, at	1,800
1 Farmer, at	1,000
1 Blacksmith, at	900
1 Carpenter, at	900
1 Physician, at	1,200
1 Miller (flour mill), at	800
2 Engineers, at	1,800
1 Miller (saw mill), at	600
1 School Teacher, at	500
2 Common Laborers, at	600
1 Head Sawyer for Saw-Mill, at	750
2 Assistant Engineers (firemen), at	800

This created twenty-six new offices, most of them with pretty fair salaries attached.

The Congressman remarked that he wanted it distinctly understood that he was to have the supplying of sixteen of the places. There was a young man sitting in the room who had taken no part in the conversation up to this time. He was the private secretary of Senator L. When the Representative made this remark he arose and said that such a distribution of these offices would never be agreed to by the Senator.

"I don't see why he should kick at that," said the Congressman. "I will have the biggest part of the work to do, in getting the appropriations through the House. I have taken ten and left six for him, and I think that he ought to be satisfied."

"I have been instructed by the Senator," said the young man, "to say that he will agree to taking twelve of these appointments and give you fourteen. He also wants the two traderships, not included in this list, who will be appointed under the intercourse law."

"I won't agree to anything of the kind," said the Representative. "I'll bust up the whole thing first. I'll do anything that is fair, but this is acting the regular hog. Besides, as I said before, I have got to work the appropriations through."

"The Senator will likely have just as much to do in getting the treaty confirmed by the Senate," replied the young man.

The Representative declared he would take nothing less than he had said, and the young man insisted upon all he had demanded, until they came to pretty hot words, and broke up without making any agreement, and both declaring they would "bust up" the whole business, rather than recede one iota from their demands.

Perkins was disgusted, and called both the Senator and Representative fools, and said they had better take what they could get, than act like lunatics. The only chance for him was to get the matter compromised in some way.

The next day he called upon the Representative, but he was still in a very bad humor, and denounced Senator L. again as a hog. He never would do anything that was fair. He always wanted to grab everything, and he had endured it as just as long as he intended to. Then he went to the young man and tried to get him to compromise, but he said the Senator would never agree to it. The fact was, the Senator was in a tight place. He had promised something to several members of the Legislature who had voted for him, and some of them he had been unable to provide for as yet, and they were getting very persistent and threatened some ugly revelations unless they got places pretty soon. There were two of them who would not be satisfied unless they got something pretty big; for these two he wanted the traderships. He was willing to let the Representative have both of the agents, but he *must* have the traderships. This information was carried by Perkins to the Representative. He replied: "That is just like him. One of his plausible stories. He knows that I can't have either one of the agents. You are to have one, and Clark got scared and gave the other one to some lawyer out at the Bluffs. You see there is nothing but skimmed milk for me, and that old sharper is to take all of the cream. I'll see him damned first. Tell him that."

Perkins went to see Mr. Clark, and told him what the Representative said.

"Well, it's your fault," said Mr. Clark. "I would never have given that agency to Wilmot if it had not been for you."

"I didn't tell you to give him the agency, I only said I thought we should have to give him something, and you went off and gave him the best thing we had. But it is no use crying over spilt milk. This thing has got to be fixed up somehow."

"What are you going to do?"

"They'll divide the patronage up somehow, or I'll make it so hot for both of them that they'll not want to stay in Washington long."

Perkins waited seven or eight days for the Senator and Representative to come to some agreement, but they both were just as obstinate as ever. Then he called on the private secretary and said:

"One tradership and eleven other places must be agreed upon for the Senator before sundown to-night, or the whole transaction with the member from Lincoln County, the amount of money paid, the place where the agreement was made, the bank on which the check was drawn, and every detail will be published to-morrow in the New York papers. I don't intend to fool around here any longer. I mean business, and you can so inform the Senator."

Then he went up to the House and sent in his card

to the Representative, who came out immediately, and said :

"This matter has come to a head at last. The Senator will send a proposition before night to take one trader and eleven other places, and you had better agree to do it."

"That's all right, I'll do it. You see, I had promised a tradership and I was bound to have it. That's what I made the fight for."

Sure enough, as Perkins had said, the private secretary called upon the Representative before sundown and the "patronage" was satisfactorily divided.

The next evening another meeting was held at the residence of the Indian commission, the same parties being present, and the details of the affair were gone into.

All the officers appointed under the treaty were to have residences built for them out of the money appropriated for the Indians. The agent's house was to cost three thousand dollars, and those of the other officers eighteen hundred each, and to be built under the direction of the agent. As they were to be the same on both reservations the contracts were to be divided equally between the two parties. A commission was to be appointed to locate the reservations and designate their boundaries. The private secretary insisted that these persons should be selected by the Senator, for, he said, it was only a temporary thing, not much money in it, and the Senator had several very respectable men who had rendered him some service in primary elections, county conventions or the legislature, who would feel it to be a compliment to be put on such a commission. The Representative said he could have them.

Then the all-important point was reached—how much should the annuities be? Perkins said that nothing less than a hundred thousand dollars a year for five years, to be gradually diminished afterward, would do.

"Now, you see," said the Representative, "that I have to furnish the money for the whole business, as I said in the first place. I am on the Indian Committee, it is true, but there are a good many more on it, and they all have something they want. What is in the Indian Appropriation Bill now runs it up to a good many millions."

"A good many millions! Why, this is only two hundred thousand, a mere bagatelle. Then if the Senate confirms the treaty, the appropriations have got to be made anyhow. The thing is to get the treaty confirmed."

"Never mind," said Mr. Clark, "we'll need all the help we can get anyhow. Now, let us go at the text of the treaty."

After working at it for some time they all got tired, and it was agreed that the private secretary and Perkins should both draw up a treaty and submit it to another meeting, and then they adjourned.

Three days afterward the drafts were completed and submitted. After both were read, Perkins's copy was adopted, with a few slight alterations. It provided for the cession of all right, title and interest in any or all lands held by the Indians to the United States, except two specified tracts which were reserved for their "use and occupancy." The title granted by the Indians to the United States was a full and entire relinquishment and quit-claim of all their interest in it forever. The title granted by it to the Indians was a fraud, no title at all, in fact, being a sort of tenancy at will, for use and occupancy. Then it specified in separate items the amounts to be appropriated by the Government, so much per annum for agent, farmer, physician, etc., through the list of appointees. This left eighty-six thousand nine hundred dollars to be spent annually for the benefit of the Indians, *in such way as the secretary of the interior might direct.* The annuities were to run for twenty years and be gradually reduced after the first five years. Another copy like this was made for the other tribe, making only such alterations as were necessary in regard to names and the boundaries of their reservations. In this way did Perkins prepare Red Iron's treaty for him.

CHAPTER XXIII.

OFFICIAL INFORMATION.

DURING all these weary days the Indians had been lodged at a miserable hotel, the whole eleven in one room. Their meals were brought to them on plates, and a tin-cup full of coffee was furnished to each one. The hotelkeeper charged full rates, two dollars a day, for each of them, it being a sort of political hotel-keeping. The Indians, being accustomed to live in the open air, which was always pure and light on the elevated plains where they had been born, soon began to feel unwell from breathing the heavy air of the sea level, vitiated as it was in the unventilated room where they were confined for the greater part of each day.

Poor old Red Iron wondered and wondered, what was the reason why the business could not be finished, and they allowed to return home; and every day he made inquiry of the man who had been detailed by the Indian Bureau to take charge of them. He was generally told that the Great Father had so much to attend to that he could not get time, but in a day or two he would see them.

Every day they were taken out for a walk, and were shown over the Capitol, the Treasury and other places which it was deemed desirable that they should see, in order to duly impress them with the greatness and power of the Great Father, and incline them to subjection to the orders of his agents. Some of these Indians had never seen a house larger than a sutler's cabin, which, before they started on this journey, they regarded as the acme of wealth. Now they were dazed and bewildered. Everything was new to them, from the paved streets to the dome of the Capitol. As they walked along the streets, looking straight ahead, one who did not understand Indian character would have supposed that they did not notice anything, but they saw everything. Red Iron stood by the open window of the hotel dining-room. To all appearance he was intensely interested in something far down the street. In the few minutes while he stood there he saw how the white people ate, cups, saucers, knives, forks, napkins, salt-spoons, butter-knives, nut-crackers, all were photographed on his mind ; and when, a few days afterward, Mr. Borden, who was greatly interested in him, took him to dine, he was astonished to see him seat himself at the table and eat with as much grace as if he had been trained in the most polite society.

Every day or two, while the Indians were waiting, the newspapers announced that they were still there, and the commission were finding great difficulty in getting them to agree to a treaty which would be of any benefit to them. Don't let the reader blame the newspaper correspondents for publishing such statements. The correspondent or reporter gets his information from "official" sources. He goes to the heads of departments and bureaus for it. If he should refuse to publish what they give him, his mission would end, his occupation would be gone, for they would refuse to give him any information, and his journal would be left without its Washington news. If a correspondent was at war with the head of a department or bureau, he could get no news at all, for from these most of it comes.

Toward the last all the Indians began to feel unwell. When the fact was announced in the papers, the comment was made that the Indian could not live after the manner of civilized life, and in consequence must soon fade from the face of the earth. This also was "official information."

When Perkins had got the "patronage" arranged and the treaties drawn up, Mr. Clark called the commission together. Mr. Borden and Mr. Hilliard gave the document the closest scrutiny. The more they had seen of Red Iron the better they liked him, and they were determined to make the best arrangement for him they could. These men were both tender-hearted, honest, Christian gentlemen, and greatly desired to do justice to the Indians. They could find nothing to criticise in the treaties, and gave Mr. Clark, whom they supposed had drawn them, great praise for the labor he had bestowed upon them.

At last Red Iron and the other chiefs were summoned before them. Shonnee and Pree-mo, whose real name among the Indians was Tangled Hair, were called upon to interpret the treaties to them. Neither of the interpreters could read or write, and the treaties were written in the stately language which is used in documents of this kind which are drawn up between enlightened and civilized nations, Perkins having copied most of the language from former treaties which were on file in Washington. They abounded in legal terms, which would not be understood by the average civilized citizen. Shonnee and Pree-mo, who only knew a few English words, and they of the commonest and simplest kind, did not understand one word in ten. Nevertheless, as Mr. Clark read it to them sentence by sentence, they instantly rattled off something in the Indian language. When they were through, the chiefs had no idea of its provisions. The interpreters had told them, in substance, that they were to have a big piece of land, one part on the Arickoree and the other on the Baha Taha, which was to be theirs forever, and that every year the Great Father would send them immense sums of money.

Red Iron inquired if they were to have teachers and missionaries sent to them, and several other questions, which Mr. Clark answered. Then the papers were presented for signature, but the chiefs refused to sign. Red Iron said they would think over it, and come again the next day; and they retired to their room in the hotel. There they had a long discussion. They tried to get some idea from Shonnee and Pree-mo of the amount of money they were to get, the number of blankets, how much rations; whether they had to stay on the reservation all the time; if they could go and visit other tribes if they wanted to; if they were to be allowed to hunt any; if their horses and arms were to be given back to them, and a hundred other things of like nature, all of which Shonnee answered in the manner which he knew the chiefs wanted the treaty to state. In fact he assured them that everything they wanted was stipulated in the treaty.

Perkins was somewhat frightened when he learned that the chiefs had refused to sign the treaty, and that afternoon he, Mr. Clark, and the Representative had a consultation over the matter in one of the committee-rooms of the Capitol. It was concluded that the best thing to be done was to send them some presents. So a purse of five hundred dollars was made up, and a lot of nice blankets, beads, tomakawks, and such other things as they thought the Indians would like was sent to them. If Perkins had only known it, this was money thrown away, for Shonnee had satisfied them on every point before, and they had already agreed to sign the treaties. The next day the treaties were signed and the Indians hustled off home. In due time the Senate confirmed them, and the appropriations were made.

Mr. Clark prepared a formal report of the work of the Peace Commission, dilating on its successful issue, portions of which were copied in all the religious weeklies and in most of the missionary journals. He did not say, however, that the whole thing was conceived in fraud and born in iniquity.

CHAPTER XXIV.

WHAT COULD IT MEAN?

CAPTAIN JACK got tired staying around the fort during Red Iron's absence, concluded to go up the country, and he got ready his outfit and started. While on the trail he met several trains hauling supplies to the fort. The Indians were still furnishing a rich harvest for the contractors.

Arriving at Council Bluffs, he stopped at the Causeland House, and went over to see Mr. Parkman and his wife. Mrs. Parkman told him that they had been appointed missionaries to Red Iron's tribe, and as soon as they were located on their new reserve they should go to live with the Indians.

Jennie asked him if he knew who was to be Red Iron's agent, and he said he did not.

"What will you give to know?" she asked.

"I'll give you a bran new pair of moccasins."

"But I don't wear moccasins."

"I'll give you an Arapahoe blanket."

"Oh, Jack! I wouldn't take that. They cost too much money."

(An Arapahoe blanket is worth a hundred dollars. They are perfectly impervious to water, will last a lifetime, and are made only by the Arapahoe Indians.)

"What do you want me to give?" asked Jack.

"I want you to make me a promise to do something."

"What is it?"

"I won't tell you until you promise."

"Well, I won't promise until you tell me."

"Now, Jack, I thought you would."

"You might want me to do something awful."

"You know I wouldn't. It's two things. One is not to do something, and the other is to do something."

"Well, if it is a thing I oughten to do, and t'other a thing I oughter do, I'll promise."

"I'll pledge you my word to that."

"I'll promise, then."

"On your word of honor, Jack."

"Yes, on honor."

"Then, when I tell you the name of Red Iron's agent you are to get acquainted with him."

"What a queer notion," said Jack.

"Will you promise?"

"Yes, I'll hunt him up if he lives anywhere in reach."

"Now, the other thing, the thing you ought not to do."

"Tell me what it is."

"You are not to shoot Perkins. Mrs. Parkman told me what you meant by having an interview with Perkins."

"Look a here, now," said Jack, "that ain't fair. Perkins ought to be killed. If ever a man lived who deserved killing, it's that Perkins. I won't make no such promise."

"Oh, Jack," said Jennie, and she began to cry.

"What are you so tender about Perkins for? Are you in love with him?"

"No, I ain't," said Jennie, "I hate him," and she stamped her foot.

"Well, now, if women ain't the queerest creatures on earth."

"Please do promise me, Jack. Now, won't you? Please do," and Jennie looked up at him in a most pleading way through her tears.

"I wish I had of sent him to kingdom come the day he was trying to make a target of me at the Causeland House."

"Oh! how I wish you had," said Jennie.

"Well, if this don't beat all creation," said Jack.

"Please do promise me, Jack. I never asked you to promise me anything before and I will never ask you again."

"Tell me why you want me to promise."

"Oh! I can't. When father comes he will tell you. Do promise me."

"Is he plotting any deviltry agin you?" asked Jack, and his eyes began to gleam.

"No."

"What under heavens is it, then?"

"I can't tell you, Jack. If I could I would. I don't know much about it, only I know it would be better for us all if you should kill me than if you killed Perkins."

Tears were streaming down Jennie's face and her voice was choked with sobs. They sat there in silence for a few minutes. Then Jennie took her handkerchief down. Her face was as white as snow. The tears were all dried up. She tried twice before she could speak. Then she said, in such a tone as Jack had never heard before:

"Will you promise?"

"I will," said Jack.

The next moment Jennie lay in a fainting-fit on the floor. Jack sprang to the door and called Mrs. Parkman, who was out in the yard talking to the next-door neighbor, and the two soon brought her back to consciousness.

Jack told Mrs. Parkman what had happened, and asked her what it meant.

"I can't imagine," said Mrs. Parkman. "All I

know is, that she has received several letters lately, which seemed to excite her very much, and as soon as she reads them, she puts them in the stove and burns them up."

Jack walked off up-town, and as he passed the Empire House he glanced in at a window, and there sat Perkins. He gritted his teeth as he looked at him. He said nothing, however, and walked on. When he got to the Causeland House, he sat down and tried to think what had made Jennie so anxious about the personal safety of Perkins. Did she know that he had come back? Were the letters which she had received from him? What possible hold could Perkins have upon her? Jack could not decide. All at once, he happened to think Jennie had not told him who Red Iron's agent was to be. How could she know, anyhow? Jack went right back to Mr. Parkman's.

Jennie was reclining on her little cot in the small room.

"See here," said he, "you did not tell me who that man was I was to get acquainted with."

"Oh, it's Mr. Wilmot."

"How did you find out?"

"Jack, you will never tell who told you, will you?" This was said with so much earnestness that it fairly startled Jack.

"Miss Walker," said he, with great seriousness of tone, "I don't like the way you talk and act about things. Now, you are young, and have no relations here to advise you or take care of you. I advise you to tell Mrs. Parkman all about this business."

"I can't tell anybody," said Jennie. "Mrs. Parkman says she has known you for years, and that you could be trusted, and I was going to write a letter to you, but you came walking in. I think it was providential. I want you to do two or three little things for me. They are all right and proper, and you may do much good that way. By and by, everything can be explained. Now don't ask me to tell, because I can't. You promised me you would get acquainted with Mr. Wilmot. I know you will keep your promise. I want you to let him know that you know he is to be appointed agent, and then I want you to say two or three things to him, which I will tell you."

Jack was worse nonplussed than before. He said nothing more, and went off to find Wilmot. He found that gentleman sitting in his office. These two men had often heard of each other but had never met before. It was not long until they were in an earnest discussion. Wilmot was surprised at Jack's conversation. Sometimes he used as elegant and well-chosen language as any man he had ever conversed with, and again, he talked the regular jargon of the frontier.

These two men were as unlike each other in every outward appearance as they well could be, but from that hour until death they were ever the closest friends.

A day or two afterward Jack intimated to Mr. Wilmot that he understood he was to be Red Iron's agent.

"Yes," said he, "I have been pressed to take the place and have agreed to accept it if it is offered to me."

Then he went on to state what he intended to try

to do for the Indians. He would try to get them to form a regular government, with courts and juries to settle every dispute which might arise. Mr. and Mrs. Parkman were to go as missionaries and he would aid them in their work all he could. He would try to have all the children go to school, and believed that in a few years he would have a self-supporting and intelligent community.

Jack called on Jennie and told her of his conversation with Wilmot.

"Now," said Jennie, "I want you to go to Mr. Wilmot and beg of him not to accept that appointment."

"How could I do such a thing? I think Wilmot a splendid man for agent. I had never hoped to get as good a man. No, no, that would not be right to go back on my old friend Red Iron."

"Jack," said Jennie, "if Mr. Wilmot goes out there as agent he will be ruined. I know he will never do what is expected of him. There now, I didn't mean to say that. You won't ever tell that I said it, will you?"

Light began to break into Jack's mind.

"I wish you would tell me all about this business. What sort of hold has that Perkins got on you? He's plotting some deviltry, I know. What interest have you got in Wilmot?"

Jennie blushed scarlet. "I think Mr. Wilmot is a very fine man. If he stays here and practices law he will go to Congress sometime."

Jack scratched his head and pulled his mustache. More light was breaking in.

"You'd better tell me or Mrs. Parkman all about it," said he.

"I wish I could," said Jennie.

The next day Jack went up to Wilmot's office. The door was closed and locked, and on it was a card. It said, "Absent from the city. Will not return for two weeks," and underneath was the date.

CHAPTER XXV.

DIVIDING THE SPOILS.

JACK made inquiry all over town about Wilmot. All that he could learn was that he had hired a team at the livery stable, telling the man that he should be absent ten or twelve days, and then went across the river, and started toward the northwest. Another thing that made his conduct more strange was, that it was the week for the session of the circuit court and court week was the lawyers' harvest. Wilmot had gone to another lawyer, told him that he was unexpectedly called away, and turned all his cases over to him.

When the grand jury were impaneled, Perkins was the first man who appeared before them. After him four or five other villainous-looking men, who were also stopping at the Empire House, were sent for.

The jury was in session two days, and when they had presented all their indictments were discharged. Perkins left town a few hours afterward. According to the rule of all courts, the indictments were kept secret until the warrants were served and the persons accused were in the hands of the officers of the court.

The district attorney, who was a first-class shyster, put on a very wise and mysterious look, but said nothing. A thousand guesses were made by the attorneys and court attendants concerning what Perkins was up to now, but none of them came anywhere near the truth.

One morning, not long after court adjourned, Wilmot drove into town. The team was jaded and worn, and had evidently been driven all night. He ate a hurried breakfast, went to his office, wrote a letter, carried it to the post-office, and then retired to his room and was not seen until the next day. Jack called upon him early in the forenoon.

"I was never so glad to see a man in my life," said Wilmot, "as I am to see you."

"I'm glad to see you too, been waiting for you two weeks."

"Do you know," said Wilmot, "that that commission of eminent philanthropists who were out here have been planning the worst piece of fraud and swindling ever attempted in this country?"

"They were a set of cowards and thieves," said Jack. "Them's the chaps that had me arrested."

"Had you arrested! What did they arrest you for?"

"I was trying to shoot a lying half-breed."

Wilmot laughed and said: "Well, why didn't you shoot him?"

"'Cause old Red Iron knocked my hand up, and the pill that was intended for him went into the ceiling."

Wilmot then explained to Jack the cause of his absence. What occurred the afternoon before he left and for the next few days was as follows:

Wilmot was sitting in his office when a gentleman came in. He was well dressed, and had a sharp business look about him. He handed Wilmot the following letter, which was dated at Washington.

"MY DEAR MR. WILMOT:

"This letter will be handed to you by Hon. A. S. Parker, who will be appointed trader at the agency which it has been agreed shall be assigned to you. As you will be associated together for some time to come he desired to make your acquaintance as soon as possible, and I have taken the liberty of sending him directly to you. Truly yours,

"H. O. CLARK."

After reading the letter Wilmot extended his hand and said he was very glad to meet him, and asked:

"Have you come direct from Washington?"

"Yes, I stayed until the treaties were confirmed and things were made safe, then I started."

"Do they intend to move the Indians to the new reservations immediately?"

"Yes, we intend to get up there and fixed up before winter sets in."

"How soon will I get my appointment," asked Wilmot.

"It will be along in the course of a month. That is all right. Everything is fixed."

A pause ensued for a minute or two, and then Parker said:

"Clark was very anxious for me to see you and get things amicably arranged. Of course you are not going out there to live among the Indians, cut off from all the benefits of society and the comforts of civilized life, for fifteen hundred dollars a year. It is about as bad as going to the penitentiary. So we might as well arrange beforehand how we are to divide, and there won't be any trouble afterward. The annual appropriation is a hundred thousand. After the salaries are all paid there will be eighty-six thousand nine hundred dollars left. The first year we will be forced to spend a good deal, for residences for the agent and employees will have to be built. That will only leave forty-two thousand three hundred dollars to feed the Indians and divide up. It is altogether too small, but it can't be helped, unless Dan (Dan was the Congressman) gets through the additional appropriation for the construction of the agency buildings—but that's not certain and we must not count on it. Now, what's your offer? How much do you want? You see how it is, we've all got to be satisfied with small slices the first year."

If that speech had been made to Jack he would have knocked the man down before he got half-way through; but Wilmot, while he was just as indignant as Jack would have been, simply leaned his head upon his hand as if in deep thought, and in a minute or two said:

"This matter has not turned out at all as I expected."

"It is rather exasperating," said Parker; "but next year we will have eighty-six thousand to divide up instead of forty-two thousand. We might have saved five or six thousand out of the construction of the agency buildings, but the Senator has laid his hands on that. It is just as Dan says, he's a regular hog."

"I'll have to take this matter into consideration," said Wilmot. "I'm not going to leave a good law practice to go out there for nothing."

"Well, it will be better next year."

"Who knows what will happen before next year?"

"Well, what's your offer? How much do you want?"

"What do you propose to give?"

"Will five thousand dollars do?"

"No."

"Will seven thousand five hundred?"

"No."

"I don't see how we can come to any agreement. Clark ought to have fixed this himself."

"How do you propose to divide the rest?"

"Well, as I have to put in a stock of goods, invest a good deal of ready money, and none of the rest are to put in any money or run any risk, I ought to have at least fifteen thousand. The Senator is to have five thousand, and Dan three thousand. That leaves eleven thousand eight hundred dollars for rations, and we can pull them through somehow on that. You see it is utterly impossible to make your share more than seven thousand five hundred."

"As I said before," remarked Wilmot, " things have taken a turn I had not thought of. I will have to take the matter under consideration. If you will call at my office early to-morrow morning, I will be able to say what I will do."

After Parker left, Wilmot put his feet up on the table, leaned back in his chair and soliloquized. "Who would ever have imagined this? A Peace Commission, too! What ever made them offer me the place?"

His thoughts for some time were confused, and led to no solution. Finally he said to himself:

"I see how it was. The gentlemen on that commission were honest, good Christian men, with one exception, and that is that man Clark. They made this treaty in good faith, and supposed they had provided for the future welfare of these Indians. There was enough money appropriated to have supplied them until they had raised crops of their own, and then to have educated the whole mass of the children. That is what they intended to do, and thought they had done. I don't blame them for thinking so, for I believed it myself. When I made that speech against large appropriations to feed and clothe the Indians, I did it on general principles, and that fellow Clark thought I understood the whole matter, and was bound to have a hand in it or make trouble. So he came around and offered me that place to keep me quiet. He's got hold of the wrong man this time. I'll follow this up until I land every one of these scoundrels in the penitentiary."

To resolve was to proceed to act with Wilmot, and he set about devising some plan to accomplish his purpose. He decided immediately that he would not take the agency, but it would not do to let them think he intended to prosecute them.

The next morning when Parker called, Wilmot said:

"I have been thinking this matter over. I can't accept of any such arrangement as you propose. I am to go out there, according to these fellows' plans, and take all the responsibility of this thing for a mere pittance. The risk is too great for the amount involved. I have a thing to propose, which, if it is accepted, will be satisfactory to me. Have you authority to arrange this matter for Mr. Clark and the other commissioners?"

"I have," said Parker, and he took from an inside pocket of his vest a large pocket-book. From among numerous papers he selected a small slip, and handed it to Mr. Wilmot. Like the other, it was dated at Washington, and contained the following words:

"Any arrangement made by the bearer, A. S. Parker, will be satisfactory to all parties interested.
"H. O. CLARK."

Wilmot could hardly resist smiling when he read it

It was a very ingeniously worded document. There was nothing in it to criminate anybody unless it was made a part of other evidence. Wilmot wanted to keep that paper very much, but he did not want to seem to want to keep it. After reading it he threw it down on the table in a careless sort of way among some other loose papers, and as he talked he took up a large package of papers, bound together with a rubber band, turned them over and over in one hand, snapped the rubber up and down until he broke it, and then tossed the loose papers on top of Mr. Clark's note. All this time he was talking, and the whole thing was done as if by accident, and as though he had utterly forgotten that little scrap of paper.

The sharp eyes of Mr. Parker had been following that paper. He wanted it too, but did not want to seem to want it. He gave a sharp glance at Wilmot, but nothing was to be learned from that tranquil countenance.

"What is your proposition?" said Parker.

"I want to name the man who is to have that agency."

"Is he known to Mr. Clark?"

"I don't know whether he is or not."

"I don't think that will be satisfactory."

"I know him, and that is enough. That agency is mine, and if I don't want to go myself, I have a right to say who shall. Let Mr. Clark try to interfere if he dares. You came upon me so suddenly that I have not had time to mention the matter to him yet, but he will be appointed agent to Red Iron's tribe, or I'll know the reason why."

"You need not get excited," said Parker; "I did not say that it could not be done, and—"

"And I say it shall be done," broke in Wilmot, with a good deal of vehemence."

"If you insist upon it, I suppose we will have to submit."

"Well I do, and most positively too," replied Wilmot.

"What is his name?"

"His name is Harkins."

Parker gave a long, low whistle.

"Do you know him?" asked Wilmot.

"I should say I did," said Parker.

"Have you any objections?"

"I don't know that it would do any good to object, as you say you will insist upon it."

"Where did you ever meet him?"

"At Hickman's, the night the outbreak occurred. I was among those who helped put him in command that night."

"Then you ought to be good friends."

"Well, we are, I guess."

"Now then, you will write to Mr. Clark the arrangement we have made?"

"Shall I tell him the matter is finally settled?"

"No, you can't tell him that, for I have not seen Harkins yet, and it will be some days before I can see him. As soon as I do, I will write to the President and ask him to withdraw my nomination and substitute

9*

that of Harkins. The gentlemen in Washington will see that it is done, or they will find out there is a hereafter."

Parker went away and Wilmot hired a team to go and find Harkins, who was off to the north-west with a surveying party. The two men were old college chums and they entered into league together, the object of which was to protect the Indians and "to send the whole outfit of contractors, Congressmen and everybody else engaged in this fraud, to the penitentiary." Harkins's contract of surveying was about finished, and he could not get another before the next season, so he thought he might as well go into this plot of Wilmot's and make a winter's job of it."

All the time that Wilmot had been telling this to Jack, he sat there getting "madder and madder," as he expressed it.

"Now, look a here," said Jack, "you'll never git them chaps convicted. The only thing for them is a dose of lead. I'd like to get a bead on that Parker. He'd never pocket any fifteen thousand dollars of old Red Iron's money, you can bet your life on that."

"Now, Jack," said Wilmot, "I have relied on you for help, but if you go to shooting anybody it will ruin the whole business. Suppose you should shoot Parker, some one else just as bad would take his place and steal just as much as he would. But suppose I should get him and Clark and Perkins convicted and sent to the penitentiary, it would put a stop to such things. The next one who comes would be afraid to try the same game. Now, I want you to promise that you won't do any shooting, but help me work up this case."

"Say, have you and Colonel Greene and Jennie Walker been putting up a job on me?"

"Why, no! What makes you ask such a question?"

"Now, there's that Perkins, that old pious fraud Clark, and that lying, thieving, half-breed Shonnee, who will never get their deserts until some man lets daylight through 'em, and you are all after me, making me promise I won't shoot 'em. Jennie Walker cried and had a fainting fit, 'cause she thought I was down here after Perkins. Colonel Greene made me swear off on Clark and Shonnie, Jennie on Perkins, and now you are awful tender on this thief Parker, who wants to steal all of old Red Iron's money. Hang me, if I can understand it. Just let them fellows come out there once, and I would clear the whole pack out in fifteen minutes, and not take any advantage of them either."

Wilmot did not hear one word of all the last part of Jack's excited speech. His face had settled into that meaningless look in which he always took refuge when excited or troubled. He made no reply at all. Jack thought he had offended him, so he stretched out his hand to shake hands with him, and said:

"Don't take it that way, pard. Of course I was joking when I said you were putting up a job on me. I know you and Jennie and Colonel Greene are all my friends and wouldn't no ways put up any sort of a job on me."

"Why is Miss Walker so very anxious about Perkins?"

"That's just what gets away with me," said Jack. "She says she hates him, wishes I'd a killed him down at the Causeland House the day he was firing that popgun off at me, and then says that she had rather I'd shoot her than Perkins."

"That's very strange."

"If it was a man who would talk that way, I'd put him down for a lunatic, but there's no accountin' for a woman's ideas. I give it up. But about this 'ere business. If I can help old Red Iron by puttin' daylight through these scoundrels, I'm in for it. If I can't do it that way, I'm in for the next best thing."

"Now you are talking sensibly. If we appeal to the law to punish these men, we must not violate it ourselves."

CHAPTER XXVI.

DYING LIKE BRAVE MEN.

COLONEL GREENE received an order to turn the Indians over to the agents of the Interior Department. Harkins was on the ground, and took charge of those who were assigned to him; but Perkins did not arrive, and the others were put under the control of the man who had been appointed farmer, as acting agent. Trains were made up, and the Indians started for their respective reservations. The Indians had no stock of their own; so contracts for their transportation had been let. All seemed satisfactory. About the time Perkins's Indians reached their destination, Colonel Greene received an order to send two companies of cavalry to their agency to preserve order. The paper stated that this was done in compliance with a request made on the Secretary of War by the Secretary of the Interior, and the troops were sent.

One morning Wilmot was greatly surprised to learn that the Judge of the Circuit Court had called a special session, to be held in two weeks. None of the lawyers in town seemed to know anything about the matter, and none could give a reason for holding a special session. The District Attorney said he supposed it was for the purpose of trying the criminal cases on the docket.

Wilmot suspected that it had some connection with Perkins's appearance before the grand jury, but could not imagine who he could want to prosecute.

Perkins was still in Washington, he learned, from a letter he had received from Mr. Clark, and did not intend to leave there for some time.

Two days before court was to convene, a military escort rode up in front of the county jail, and turned over to the sheriff five Indian prisoners. They were Badger, Meha's uncle, and three others of the same band. They had been arrested for the murder of the passengers in the stage-coach.

Wilmot was furious when he heard the news, and resolved to offer his services to defend them. When he made an effort to see them, he was informed that they could be seen by no one except their counsel, and the Government had furnished them with counsel. He got the names of these lawyers and went to call on them, to offer them his assistance. On going to the Empire House, he was introduced to two as villainous-looking men as he had ever seen. Both of them were very much under the influence of liquor, and declined his offer of aid in the most insulting manner possible. Wilmot found that he was unable to render the Indians the slightest assistance. The next day Colonel Greene, accompanied by an aid, and the Judge Advocate of the department, arrived, and took rooms at the Causeland House.

How all this came about may seem very strange to the forty-nine million five hundred thousand people in the United States, who know nothing about our Indian system. So it will have to be explained.

When Perkins was with the Peace Commission at the fort on the Little Blue, he was very much enraged at the earnest protest made by Badger's band against his appointment as agent. He had a talk with Shonnee about it. Shonnee said, "Injun heap mad. Kill 'em, sure."

"What are they mad about?" asked Perkins.

"Badger say you cheat heap. No play fair. Steal Injun blanket, money, everything. Badger heap mad. Kill 'em, sure."

Perkins was very badly frightened about this, and took measures to get rid of Badger and the leaders of this movement against him. So he laid the plot to have them arrested for murder, and knowing he could not carry it out as long as they were under the control of the military as prisoners of war, he had waited until they were turned over to the Interior Department. Then he went down to Hickman's and hunted up some of the gamblers and roughs who infested that neighborhood, and took them as witnesses before the grand jury, who, on the evidence presented (for these men swore they knew these Indians, and had met them as they were returning from the assault on the stage-coach, having hid in the brush and saw them go by), found a true bill against them. As soon as they were indicted, Perkins went to Washington and laid the matter before the Secretary of the Interior. He took a letter from the Senator, and the Representative went with him to the office of the Secretary.

"This gentleman," said the Representative, "desires to call your attention to a very important matter. He has long been known as a friend to the Indians, and it is owing to his unselfish exertions, more than to any other man, that the troubles on the Little Blue have been satisfactorily settled. I ask for him a patient hearing."

"What is the nature of your business?" asked the Secretary.

"I reside," said Perkins, "near the scene of the recent war. I know a great many of those Indians personally, for they have been in the habit, for a long time, of coming to me for advice and assistance. I am very much attached to some, for they are trusting and childlike, and want to do what is right, but there are others among them who are very desperate characters, blood-thirsty and cruel. They are very much opposed to any change in their habits, despise work, and look upon any Indian who is willing to work as degraded. There will never be any chance to do anything with them, until some of them are punished for their crimes, and taught that murder is not a thing to be proud of. This whole war was caused by the cold-blooded murder of the people in the stage. Not being satisfied with murder and robbery they scalped and mutilated the bodies of their victims beyond recognition, some of their work being too horrible and indecent to be related. Only five Indians were engaged in this. They are well-known, and these are not the only murders they have committed. No white settler within a hundred miles of the new agency will be safe while these Indians are at large. The grand jury at Council Bluffs has indicted them in due form. If taken there they will have a fair trial."

"There is a general demand in that section of the country," said the Representative, "that these Indians should be punished."

"What do you desire should be done?" asked the Secretary.

"Well, if any civil officer should undertake to arrest them, his scalp would be dangling at some of their belts inside of five minutes, so the people there desire that they may be arrested by the military and turned over to the sheriff of the county."

"I see no reason why this request should not be granted," said the Secretary.

"I am very anxious," said Perkins, "that the Indians, if they are turned over to the civil authorities, should have a fair trial and be well defended. It may be possible that some one of them may not be guilty, or not as guilty as others. They are the wards of the Government, and ought to have counsel to defend them. I think you have authority to appoint such counsel?"

"Yes," replied the Secretary, "that is always done in such cases. Have you in mind any lawyer you would like to recommend."

"I would recommend two smart, active lawyers, who live not far from there. They are partners. The firm name is Bledsoe & Dosier. Perhaps our Representative has some one else to suggest."

"They are the best criminal lawyers in that section, and would be an excellent selection," said the Representative.

Then the Secretary wrote a formal request to the Secretary of War, asking that the nearest military commander be instructed to furnish a detail of soldiers, sufficiently large to arrest these Indians and convey them to Council Bluffs, there to be turned over to the civil authorities and be tried for murder.

The Secretary of War issued the order, which was forwarded through the regular channels to Colonel Greene.

When Colonel Greene received that order, he was astonished and chagrined beyond the power of expression. More than that, he felt humiliated and disgraced.

But Colonel Greene was a soldier, and of soldiers it is said:

> "Theirs not to make reply,
> Theirs not to reason why,
> Theirs but to do—"

When such facts as these have been related it is often asked "Why didn't he resign?" Colonel Greene had this order. If he did not obey it he would be court-martialed. If he had sent in his resignation the moment he received the order he would not be relieved, if it was accepted, for months, and meantime he must do his duty as an officer of the army. If it was accepted what good would it have done? Another officer would take his place, and the same system would still endure. There was but one thing that Colonel Greene could do, for he had taken a solemn oath when he entered the army to obey the orders of his superior officers, and that was to make the detail and send these Indians to Council Bluffs.

It was with a sad heart that Colonel Greene wrote the necessary orders. He made a detail of only one Lieutenant and three men, and gave them their instructions. The Lieutenant went to Badger's tent alone and told him that he had orders to take him to Council Bluffs; that he was charged with the murder of the people in the stage-coach, and that four others must come with him. Then the Lieutenant went away. Word was sent by the Indians to all the band, and they assembled together. Badger arose and addressed them. After stating the message he had received, he said:

"We will have to obey this order. We are utterly helpless. All our horses and all our arms have been surrendered on the promise that our lives should be protected. The white officer has violated his promise. We cannot resist. To flee on foot out on the prairies is but to die, with all our women and children. When the white officer sees our dead bodies, perhaps he will be satisfied, and he will let the rest of you live. To-morrow morning come to my tent, and we will go together with this officer."

The five victims sat down and drew their blankets over their heads. They spoke not one word, nor made any sign of the woe that was in their hearts. It was not so with their friends and relatives. They wept and wailed aloud for hours. After awhile the men got up and went to their tents, and their wives and children gathered around them. They did not express their grief then in the same form that white women and children would have done, but their sorrow was just as deep and agonizing. Swift Walker, Meha's uncle, took his accustomed place in his tent. His wife spread out the best robe she had for him to sit on. Then she sat down beside him. For a long time not a word was spoken. At last Swift Walker said:

"It seems but a little while ago that you came to live with me; but many summers have come and gone, and we are now getting old. You have always been good to me. It would be a little while, not many summers, before we must die, if the white men would let us live our full length of days. The Great Spirit seems to be angry with his red children, and takes us away before our time. We did wrong to give up our horses and our guns to the white officer, and the Great Spirit is angry. He gave us these things to defend our women and children, and we, like cowards, surrendered them up. If we had horses we might flee away. If we had arms we could subsist on the plains; but now we are at his mercy, and what the white man calls mercy is to kill the innocent, and break his word to those who have trusted in him."

The tears streamed down over his wife's face, and she rocked herself backward and forward, but uttered not any sound.

After awhile the Indian woman got up and went outside the tent. If a stranger had passed by he would never have guessed from her appearance that her heart was breaking. Then she cooked her husband's supper. Every delicacy which she had she spread before him. But Swift Walker ate but little. After supper she spread his couch for him and laid down by his side. When he was asleep she arose and sat by his side through the long hours of the night, bending over him and weeping. Early in the morning she prepared his breakfast. Swift Walker did not come out of his tent. When she thought that this was the last time she would ever eat with him it seemed as though she would die. She put her hand on her heart and said, "I have a great pain here."

Her husband spoke but one word. Translated, it could be rendered only, "be brave," but it had a deeper meaning than that, a religious meaning, which seemed to give her strength to endure with fortitude the great trial of a final parting. About sunrise the doomed five assembled at Badger's tent. Similar scenes had been enacted at each of their homes. They knew that they were going among those who thirsted for their blood, and that they were going to their death, and that death the most ignominious that could be accorded to a red man. The Indians gave one long look at their tents, but no word of complaint ever came from their lips. Badger led the way to the place where the Lieutenant was stopping. They were given horses to ride, but no guard was placed over them. They rode into Council Bluffs with heads erect and with the bearing of senators, amidst the jeers of a brutal crowd, to the jail which was to be the last covering they would ever have over their heads.

The trial came on. The jury was impaneled and they were shown the two villains, called lawyers, who were to defend them. To none of it did they pay any heed.

At this stage of the proceedings, Wilmot arose and addressed the court. He said that Colonel Greene was present and desired to make a statement through the Judge Advocate of the Department, who was an attorney and entitled to address the court. The Judge said he would hear what he had to say.

The Judge Advocate then stated that these prisoners were among the number of Indians who had recently surrendered to Colonel Greene as prisoners of war; that Colonel Greene, being in command of the forces sent to subject them, was authorized by the laws of war, and by direct orders from the General-in-

Chief of the army, to make the conditions of surrender. The arrest of these parties was a violation of the conditions under which they surrendered, and he did not believe that their prosecution by the civil authorities, for acts committed during the progress of the war, was legal. He asked the Judge to dismiss the cases against them, and decree that Colonel Greene was acting legally and in accordance with the laws of the United States, as well as the law of nations, in making these conditions of surrender.

The Judge said these cases came before him as any ordinary case. An indictment had been found in due form, the cases had been called, a jury impaneled, and the prisoners interrogated as to whether they were guilty or not guilty. They had plead not guilty. They had counsel employed by the Government. He could not see how, at this stage of the proceedings, he could dismiss the case on an ex parte statement. If their counsel desired to make a motion to quash the indictments on this ground or any other, he would hear argument upon it.

"We are capable, we think," said Mr. Bledsoe, " of managing this defense without any instructions or interference from the military or anybody else. We do not desire to make any such motion."

" Then," said the Judge, " I see no way but to proceed with the trial. The District Attorney will call his first witness."

" John Hildreth," said the attorney, " come forward and be sworn."

A low-browed, short-haired, dark-complected, stout-built man pressed his way through the crowd to the witness-stand.

"Be sworn," said the judge.

He held up his hand, and the clerk of the court administered the oath.

"What is your name?" asked the attorney.

"John Hildreth."

"Where do you reside?"

"In St. Louis."

"Do you know these prisoners at the bar?"

"I do."

"Tell to the court where you last saw them, and all the circumstances, as far as you can remember them."

"In the month of June, last year, I was coming up from St. Joe with four other men. We passed by Hickman's——"

Here Mr. Bledsoe arose and said, that as his clients could not speak English or understand it, he asked of the court that an interpreter might be appointed to interpret the evidence to them.

The Judge said that he would appoint one, if one could be had.

Mr. Bledsoe replied, that they had made every effort to prepare for a vigorous defense, and had not overlooked this. They had a reliable interpreter present, and he brought forward Shonnee. Then the witness proceeded.

"As I was saying, we passed by Hickman's the morning after the outbreak. Hearing the news, we kept a sharp look-out for Indians, and where the underbrush was thick and likely to be made an ambush by them, we did not keep in the open road. As we were passing carefully through the timber, we heard a noise and concealed ourselves. Shortly after these five Indians passed by, within a few yards of us. They had fresh scalps fastened to their belts, and an extra horse on which was strapped several mail bags. That's all I know about it."

"Have you anything else to ask him?" said the Judge to the District Attorney.

"Nothing," replied the attorney.

"Take the witness, Mr. Bledsoe," said the Judge.

"You are certain that these are the same men whom you saw on that June day a year or more ago?" asked Mr. Bledsoe.

"Yes, sir," said the witness.

"Don't all Indians look very much alike?"

"Well, they are all red-skins, but there's a good deal of difference in them after all."

"How can you tell one Indian from another?"

"Pretty much in the same way that you tell one white man from another."

"Was there anything peculiar about those Indians so as to make it possible to recognize the identical persons when you saw them again?"

"Well, yes; two of them were very tall, and the others short. One was inclined to be fleshy. One had a large, long scar on his right arm. The tall one had a slit in his ear that was next to me, which went almost clear around the whole ear."

"Mr. Hildreth," said Bledsoe, in a very rough tone, "do you come into court, and pretend to swear positively, after a whole year has intervened, that these are the same Indians you saw that next day after the outbreak at Hickman's?"

"I do," said Hildreth.

"Well, you can step aside," said Bledsoe in a disgusted tone.

"Mr. Sheriff," said the Judge, "adjourn court until 6 o'clock," and that ended the first session of the court.

About half-past one o'clock, Wilmot called on Colonel Greene at the Causeland House. His face was flushed and he was in a towering rage.

"Do you see what they are doing?" said Wilmot.

"I see that they don't intend to pay any attention to the terms of that surrender," said Colonel Greene.

"I know that," said Wilmot, "but don't you see what Bledsoe and Dosier are doing, while they are pretending to act as counsel for these Indians?"

"No, I didn't see anything wrong. Bledsoe did more than I expected to see him, in cross-examining that witness. I should think that a very doubtful point about identifying these particular Indians."

"Well, Colonel, you would never make a lawyer, that's one thing sure."

"I don't think I should. But what is wrong about that defense?"

"It's a fraud, a most damnable fraud," said Wilmot, and he brought his fist down on the table with a force that made everything in the room rattle. "Can't you see what that fellow was deliberately doing? The only ground for a defense which was left was that these were not the persons who committed the crime; and he went to work with malice and deliberation to put that point beyond dispute. When he commenced to question the witness on points not mentioned in the examination in chief, he made him, in law, his own witness. Now, you can't introduce testimony to impeach your own witness. So what he says, if it is against you, must stand. Now, after he had made him his own witness, he goes to work and proves that these are the identical Indians. He can't impeach that witness now. His testimony must stand. It seals the fate of every one of them. Every question he asked was asked for the purpose of proving that these were the very parties and no mistake. It's a fraud, a most damnable fraud, and Bledsoe and Dosier ought to be hung, drawn and quartered. They have deliberately sacrificed the lives of their clients. Why did not they ask for a continuance, summon witnesses and prove an alibi? They never could have convicted these Indians in the world if they had made half a defense. A lawyer who will betray his client—well, there is no place in the infernal regions half hot enough for him."

"I see now," said Colonel Greene, "the object of those questions. I came down here to see if I could aid these poor men in any way, but I guess the case is hopeless. I don't think, though, that these lawyers have betrayed their client. The Secretary of the Interior is their client, and not these Indians. He hired them, and I suppose they are trying to carry out his wishes, and perhaps his instructions."

"Oh, no," said Wilmot, "it is impossible that the

Secretary of the Interior should do such a thing. He is a statesman of national reputation, and that he has the good of these Indians at heart I have no doubt. It is impossible that he should know anything about the circumstances of this case. I have a notion to go to Washington and lay the whole matter before him."

"That would be a waste of time. He knows a good deal more about it than you do. They have all the facts down to the smallest details in Washington. All my official reports have been laid before the Secretary of the Interior for his information, and I have been very careful to make them full and explicit. I sent all the facts about the attack on Hickman's and the robbery of the stage-coach, with the evidence showing that the crime was committed by white men, over a year ago, and it was sent to the Secretary's office the very day it was received in Washington."

"Is it possible?" said Wilmot, "you astonish me beyond measure."

"You see it is only a waste of time and money for you to go there to give him information."

"What is to be done then?"

"There is nothing which can be done that I know," said Colonel Greene. "These men, though innocent, will have to suffer death."

"It is perfectly awful," said Wilmot.

"I have seen the same scenes enacted, over and over again, ever since I have been in the army. I only know of two ways that this cruelty can be stopped. One is to make the Indians citizens and treat them like all other persons, and the other to put them entirely under the control of the army. If these Indians who are under arrest here were citizens, they would have the right to choose their own counsel, but as they are 'wards' of the nation, the Secretary of the Interior is their guardian, and he employs their lawyers for them."

"Shall you make any further effort to assist them?"

"No, I shall start for the fort in the morning. I sent a courier the moment I received the order for their arrest, with a report, containing a protest against the violation of the conditions on which these Indians surrendered, to the department commander, but nothing can be done."

When court was called that afternoon a great crowd was in attendance. Another witness was called and the scene of the morning was re-enacted, and so it went on for two or three days. At last the case was submitted and the jury found them guilty without leaving their seats.

Long afterward Colonel Greene wrote the following account of the last scene in this tragedy:

"The trial was over and, of course, the Indians were condemned to be hanged. Without a murmur or sigh of regret, and with a dignity that would have impressed a Zulu with profound pity, these men walked to the gallows and were hung, while a crowd of 'civilized' Americans,—men, women and children of the nineteenth century,—looked on and laughed at their last convulsions.

"We have read of heroes of all times, but never did we read or believe that such heroism as these

Indians exhibited could exist. They knew that to be accused was to be condemned, and that they would be executed in that civilized town, just as surely as would a poor woman accused of being a witch have been executed in the civilized town of Salem, in the good State of Massachusetts, two hundred years ago.

"Many years have passed away since the execution or murder of these Indians. Bledsoe & Dosier still live, and the intelligent jury, no man of whom dared to utter a word of pity or admiration of these poor Indians, with the spectators of that horrid scene, are either dead and damned, or they are sunk in the oblivion that is the fate of those who are born without souls. But while history is read, or men admire that which is heroic, noble and unselfish, will these brave sufferers under a system more cruel and relentless than the iron rule of czar or sultan, be remembered and honored."

CHAPTER XXVII.

COLONEL GREENE DISGRACED.

ARKINS had conducted the Indians to their reservation. He was active, prudent and energetic. The first thing to be done was to build the necessary agency buildings. The spot chosen was on the bank of the river. Near by was a large bottom covered with a heavy growth of timber. The houses for the agency employees were strung along the bank without any regard to order. They were one-story frame houses, except the agent's, which was two-story. Then there was a blacksmith-shop, a carpenter-shop, the trader's house and store, the council-room, and the agent's office. Their erection cost the full amount estimated by Parker. This gave active employment to Harkins for many weeks, but when they were finished a dull monotony settled down over everything. He was, as it were, out of the world, no occupation, no kind of amusement. A constant tattle went on between the families which constituted the little white colony. It was, "she said," "he said," "they did this," and "they did that," from morning until night. Nobody had anything to do, so they spent their time in tattling.

One day Red Iron and two or three leading men appeared at the agent's office, and requested a pass to go down to the fort on the Little Blue. Red Iron said that he had heard that the conditions of the surrender to Colonel Greene had been violated and he wanted to go and see that officer. Harkins granted him permission and the chief started forthwith.

The morning that Red Iron came to Harkins's office, was just three days after the Lieutenant had appeared at Badger's tent. The agencies were two hundred and fifty miles apart. Badger had sent a runner and he had traveled that distance on foot. When the runner arrived at Red Iron's tent, he was so much exhausted that he fell at the door as he stooped to come in. The long journey to the fort on the Little

Blue was made by the chiefs on foot, and when they arrived, they found that Colonel Greene was absent. They waited ten days for his return.

When Colonel Greene was informed of their presence, he said,

"I never was in such a humiliating position in my life. I don't see how I can meet this old chief or even look him in the face."

However, a council was arranged and the two men came together. Red Iron spoke as follows:

"When I came in from the Arickoree to make peace, I did it because I thought it would be best for my people. I then had with me a large number of warriors. They were all well armed and we had many horses. I could have carried on the war for a long time. We did not make peace because we were conquered. In doing so, I stipulated, first of all, that none of my people should be killed. I was particular to mention Badger and his band, for he had had a fight with the soldiers and killed a great many. You promised me that their lives should all be spared, that not one of them should be hurt. Now, I have heard that you have arrested Badger and four others and sent them across the river, where the white people are going to hang them. Worst of all is, you have charged them with killing some people in a stage-coach, and they did not do it. All this is a direct violation of the promise you made to me when we surrendered. I have come to talk to you about it. I want to save the life of Badger and the others whom you have arrested. I want you to keep your promise. I am as a prisoner now. I cannot go to war to avenge this wrong. My young men have no arms. We have no horses. We are perfectly helpless. You can arrest us and hang us all, and we cannot resist. I believed what you said. I trusted in your word, and I gave up all my arms and horses. I have come to ask you to keep your word."

Colonel Greene had felt humiliated before; now he felt disgraced and dishonored. What reply could he make? What could an honorable man do under such circumstances? He bowed his head in his hands and sat in silence. At last he replied (Jack had returned with him, and was acting as interpreter) as follows:

"What you have said is true. Every word you have spoken is true. When I made you that promise I expected it would be kept. It is like this: if you sent your head warrior out to fight with another tribe, and tell him if they desired to surrender to him that he might promise that you would treat them well, and adopt them into your tribe, and he should go and make such terms with them; and when they were brought into your camp you should change your mind and kill them all, the head warrior would not be to blame. That is just the way it was with me."

"But no Indian would do such a thing as that," said Red Iron. "If I sent my head warrior out to make a promise, I would keep it."

"Jack," said the Colonel, "you know how all this came about. I wish you would explain it to him fully."

"It's no use," said Jack; "you can't never make an Injun understand why, when the Government, through its officers, makes a promise, that that promise should not be kept. This is the way he thinks about it. Badger surrendered, and did everything he promised. He was living peaceably on his reservation with his family. All at once the soldiers come and arrest him, and take him off and hang him. You are the head soldier, and you give the orders. If you did not want Badger hung, you should not give the orders."

"Does the Great Father know about this?" asked Red Iron.

"I don't think he does," said Colonel Greene.

"Then why don't you write a letter and tell him?"

"There it is again," said Jack. "How do you suppose that I can make him understand that the President can't interfere with the process of the courts and the verdicts of juries? I tell you it can't be explained to him."

"Tell him," said Colonel Greene, "that there are millions of white people, and every day there are a great many men tried in the courts, and it would be utterly impossible for the Great Father to look into all these cases, and it must be left to the courts."

"How do you suppose I can tell him that?" said Jack. "In the first place, there is no word in the Indian language for 'million.' They can only count as high as ten thousand with certainty, and a hundred thousand is the uttermost limit of their enumeration, and in the second place there is no word for 'court.' He don't know anything about courts."

"Well, what does he know?"

"He knows as much about the eternal principles of

right and wrong as any man, and he knows when a promise is broken and when it is kept."

"Well, can't you tell him in some simple way that I am his friend, and that I have done all that I could to have the terms of the surrender kept sacred."

"Yes, I can tell him that," said Jack, and he interpreted it to Red Iron.

"He is a great chief," said Red Iron. "He told me that all the soldiers in this part of the country had to obey his orders. He told me that he had authority to make the conditions of the surrender, and that the Great Father would do what he promised. Ask him if he did not tell me that?"

"I did," said Colonel Greene.

"Now, then, he tells me that somebody has more authority than he has, and that they ordered him to have Badger hung. If he is my friend why did he not tell me that there was a man somewhere who could issue orders that he would have to obey?"

"Can you explain to him," asked Colonel Greene, of Jack, "how that, as long as I held them as prisoners of war, I could see that my promise was kept, but when the Secretary of the Interior took charge of them, they passed under the control of another department of the Government, over which the military have no control?"

"Now, Colonel," said Jack, "there ain't more than five hundred white men in the United States who understand the relations existing between the Interior and War Departments in regard to Indians, and I am not one of that five hundred. How can I explain to an Injun what I have been trying to understand for ten years myself and never could find head nor tail to it. I'll do my best to interpret anything you have to say, but I've got nothing to say myself on that subject. I give you warning though, before you commence, that there ain't no words in the Injun language for such things as departments of government, secretaries of war and the interior."

"I guess it can't be done."

"No, I said it couldn't in the first place. This Injun will always think you broke your promise, and I can't help it."

This ended the council. The next day the chiefs started back to their reservation and Jack accompanied them. One of the chiefs who was with Red Iron was Badger's brother. All hope seemed to have died within his bosom. He longed very much to make a personal plea for his brother's life to Colonel Greene, but the formalities of a council, according to an Indian's idea of etiquette, forbade it. If he could have spoken English he would have gone to Colonel Greene privately, but to plead for his brother's life through an interpreter he could never do. When this fact became known, some of the officers, who had great sympathy for all of of them, collected a little sum of money and gave it to them. They also met at the fort another band of Indians who made them presents of horses, and so Jack and the chiefs returned on horseback.

CHAPTER XXVIII.

AN AGENCY SCHOOL.

AS day after day passed away, Jennie Walker grew more and more anxious. She would go to the post-office the moment she saw the stage coming and wait until the mail was opened and delivered. For a while she got letters about twice a week, and then they ceased to come at all.

Mr. and Mrs. Parkman were getting ready to go to the new reservation as missionaries. One afternoon Jennie put on her hat and went to the Causeland House and asked for Mr. Harkins. When that gentleman came into the parlor she made application to him for the position of teacher on the reserve, and referred him to Mr. and Mrs. Parkman as to her character and qualifications. Mr. Harkins was very favorably impressed with her, but wondered much why a young lady of her appearance should desire to go and live on an Indian reserve, and asked her what her motives were in desiring to undertake such difficult and dangerous work.

"I have felt it my duty," she said, "to become a missionary, and I think it is our duty to teach the way of salvation first to the heathen in our own land."

"That is so," said Harkins. "I have often wondered why it was, that the churches sent missionaries away off to the South Sea Ilands, to Africa and India, while the Indians were almost entirely neglected. I will see Mr. Parkman and let you know in a day or two."

When Mr. Parkman was ready to start Jennie went along.

In constructing the buildings at the agency no school-house was built. The treaty said that the money should be expended under the direction of the Secretary of the Interior, but the orders to Harkins came from the Commissioner of Indian Affairs, and he set apart no money for a school house. The missionary and his family did not have a house built for them by the government. Mr. Parkman had a salary of five hundred dollars a year paid to him by the Missionary Society, and out of that he could not build himself a nice house like the agency employees had provided for them. He had a small tent and the covered wagon in which he had moved, and in these he lived. The Indians often wondered why it was that the man who came to teach them about God did not have a nice house like the other white people. One day Red Iron came to the little tent. Jack was along with him, and he had a pony pretty well ladened. He unpacked the pony and then called to some Indian women near by. After he had spoken a few words to them, they untied the bundle, separated the poles and set up a nice large tent. Then he said to Mrs. Parkman,

"I have brought you a big tent, one that it will be nice for you to live in. The one you have is too little."

The tears came into Mrs. Parkman's eyes, and she said:

"Red Iron, I don't see why you do this act of kindness to us. After all the white people have done to you I should think you would hate us."

"I know," he said, "that there are good white people as well as bad ones. You came here to do us good. You did not come because you would have a fine house to live in," and then he went away.

Mr. Parkman was hard at work in the woods cutting logs to build him a house. The Indians watched him with a great deal of curiosity, and sometimes they would take an axe and try to chop, but they made poor work of it. There was one young Indian who went with him nearly every day. His name was Gray Cloud. Little by little he learned to handle tools, and when the agent let Mr. Parkman have the agency team to haul the logs to build his house, he was of great assistance. It took Mr. Parkman several weeks to build his house. When finished, it was twenty-four feet long, sixteen feet wide, had two rooms, and was covered with dirt.

Meantime Jennie had made a school-house out of Red Iron's big tent. She did not have a book, slate, desk, map or any appliance whatever for teaching. She could not understand one word the children said, they could not understand her, and she had no interpreter. She told Jack to tell Red Iron that she wanted some of the children to come and she would teach them how to read. The next day about a dozen came, accompanied either by their fathers or mothers. One of the first things Harkins did when he arrived there, was to make estimates for the school-house, furniture and books, and he had written repeatedly to the Commissioner urging that they be sent on, but he never made any reply. Jennie asked him to have a blackboard made for her, and the carpenter made one. This was fastened to two sticks stuck in the ground. Jennie hunted up and down the bank of the river until she found some soft red stone, called "keel," and this she used in place of chalk.

The children came into the tent; all sat down on the ground in Indian style, and the first school on the reservation was opened.

Jennie made a picture, on the blackboard, of a horse. She pointed to it and said, "What is it?" The children were all silent. Then she put her fingers to her lips and said again, "What is it?"

One bright little girl said, timidly, "Shonga."

Jennie did not catch the word exactly, and said, "Shonnee."

The children looked bewildered. Then she pointed to the picture again, and a boy said out strong and loud, "Shon-ga!"

Jennie pronounced the word just as he did, and three or four of the larger boys said—there are no English letters which will spell it phonetically, but it is usually written "how"—being their way of signifying their approval or assent to what is said. Then Jennie said it and they said it two or three times over. After that exercise was over she pointed to the picture again, and said "horse."

There being no sound of "r" in their language, this word was too hard for them; several tried it, but did not get it right.

While this was going on, a little fellow unseen by Jennie had crawled out under the edge of the tent. He came in with a handful of sugar. Jennie was somewhat surprised when she saw him, and was just going to say to him that he must not go out again without permission, when she thought "Why, he can't understand."

The little boy came up to her and pointed to the sugar in his hand, and said, "Shonnee." Then he pointed the picture on the blackboard, and said, " Shonga."

At first Jennie could not imagine what he meant. All at once she thought, " Why, 'Shonnee' is sugar, and 'Shonga' is horse."

Then she said "sugar." They tried that, but there was another " r," and they could not get it quite right.

An Indian was sitting by the tent door, filling his pipe. Jennie went up to him and took up a small bit of the tobacco and held it up. They all said " neenee." Then she said " tobacco." To her surprise they pronounced that long word perfectly correct. There was no sound in it which was not in their own language. Thus the lesson went on for two hours. Then Jennie sang a Sunday-school hymn, which very much pleased the children. At the close of the hymn she looked down on the group of little, anxious, upturned faces, and thought how they were shut out from all the knowledge which had made her race rich and happy, and tears came into her eyes. In a moment more she kneeled down, clasped her hands over her bosom, and prayed. That prayer was full of all the loving and tender sympathy of woman.

Although the children could not understand a word they whispered to one another, "She is talking to God."

When the children went home they had many wonderful things to tell their mothers about the white teacher.

CHAPTER XXIX.

THE MIGHTY MONARCH.

WILMOT was a strict believer in the maxim "Better travel a thousand miles than write a letter;" but he could not always follow it out. In working out his plans to convict this ring of thieves it was necessary that he should keep up a correspondence with Harkins. So he arranged a cipher to be used between them, thinking that if any member of the ring should happen to intercept one or more of the letters, they would be none the wiser.

In an ordinarily friendly letter Wilmot inclosed a small slip, on which the following words were written:

"Fosse bypath privately messuage abacuses corrector anemography accouple offenseless allege expensiveness toadies data, withdrawment nankeens offenseless parvanu toadies whortleberry moneysworth washdown painful, amphribology offenseless annular anemography rationality soapstone faring recent. Statement quandaries. Maladministration carelessness inspirable of fenseless suggestion, cogged, flow, been anemography porphybitic. Repository **firth** indict offenseless fraudulent."

The post-office is always located in the trader's store at every agency. Sometimes he is a regularly appointed Postmaster and sometimes he is not, the letters being directed to the nearest post-office, and forwarded there for distribution to the employees. Parker had been suspicious of Harkins from the first, and he had kept a sharp look-out from the time he had opened his store. He had a little round piece of wood, which he could insert under the sealed edge of an envelope, and by rolling it along he could open almost any letter without mutilating it in the least. Then by applying a little mucilage he could seal it up, and no one would ever suspect it had been tampered with. He applied his "little joker," as he called it, to Wilmot's letter, and discovered the slip with the cipher message upon it. He copied the words very carefully, and then sealed up the letter again.

Up to this time Harkins had not discovered even an indication of fraud. It is true that the construction of the agency buildings had cost more than he thought they ought to, but the contracts which had been made were carried out to the letter. The flour, beef, pork, sugar, coffee, in fact everything, had been of fair quality. Harkins began to think that Wilmot had been mistaken, and an agent of the department had only been testing him, by the propositions which were made to him, to see if he was honest, when one day the cattle for beef did not arrive. The consequence was that several thousand Indians were left almost without food. They had no way to procure food for themselves, for an agency Indian is entirely dependent on the Government. There was no game in the reservation, and they had no arms or ammunition to hunt with if there had been. To stop the rations for one day only was to leave men, women and children without food.

Harkins sent out scouts to find where the herd was. They came back after two days' absence and reported that they were sixty miles away, and traveling about fifteen miles a day. It would take four days for them to reach the agency. Hungry men, women and children were hanging around the agency, so hungry that they stood around the doors of the houses of the white employees and picked up every bone and scrap that was thrown out, and gnawed at it ravenously. Sickness commenced. Starvation always brings sickness. Harkins found that the medical supplies were exhausted. He reprimanded the physician for not having forwarded his estimates in time, but when he came to look over his own papers he found that the estimates had long since been forwarded, but only one quarter of the amount estimated had been contracted for. The Secretary of the Interior had exercised his "discretion," in accordance with the terms of the treaty. He thought the estimates were too large and had cut them down. Harkins wrote a most urgent letter to the Commissioner, asking that medical supplies be sent immediately. No attention was paid to it. He then invited Colonel Greene to send a board of army medical officers to inspect affairs at the agency. The surgeons came and made a report, setting forth the extent of the sickness and suffering for the lack of medical supplies, and this was forwarded. Upon the receipt of this the Commissioner, representing the Secretary of the Interior, in the exercise of his "discretion," ordered five ounces of quinine to be purchased and forwarded.

When the beef cattle finally arrived, a portion was slaughtered and six days' rations were distributed. The Indians, being ravenously hungry, ate the most of it the first day, and at the end of three days had none left. Three days of starving ensued, and when the next issue was made the same scenes were enacted again. This alternate gorging and starving produced still more sickness.

Harkins represented things just as they were in his report to the Commissioner. The last herd of cattle driven in were almost gone. Harkins feared another repetition of the starving which he had witnessed, and wrote to the Commissioner urging that the contractors be forced to deliver the beef on time. In reply to this, he got a note from the Commissioner saying that he would do all that was possible to push the contractors, but if they should fail again, not to let the Indians starve, but instruct the trader to furnish them such things as they actually needed from the store, keeping an account with each head of a family, and the money could be paid by them when they received their cash annuity. Not a word was said about the medical supplies.

Harkins sent Jack to Council Bluffs with a full report of the state of affairs, and closed it by saying that he did not believe they intended to furnish the Indians with any more rations, except through the trader. He had also discovered that a great many of the Indians had obtained firearms of the most approved pattern. On inquiry he had found that the guns had been sold to them on credit by the trader. The trader had a very large stock of goods on hand.

The next day after Jack left, an Indian inspector arrived at the agency. An inspector is one of the numerous officers appointed by law in the Indian service, and is under the control of the Secretary of the Interior. Of course, if he should do anything displeasing to the Secretary he would be instantly dismissed. The salary is a pretty liberal one. All of his acts and reports are in line with the Secretary's " policy."

Inspector Brown held a long consultation with the trader. He then called at Harkins's office, and examined his books and accounts. He left the agency without making any suggestions or giving any directions. Three days after that a company of troops arrived and camped near the trader's store. They were under command of Lieutenant Blake.

Harkins called upon him, and asked:

" Why did these troops come here?"

" They were ordered here," said the Lieutenant.

" How long will they remain?"

" Until they are ordered away."

" Everything is peaceful here. What is the object of their coming?"

" My object was to obey my instructions."

That day a detail was sent out, and they made a search through all the tents for arms. Not a gun was found. That night several of the soldiers got drunk, and made a raid on a tent, captured two Indian girls, and carried them off to the woods. They were allowed to return about daylight. Nobody could tell where the soldiers got their whisky. The four soldiers who were engaged in this outrage were arrested in the morning, by order of Lieutenant Blake, and each of them tied fast to a wagon wheel, in which position, with a few moments of intermission at a time, he kept them for four days.

This affair created a great uproar among the Indians. When the chiefs called on Lieutenant Blake in regard to the matter, he pointed to the men tied to wagon wheels, and told them that he should take them back to the fort when he went, where every one of them would be shot, by order of the Great Father. The chiefs thought that was sufficient, and were satisfied. The four days tied to a wagon wheel, however, was all the punishment they ever received.

A few days after this, Inspector Brown returned to the agency. He went direct to Harkins's house, and summarily dismissed him as agent, and took charge of the agency himself. Half an hour afterward, Harkins found himself under arrest by a deputy United States Marshal, who had a warrant for him. He was informed that Brown had sworn out a warrant for his arrest, and it had been placed in his hands; and the Marshal politely put a pair of handcuffs on him. He had been charged, on the information filed by Brown, with stealing several hundred head of cattle belonging to the Indians. Harkins was marched off to the guard-house, which he had built himself, under orders from the Commissioner.

About the middle of the afternoon of the same day Harkins was arrested, Wilmot and Jack arrived. Wilmot was instantly arrested.

Inspector Brown read to him an order from the Secretary of the Interior, dated at Washington, and duly signed by that official.

"What crime am I charged with?" asked Wilmot.

"You are not charged with any crime," said Brown, "but under the Revised Statutes of the United States the Secretary has the power, according to law, to arrest any person he may choose, found upon an Indian reservation. He has directed your arrest if you came upon this reserve, and I am simply obeying orders."

Two soldiers, under the command of a corporal, marched Wilmot off to the guard-house. He was handcuffed to Harkins, the door was shut and bolted, and they were left alone. There they stood with the irons upon them, looking into each other's faces. Before they had time to speak, a fiendish face appeared at the little aperture which alone admitted light and air to the dungeon. It was Parker, the trader.

In a voice full of hatred and malice, he asked:

"How do you like the working of your little plan to send us all to the penitentiary?"

Of course, Harkins and Wilmot, chained together in a cell, were furious with rage.

"I wonder whether this is Russia or America," said Wilmot.

They were only suffering a just punishment for trying to interfere with the "policy" of that almighty monarch, the Secretary of the Interior.

CHAPTER XXX.

WREAKING VENGEANCE ON A WOMAN.

ILMOT and Harkins were confined in the guard-house. Early next morning Jack's face appeared at the hole in the wall. Wilmot and Harkins were walking up and down the cell chained together.

"What did I tell you?" said Jack. "Nothing but cold lead will do for these fellows. Perkins is at the bottom of the whole of it, and I know it. How're you going to git out?"

"Hang me if I know," said Harkins. "Ask Wilmot. He got me in here and he must get me out."

"Jack," said Wilmot, "can you get me some paper, pen and ink?"

"Don't know. All the paper there is around the agency is at the trader's store, and I hardly think Parker would let me have any. Besides, if I should undertake to put anything in at this hole, I'd get a bullet through me. There's a guard out here watching."

"What do you want with paper, pen and ink?" asked Harkins.

"I want to write a note to Dawson, he's the best lawyer in Council Bluffs, and have him sue out a writ of *habeas corpus*."

"Say," said Jack, "I think I know where I can get some paper. I'll bet Mr. Parkman has some."

"Well, go and get it quick," said Wilmot.

Jack had four revolvers stuck in his belt, and carried in his hand a repeating rifle. He walked down to the trader's store, went in, bought a plug of tobacco, and then walked out. Brown and Parker were standing near the door. A little to one side there was a small ground-squirrel. It was running around, stopping every moment or so, standing on its hind feet and looking about.

"See thar, stranger," said Jack, to Inspector Brown. "Now see me knock that chap's head off."

He pulled out his revolver, fired, and the squirrel's head was gone. Jack put another cartridge in his pistol and walked away.

"That's a desperate-looking ruffian," said Brown.

"He is the worst desperado on the plains," said Parker.

"Why don't you get rid of him?"

"That's easier said than done, you see how he can shoot. Besides that, he is a member of the tribe."

"I wish I had known about him before I came back. I would have got orders for his arrest too, and sent the military after him. I always go on the principle of letting them take the risks. That's what they are paid for."

Jack went around to the carpenter-shop, and then

to the blacksmith-shop, giving them all exhibitions of his skill with a pistol. Then he mounted a wild mustang pony, and rode at full gallop up and down and around the agency, yelling like a demon, and firing off his pistols. After he got tired of that, he called up an Indian, gave his horse to him, and told him to lariat it out. Then he went over to Mr. Parkman's log-house. The school had been moved from the tent into one of the rooms of Mr. Parkman's house, and there were just as many children present as could well be crowded in.

Jennie was standing up by her blackboard, with a piece of "keel" in her hand. There were no pictures on the board now, but "words." The children had advanced so that many of them could write small words quite nicely. Gray Cloud was there. He had a small blackboard of his own, but his was covered with figures. He had made the board himself.

Jack sat down on the ground with the children and looked on. He had not been there many minutes until Jennie asked him if he would please interpret for her a little.

"I have never been able to talk with them but once," she said, "and then only a few words. I asked Mr. Harkins to send me the Government interpreter, and he did, but he was so rough and insulting to me that I never wanted him to come again." (The Government interpreter was a half-breed, who had been hired by Harkins by the express order of the Commissioner.)

Jack said he would with pleasure. Then Jennie spoke as follows:

"I am so sorry I can't talk with you every day; but

I am trying very hard to learn your language. I can speak a few words now. I want to tell you about Jesus. He was God's son, and he came into the world to teach us what is right. He loved little children, and took them in his arms and blessed them. He said we must love one another, and do good to one another. I read this in his book, and that is why I came to teach you. I love you all very much, and I want you all to be good. By and by, when I can talk to you myself, I will tell you more. I want to talk to your mothers, and tell them how good you have been."

Jennie then dismissed them, and they went away for their two hours' recess, which she gave them at noon. She found that it was necessary to have short sessions, for they could not endure too much confinement.

After the children left, Jack and Jennie went into the other room. Mr. Parkman was seated at a rude table, which he had made himself. Several large sheets of paper were spread out on the table, on which there were lists of words, some in English and some in the Indian language. He was engaged in learning the language, and reducing it to writing. The papers were speedily put away, and the all-absorbing topic of the removal of the agent and the imprisonment of Wilmot was introduced.

Jack told Mr. Parkman that Wilmot wanted some paper and pen and ink, to write to a lawyer in Council Bluffs to get him out of jail.

"But," said he, "I don't know how I am to get it to him. Brown will never give permission for him to write, and there are two guards stationed there, and you can't get it in without one of them seeing."

Jennie arose and put on her hat.

"Where are you going, my dear," asked Mrs. Parkman.

"I am going to take writing material to Mr. Wilmot," she replied.

"How will you do it?" asked Jack.

"I don't know," said Jennie. "I can only pray that God will help me."

She rolled up some paper, took a pen and a small bottle of ink, placed them under her shawl and walked out.

She went direct to the guard-house. A soldier stood a short distance from the little opening.

"Good-day," said Jennie.

"Good-day, mum," answered the soldier.

"Isn't it very tiresome standing here?"

"It's a kind of duty we have to do."

"How long do you have to stand here?"

"Two hours on and four hours off."

"When do you go off?"

"At twelve o'clock. That's pretty soon now."

"May I talk to the men inside?"

"Do you know them?"

"Oh, yes. I know them both."

"Yes, you can talk to them through that hole, but you must not give them anything; that's the orders."

"You won't look at me all the time, will you?" and Jennie smiled and blushed.

"I reckon you don't want me to hear either, do

you?" said the soldier. Think a good deal of them, don't you?"

"Yes," said Jennie; and then, in a lower tone, "That is, one of them."

The soldier laughed and said, "What will you give me if I turn my back?"

"Oh, I'll give you anything!"

"Well, I won't look."

"Won't you now?"

"No, 'pon honor I won't. If I was in the guard-house, and my girl came to see me, I wouldn't want anybody to be looking. Now, see here, I'll go off to the other end of my beat, and stay there while you talk to him."

Jennie went up to the opening. She stood on her toes and peeped in. There, sitting on the floor, hand-cuffed together, were Wilmot and Harkins.

"Mr. Wilmot," said she, timidly.

"Who's there?" he answered.

"It's Jennie Walker. I have brought you the writing materials. Take them quickly and write what you want to. Don't stop to talk, for the guard may interfere. Don't say a word. Just write."

She passed the paper, pen and ink inside. She could not see in without standing on her tiptoes. Near where the soldier stood was a block of wood. She went and got it to stand upon.

"She couldn't quite kiss him standing on the ground," the soldier said to himself, but he kept his word and didn't look.

It didn't take Wilmot long to write what he wanted

to say to Dawson. He handed it to Jennie, and said,

"Take that to Jack and tell him to put it into Dawson's hands just as soon as he can get it there."

"I will do it," said Jennie.

"Miss Walker, I hope we will meet under more favorable circumstances before long."

"I hope we may. I have wanted to talk with you, oh! for so long."

"Have you?"

"Indeed I have, but I could never get an opportunity. I wanted to apologize for the rude manner in which I treated you, just as you were starting off for the Indian war."

Wilmot began to wish that Harkins was in Halifax or some other place, but there he was, chained to him, with no chance to get away.

"Miss Walker," said Wilmot, "I will try and see you just as soon as I am released by this writ."

"I'd like to know how you are going to see her," said Harkins, as Jennie walked away. "If you come out here, there's a standing order of the Secretary of the Interior to arrest you and put you in confinement."

"That's so. I didn't think of that. What an infernal thing this Indian system is anyhow. Think of it! Here we are, two American citizens, chained together in a miserable dungeon, never having committed any crime, denied bail. I tell you what, Harkins, this whole thing is unconstitutional. Is the Secretary of the Interior an absolute monarch? Can he arrest and put in chains any man he sees fit?"

"Well, he has seen fit to arrest and chain you anyhow. What are you going to do about it?"

"I'll sue this Brown for fifty thousand dollars for false imprisonment. I'll let them know whether an American citizen, who has never committed a crime, can be handcuffed and imprisoned without any process of law whatsoever, at the dictate of some individual in Washington. There is not a monarchical government in Europe to-day that can do such a thing."

"I don't care anything about the governments of Europe. I want to get this handcuff off, and out of this jail. The next time you get me to go into a plot against the Indian Ring, you'll know it. I've had enough of it."

As Jennie was going back to Mr. Parkman's, she met Inspector Brown.

"You have been up to the guard-house?"

"Yes, sir," said Jennie.

"Are you acquainted with Mr. Wilmot?"

"Yes, sir."

"How long have you known him?"

"I have known him since the beginning of this war."

"He's a friend of yours?"

"Yes, sir. He saved my life at the time Red Iron made the raid on the west side of the river."

"Have you seen him frequently since that time?"

"Only once or twice." The Inspector passed on, and no more was said.

When Jennie came back to Mrs. Parkman's, Jack was still there, and she delivered Mr. Wilmot's letter and request that he should take it to Mr. Dawson immediately.

As he was going out she said:

"Jack, I wish you would not be so rough. See how you were riding around and shooting this morning. You frighten people half to death."

"Were you afraid?" asked Jack.

"No, because I know you, but people who don't know you will think you're awful."

"If you won't tell anybody, I'll tell you why I did it."

"I won't."

"Well, you see there ain't any law or government of any kind here, and these inspectors and agents can do just as they please, arrest anybody they take a notion to, and keep 'em in jail just as long as they want. I knowed one feller an agent kept locked up and chained for nine months, and it so worked on him that he died a little while after he got away. The fact was, I and some other fellers made a raid on the old pen he was shut up in, tore it down, and let him go. Now, I had a sorter of an idea that this 'ere inspector had his eye on me, and I thought I'd let him know the kind of metal I was made of, and what he might expect if he undertook that sort of a job. I think they'll give me a wide berth."

"You wanted to scare them," said Jennie.

"That's just it," said Jack.

The next day, Jennie was teaching in her school, as usual. Very suddenly, and very much to her surprise, the government interpreter walked in. He said a few words to the children in the Indian language, which Jennie did not understand. They sprang to their feet, and all rushed out of the room, and ran home as fast as their legs could carry them. He then handed Jennie the following letter:

"Miss J. Walker:

"Your services as teacher at this agency will be no longer required. Please call at the office and receive your salary, which will be paid up to last night.
"Yours truly,
"J. Young Brown,
"United States Indian Inspector and Acting Agent."

For a moment after reading the letter Jennie stood speechless, her face as white as snow. Then she burst into a flood of tears, and sobbed and sobbed as if her heart would break.

"Oh, my poor, dear little ones," she said, "you will have no one to teach you now."

She stood leaning her head against the wall for a long time, weeping most bitterly. At last Mr. Parkman came in.

"Where are the children? What is the matter?" he asked.

"The Inspector—" said Jennie, and then she could speak no more for sobs and tears.

"What has the Inspector done?"

"He has broken up my school and discharged me."

"What reason has he assigned; what did he do it for?"

11*

"I don't know. Here is his letter."

Mr. Parkman read the letter.

"This is very strange," said he.

"I don't know what I have done," said Jennie. She sat down on a little stool which Gray Cloud had made for her, and sobbed as if her heart would break.

Presently they went into the other room. Jennie put her arms around Mrs. Parkman's neck, and tears streamed down over both of their faces in silence. Presently Mrs. Parkman reached out her hand, took up a well-worn pocket Bible, and read:

"Let not your heart be troubled; ye believe in God, believe also in me."

"And God shall wipe away all tears from their eyes, and there shall be no more death, neither sorrow nor crying, neither shall there be any more pain."

"Though I walk through the valley of the shadow of death, I will fear no evil, for thou art with me."

After reading these words it was silent for some minutes in the missionaries' room. Mrs. Parkman began to sing. How many weary, heart-broken ones have found relief in sacred song! These were the words:

"Though troubles assail and dangers affright,
  Though friends should all fail and foes all unite;
  Yet one thing secures us, whatever betide,
  The promise assures us the Lord will provide."

Again it was silent. Finally Jennie's sobs ceased. She raised her head. A calm and heavenly look had come into her face. She sang in her clear, pure voice:

> "There is an hour of peaceful rest
>   To mourning wand'rers given ;
> There is a joy for souls distressed,
> A balm for every wounded breast—
>   'Tis found above in heaven.
>
> "There is a home for weary souls
>   By sin and sorrow driven,
> When tossed on life's tempestuous shoals,
> Where storms arise and ocean rolls,
>   And all is drear but heaven."

As Jennie sang, a look of joy and triumph came over her. Timid, weak and cowardly as she was by nature, she would at that moment have walked to the stake and burned, and have counted it a joy, if by that means she could have brought the Gospel to these Indians. The fear of death had been taken away. From this hour she was ready to suffer all things and endure all things. Whatever men may think, whatever explanation they may give, the fact cannot be disputed, that many missionaries, very cowardly and timid by nature, live always in this state of mind, and meet death with a calmness, fortitude and courage not excelled by those whom we denominate the bravest of the brave.

It was decided that Jennie should remain with Mr. Parkman. He would write to the missionary board, represent her case, and request that she be appointed and paid as a missionary.

CHAPTER XXXI.

JACK'S STRATAGEM.

THE next morning dawned on the agency as many had before. The farmer, carpenter, blacksmith, miller and other employees were lounging about here and there, some at the trader's store and some in other places. Nothing was to be seen save the dull, listless, lazy life which agency employees led. There was nothing for anybody to do, except the days when rations were issued. During the morning some of them pitched quoits, and a party were in the back room of the trader's store playing cards. About eleven o'clock two naked Indians (save breech-cloth and moccasins), covered with perspiration and out of breath, running at the top of their speed, rushed by the store and up to the agent's office. Inspector Brown was sitting there quietly looking over some papers. The Indians gesticulated wildly and talked rapidly, but of course he could not understand a word. He rushed out and called for the interpreter. He was nowhere to be found. After inquiry it was learned that he had gone off to a camp about ten miles away. An employee was put on a horse and started after him. There was great excitement among the Indians. All who were located to the southwest came rushing to the agency. Many of them began to put on their war-paint. The agency employees were frightened half out of their senses, for nobody could tell what the matter was. Lieutenant Blake had his whole command under arms, and had moved his train to a position on a hill near by. It was three o'clock when the interpreter returned. Then it was learned that the Comanches were coming. Shortly afterward, Indians on horseback could be seen on the hill-tops to the southwest. An hour later great volumes of smoke rolled up toward the sky to the northeast. The prairie was on fire, and the Indians had surrounded them. Lieutenant Blake had taken the soldiers away who were guarding Wilmot and Harkins, and they were left to themselves. He set his men to work throwing up some slight earthworks, and a defense made of brush and pieces of timber found around the agency. When night came, all the white people, except Mr. Parkman and his family, took refuge there. Nothing was heard or seen until about midnight, when the prairie was fired to the south. When daylight dawned, no Indians were in sight except those who belonged to the agency. The white people went back to their houses, and then it was discovered that the guard-house had been broken open and Wilmot and Harkins were gone.

Scouts were sent out in all directions, but there had been so much running around, it was not possible to discover any trail. The prairie had been burned over in the direction which the Indians on horseback had been seen, and so nothing could be discovered there. An examination of the guard-house showed that some one had furnished the prisoners with a saw, and they had sawed a log out and thus escaped.

The agency people had something to talk about for a long time afterward, but no one ever learned what was the cause of the disturbance. It was thought Gray Cloud, who had been a great favorite with agent Harkins, had furnished the saw.

The true cause of all the trouble was as follows:

When Jack left Mr. Parkman's, instead of starting for Council Bluffs with the latter, he went off to Red Iron's camp, which was ten miles away. He did not fancy riding back to Council Bluffs, for he had just come from there. He hadn't any faith in a writ of *habeas corpus*, so he said to himself,

"I'll serve a writ of *habeas corpus* on 'em such as no lawyer ever heard of before. I won't file any papers, or argue any motions before the court either, but I'll bet it'll fetch 'em."

Arriving at Red Iron's tent, he explained the situation, telling him that the inspector and trader would steal every cent of the money which was coming from the Great Father, unless Wilmot and Harkins could get away. If they could they would tell the Great Father all about this matter, and perhaps he would send Harkins back, or stop the stealing some other way.

Red Iron, who had not forgotten the days without rations, was willing to do anything he could do, with safety. So the two plotted an Indian raid, to draw the guards away and give an opportunity for them to escape.

The Indians who were seen on horseback were Red Iron's warriors, who were operating under his instructions, and so also were the excited runners who came into Brown's office. All but about half a dozen Indians, however, really thought there was a raid by the Comanches.

The first thing that Wilmot knew about this plot was when Jack appeared with a saw at the opening in the guard house.

"Here," said Jack, "I've got a writ of *habeas corpus*. You just file it on that log for awhile."

"I won't do any thing of the kind," said Wilmot, "I'm not going to break jail."

"Don't act like a fool," said Jack.

"Here, give it to me," said Harkins. "I've had enough of this. I'm going to get out if I can. You can stay here if you want to, but I won't."

"Where's the guard?" asked Wilmot.

"Where's the guard!" said Jack. "Didn't you know the guard had gone? Good heavens, go to work there and saw out that log, while I watch. Hain't you heard that the Comanches are comin', and the soldiers are all withdrawn to protect the trader's store, and you have been left in here to be scalped. You'll have your hair lifted inside of six hours if you stay in there."

When they heard this, Harkins and Wilmot went to work with a will, and were soon on the outside. Their fetters were sawn apart, they mounted the horses Jack had in a ravine close by, and rode away.

CHAPTER XXXII.

A LEGAL TANGLE.

WILMOT recognized the truth of the maxim, that "the lawyer who pleads his own cause has a fool for a client," and so he made up his mind that on his arrival he would engage Dawson to conduct his case for false imprisonment against Brown, and he would manage Harkins's case himself. Harkins, by his advice, upon his arrival, went directly to the magistrate who had issued the warrant for his arrest, surrendered to his jurisdiction, and gave bail in the sum of five thousand dollars for his appearance at the next term of court. Wilmot went to Dawson and laid his case before him.

"So you want to sue Brown for twenty thousand dollars damages?" said Dawson.

"Yes."

"What court will you bring your case in?"

"The United States District Court."

"Let me see how that will work. That reservation is not in this district."

"What district is it in?"

"I'll have to look," said Dawson.

The two lawyers took down the United States Statutes at Large and commenced to search. Not a word was spoken for half an hour. At last Dawson said:

"That reservation is in the heart of the Indian country, and is not included in the jurisdiction of any circuit or district court of the United States."

"I believe you are right," said Wilmot.

"Suppose we bring the case in the Territorial Court?"

"You can't do that, for Indian reservations are excluded from their jurisdiction by statute."

"The United States Courts must have jurisdiction," said Wilmot. "Harkins was arrested on a warrant issued by a Commissioner of the United States District Court, served by a deputy United States marshal. If that is so, the court must have civil jurisdiction also."

"I don't see how a court can have jurisdiction outside of the boundaries of the district as prescribed by law. I don't believe that marshal had any authority for arresting Harkins. At least that is the way it looks to me so far as I have examined it."

"You must be wrong," said Wilmot. "Congress could never have left millions of square miles of country without any form of government, a place where men can commit murder or any other crime, and they can't be arrested or tried in any court. That sort of a proposition will never do. Suppose I had shot the marshal when he attempted to arrest me, wouldn't I be guilty of crime, and do you mean to say I couldn't be tried in any court for it?"

"I say that is the way it looks to me as far as I have been able to examine it. I see this is a very knotty question. I will have to take time to look into it. Now you go home, study up your own case, and clear Harkins. I will attend to this."

Five days afterward Wilmot called again.

"Well, Dawson," said he, "what have you found out?"

"I never studied so hard in my life as I have during the last five days," said Dawson, "and I am about as much in the dark as I was I commenced. That reservation is not in the jurisdiction of any court, State, Territorial or United States. I've settled that. A court *can't* have jurisdiction outside of the limits prescribed by law, and that country is not included in the limits of any district or circuit. The Supreme Court of the United States has jurisdiction, but you can't commence such an action in that court."

"Well, how could they arrest Harkins then?"

"I said before I don't believe that they had any authority to arrest him, and you can move to dismiss the case on the ground that the crime charged was not committed within the jurisdiction of the court."

"But I don't want to dismiss the case. I want to try it, and ventilate this whole business."

"Well, you needn't make the motion then, and go on and try it. But I am not done with your case. I am going to look further. There must be some special statutes which I have not found."

Three days after this Dawson came into Wilmot's office.

"I've found it," he said. "There is a statute which extends the jurisdiction of the United States Courts over these reservations in relation to specified crimes, and Harkins's case comes under it. It's a peculiar sort of a thing."

"Peculiar!" said Wilmot. "In what way?"

"Well, I've studied it a good deal. You can arrest an Indian for a crime committed against a white man, but you can't arrest a white man for a crime committed against an Indian, or an Indian for a crime committed against another Indian, and there's several other things somewhat peculiar about it. I've done more reading in the last ten days than in a year before, and the more I look into this legislation affecting Indians, and the decisions which have been rendered by the Supreme Court, the deeper I get into the fog. Some of the decisions recognize them as nations. If they are nations, then our courts and law officers have no more right to go into their territory than into Canada. Then the intercourse law of 1838 and other statutes passed since that time, seem to put them completely into the jurisdiction of the United States. It's too big a question for me. I give it up."

"You don't mean to give up my case?" said Wilmot.

"No, not at all. I can sue this fellow Brown for twenty thousand dollars damages for false imprisonment, providing I can get service on him. How are we going to get service?"

"By publication, if no other way."

"Suppose I commence the suit in the United States District Court, and send a deputy marshal out there to the reservation to serve a notice, and then make notice by publication also."

"Go ahead. Do anything you like. You're running the case."

"Will you take my advice?"

"Of course I will. What did I engage you for?"

"Well then, I advise you to drop the whole thing. This suit will cost a good deal of money. Brown may not be worth a cent, and if you should get judgment against him, what good will it do? My opinion is, that he will pay no sort of attention to the case, let it go by default, and here you will be with all the costs to pay and never get a cent. I tell you you can't make anything out of it.

"Dawson," said Wilmot, "I am an American citizen, free-born, and I thought I lived in a free country, under a Constitution which guarantees the liberty of all men. Now, I have been arrested, imprisoned, chained like a felon, by the arbitrary order of one man, without any crime being charged against me and without any process of law. I'll be d——d if I will stand it. Is this Government a fraud?"

"All that you say is true, but show me the remedy. Tell me the process and I'll sue it out, and fight it to the bitter end."

"I say, sue him for false imprisonment. That's your process."

"All right, if you say so; I'll make out the papers and file them with the clerk of the District Court to-morrow; but I want to read you a few words from a decision of this same judge before whom your case will come. He says:

"'Laws passed for the government of the Indian

country, and for the purpose of regulating trade and intercourse with the Indian tribes, confer upon certain officers of the Government *almost unlimited power* over the persons who go upon reservations without lawful authority. Section 2,149 of the Revised Statutes authorizes and requires the Commissioner of Indian Affairs, with the approval of the Secretary of the Interior, to remove from any tribal reservation any person being there without authority of law, or whose presence within the limits of the reservation may, *in the judgment of the Commissioner*, be detrimental to the peace and welfare of the Indians.'

"Now, no person has any legal right upon a reservation but the Indians who belong to the tribe and the officers and employees of the Government. This being the case, the Commissioner had a legal right to order your arrest."

"Which side of this case are you arguing anyhow?" asked Wilmot. "I guess there is some law on the other side. There's another section of the Revised Statutes which says that 'no person shall be deprived of life, liberty or property without due process of law.' I tell you that this whole system of legislation, giving to the Commissioner or Secretary of the Interior absolute control over the life, liberty and property of individuals, is unconstitutional, and if you knew any law at all, you'd know it."

"It's a good thing that you had sense enough not to try and manage this case yourself. You've got so mad over being arrested that you can't keep cool enough to talk decent to your own counsel. You act just like any other client who wants to sue somebody, and when the attorney, for the good of the client, points out the difficulties to be met, he always thinks the attorney is in sympathy with the other side and arguing against him."

"I guess if you had been arrested, and confined in a dungeon for days, chained to another man, you wouldn't be in a very good humor, either."

"Perhaps not, but if I had employed an attorney to manage a case, I'd let him manage it."

"Didn't I tell you I'd follow your advice and for you to go ahead?"

"And I, like an honest lawyer, tell you, you will have the costs to pay, and make nothing out of it."

"I don't care if I do. I want Brown sued."

"All right. I'll sue him."

As Dawson passed out he noticed a man standing by the door of the office. He seemed intently reading a newspaper. Dawson gave him a sharp look and passed on. After walking down the street a short distance, he turned and looked again. The man still stood there intently reading.

Dawson was not superstitious, but he *felt* there was something wrong about that man. After he got to his office he could not drive him out of his mind. Such things as this happen a great many times. I don't pretend to account for them, but because I cannot account for them, I do not think that a good reason why I should deny the fact, for there are a good many things in this world I have never been able to account for.

Dawson tried to drive this fellow's image out of his

mind, but he could not. At last he got out of temper and called himself a fool. Then he put on his hat and went out to look for the man. He found him sitting at a table in the Empire House, writing. Then Dawson got intensely interested in a newspaper. The man went on writing. After awhile he folded up his letter and, just as he finished, addressing it, Dawson walked behind him and passed out of the door. On the back of that letter was written, "Secretary of the Interior, Washington, D. C."

Dawson went straight to Wilmot's office and told him about the man and what he had seen.

"What does it mean?" asked Wilmot.

"It's beyond my comprehension," said Dawson, "but I want you to keep a sharp look-out for this fellow. I'll see if I can find out who he is."

CHAPTER XXXIII.

INDIANS DISCUSSING THE WHITES.

AFTER Harkins and Wilmot escaped, Jack spent his time in the camp of Red Iron's band. Both he and the old chief seemed to be in a particular good humor. The camp was on the "second bottom" of a little stream, near by a large grove of timber. The tents were pitched in a semicircle. Four or five horses were picketed out. Large camp-fires were burning in several places, and the Indians were lounging around, some of them asleep on the ground in the open air, and some in the tents. In one part a lot of young fellows were having a dance, the music being made on a rude drum and by singing. Around Red Iron's fire quite a crowd had gathered, for the old chief was in a story-telling mood. His first story was about a raid which he made on another tribe when he was a young man, when they stole and carried away over a hundred horses. Finally he got on to his favorite topic of what he had seen among the white people when he went to Washington. He said the white people were always talking about how bad it was to take scalps, but they were the worst scalpers in the world. He saw two or three stores full of scalps (hair stores). They had them hung up, two or three hundred in a window, and sold them for so much each.

"A great many of the white people," said he, "haven't any hair, and they buy these scalps, and wear them on their heads. All these scalps were scalps of white people. I did not see one Indian's scalp. I said to the man that I thought the white people must go to war a great deal against one another, and then he told me that these scalps were taken from the heads of persons who had died from sickness. Now, what do you think of that? No Indian who ever lived was mean enough to scalp one of his tribe who had died from sickness. I think in some things the white people are the meanest people who ever lived. But they have got lots of nice things. They build great big, high houses, like one tent above another, and then they put the prettiest cloth you ever saw on the floors to walk on. They have knives and forks and spoons made out of pure silver to eat with. But they are the dirtiest people that ever lived. They eat nasty, slimy bugs (oysters). These bugs grow in a kind of a shell in the water. They are the nastiest-looking things you ever saw, and they taste just as nasty as they look. I tasted of some once. They eat worms too. It's a little white worm. They put great handfuls of them in a pot and make soup of them (vermicelli). I asked a man where they got so many of them, and he said they brought them from across the great water in their big canoes. Everybody eats these worms. I saw the women and children eat them.

"They always eat their meat raw. They don't cook it at all, they just make it warm, that's all. When they cut it up, the blood runs out of it. Everybody knows that raw liver is good, but just think of eating raw meat!

"Then they eat snakes. They have a great big store, or rather a great many stores together in one place, where they sell all kinds of things to eat. The man took us down there one morning and I saw a great big box full of snakes (eels). They don't eat all kinds of snakes, but just one kind. It is a water snake. They eat frogs too. I saw a lot of frogs in that same place. The white people are terribly dirty and nasty about some things.

"Their houses are all like sweat houses. The first thing they do when they want to build a house is to dig a big hole in the ground. After they get the house built they have some sort of a place down in that hole where they make a big fire and the heat comes up through a hole, and it is just like a hot wind in the summer time. They make the house just as hot as summer all the time. We used to take off our blankets and leggins, and sit there and sweat just like as if we were in a sweat house. Then when we went out-doors it made it feel awful cold.

"I think the sides of the white people's houses must be hollow, and filled with water, for they have little hollow pipes which come out of them, with a little handle. When you want a drink all you have to do is to turn the handle and the water runs out. I don't see where so much water comes from.

"The white people don't know anything about good manners. I used to think that these people we met out here were the worst ones, and that they didn't know much, but they are all alike. There are none of them who know what good manners is. If they see anything strange, they will stop, stand and look at it. They will stop and stare at you when you go along.

"When any one comes to pay us a visit we give him something to eat, and he eats it all up. When one comes to visit them, they give him something to eat, and when he eats it up they give him more and more and more, just as long as he can swallow. It is enough to kill a man. One of the Commissioners invited me to a feast (took him to dine). The women and men all sat down together. Then they brought some soup. It was warm soup. I told Shonnee to tell them I didn't like soup. Then they took everything away and brought fish, and then they took everything away again and brought meat. They kept giving me meat until I couldn't swallow any more. I didn't know what to do. I told Shonnee to tell them to stop. I was afraid they would be insulted. They don't seem to know how much a man can eat at all."

(Indians give to a visitor just what they think he can eat; and if he don't eat it all, they take it as a grave insult.)

"After that they wanted me to eat a lot of other things, sweet things, and a kind of white stuff as cold as ice (ice cream). Then they brought apples as big as your fist, and some long yellow things and nuts. I thought I should die. The white people are the worst gluttons in the world. Every one of them will eat more than a horse."

(That was just what the gentleman who took Red Iron out to dine said of him.)

"But the strangest thing of it all was that they had some men to bring us the things to eat. These men were perfectly black, and had short hair, not as long as my finger-nail."

"Wah," said Little Duck, "don't tell us any more. Men perfectly black!"

"What do you know?" said Standing Hawk. "There are black men. I saw one once myself."

Here a great discussion arose, some saying there were black men, and some saying it was a lie, and that these men who brought the things to eat were painted.

Little Duck said that when he was a young man he went to visit a tribe of Indians, who painted their faces all black when they went on the war-path, and that the white people had learned this from them.

"Did you see the Great Council?" asked one of them.

"Yes," said Red Iron. "I went in there two or three times. They have two councils, but the Great Father don't go there at all. When they do anything they write it in a letter and send it to the Great Father. If he don't like it he writes 'No' on it, and then it is no good. They dare not do anything the Great Father don't like. I don't see any use of a council like that. In both councils there is a sort of head chief, and he sits in a high place. Sometimes the chiefs quarrel like everything. I was in there one day when they were quarreling. The head chief had a little wooden tomahawk, and he pounded on a board with it with all his might. After that he made a speech. The man said he was scolding them. They all sat down and quit quarreling."

"How many chiefs were there?" asked Little Duck.

"They have one little council and one big one. I guess there are a thousand chiefs in both of them."

"Was the Little Great Father there?" (Secretary of the Interior.)

"No. He's a bigger chief than those, and has a big council-house all by himself. These little chiefs have to do what he says. That is what the man told me."

"Well, he's got to do what the Great Father says."

"I don't know. They told me that the Great Father had so many things to attend to that he told this man he must attend to the Indians; and that whatever he said the Great Father always did. The Little Great Father is a very lazy man, for he does not attend to these matters at all. He turned it all over to another chief. That is the man we made the treaty with. I think the white people have some very queer ways of doing things."

Just here a runner from the agency came in, and the old crier went yelling around the camp, telling them that there was news to be heard at Red Iron's tent. Soon the whole band assembled. After due formalities had been gone through with, the runner said that two white men had come to the agency that afternoon, and the Inspector had arrested one of them and put him in the guard-house. The other man went to the Inspector's house, and seemed to be a friend of his. This one was a minister. (Of course the Indians have no word in their language for minister, preacher or clergyman, so they designate them as "men who talk about God," or "the men who teach about God," and sometimes as the "white medicine man.") The Inspector had said that this man was to take the place of Mr. Parkman and his wife, who were going away.

Upon the announcement of this news a different mood came upon the Indians. Some of them said there was trouble ahead, but no one could guess what. One by one they went to their tents, and silence reigned in the Indian camp.

CHAPTER XXXIV.

THE EXILES.

THE presence of the two men of whom the runner brought news, at the agency, came about as follows :

Dawson commenced the suit, and a Deputy United States Marshal had been sent to serve notice on Inspector Brown. Brown had been informed of his coming, and stationed a guard some miles out of the agency, and the moment he appeared he was arrested, handcuffed and brought into the guard-house. When he was safely locked up he was searched, and all his papers taken away. Then Mr. Brown called upon him.

"I am sorry," said he, "to meet you under such unpleasant circumstances; but I have adopted a set of rules for the good of the Indians on this reservation, which I cannot suffer, under any circumstances, to be violated. One of them is, that no whites shall be allowed upon it except the employees of the Government. You were found within the limits of the reservaiton, and it became my painful duty to order your arrest."

"I am an officer," said the marshal, "of the United States District Court, and came here on official business. I'd like to know where you get authority to arrest an officer in the performance of his duty in this arbitrary manner."

"I am acting agent of this tribe. I have control of this territory. The safest place for all meddlers is outside of the reservation. I arrested the man you represent, and I will arrest any of them who are meddling with matters which is none of their business, who dare set foot inside of this reservation. Wilmot broke jail and got away. So did that thief Harkins, but I rather think you won't get off quite so easy. Any man who is fool enough to be made a tool of by Wilmot, must expect to suffer the consequences. I know all about your plans. I knew when you started, the route you came by, just where you entered the reservation and what you intended to do. The Government is perfectly capable of taking care of its own interests, and meddlers better keep their hands off."

"How long do you intend to imprison me here without process of law and without cause?"

"Long enough to make you and your thieving set understand that it is not a pleasant business to be meddling with what don't concern them. If I gave you your just deserts I would call in half a dozen Indians and tell them to swing you up to the nearest tree, you low-lived, thieving vagabond you."

The marshal raised himself up to his full height, took a step or two forward, looked Brown straight in the eye, and said:

"You have got me here a prisoner, unarmed and handcuffed. Of course you can talk to me just as insultingly as you please, but, sir, no gentleman, no, sir, no one but the most consummate coward would insult and abuse an unarmed prisoner. Now go on, say what you please. I'll meet you in the States some day, where we are on equal footing, and I'll make you wish you had never been born."

"You will, will you? I heard chaps talk that way before, but they generally got very humble before I got through with them."

The Inspector went from there to his office and wrote a short note to Mr. Parkman, inviting him to call immediately.

Mr. Parkman went to the Inspector's office.

"I am directed by the Secretary of the Interior to inform you that this reservation," said Brown, "has been assigned to another denomination, and notify you to leave, as a clergyman of the denomination to which it is assigned will take charge immediately. You will therefore leave within five days."

Mr. Parkman looked at the Inspector in astonishment. He did not say a word.

"The 'policy' of the secretary is to make no distinction between the different sects, to treat them all alike, and to prevent any controversy between them about their different creeds, modes of baptism and forms of worship, which might arise if different denominations were allowed to propagate their beliefs upon the same reservation, he has divided the Indians up between the different sects, and this tribe has fallen to another denomination. You will, therefore, prepare to leave immediately. I have thought that five days would be sufficient time for you to prepare to leave. I therefore give you official notice to leave this reservation within that time."

Mr. Parkman turned on his heel, walked out of the office and made no reply. He went back to his little cabin, sat down at his table and wrote a letter to the Secretary of the Missionary Board. He did not mention the matter to Mrs. Parkman. This is why he did not speak to her about it.

One day, two Indian women were sitting under the little window of Mr. Parkman's house. One of them heard the crying of a tiny baby.

"Did you hear that?" said one.

"Yes. There's a little white baby in there," said the other.

"Did you ever see a white baby?"

"No. Let us go in. I wonder if they will let us see it?"

"Why wouldn't they? Do you suppose they would think we would want to hurt it?"

"I don't know. White people have such strange ways."

One of the Indian women was old and the other was under middle life. They arose, walked into the room and went up to the side of the bed. They stood in silence for a minute or two and then one made a sign that she wanted to hold the baby.

Mrs. Parkman turned down the bedclothes and the Indian woman took the little babe in her arms.

"It is so white, and so fat, and so pretty," she said.

"Just look at its eyes! They are not like our babies' eyes. See its hair! How fine and soft it is. Its hair is almost white, too."

"It ought to be put on a board. I wonder why

they haven't put it on a board. I don't see any board around here."

"Don't you know," said the other, "that the white people don't put their babies on a board?"

"Oh! I forgot."

"See its little feet. Arn't they pretty?"

The younger of the two women pressed the baby to her bosom and rocked herself to and fro. Mrs. Parkman looked at her and saw that tears were in her eyes. Presently she laid it down in the bed and gently covered it over, and her tears fell on its forehead—baptizing it with an Indian mother's love.

She then stood up by the side of the bed and held up her right hand. One finger was gone. Mrs. Parkman did not know what she meant. There was no one there to explain the sad sign. The Indian woman's baby was dead. She had loved it with as tender a devotion as any white mother ever did. After it had been buried in the trees, in her great grief she had cut off the finger in remembrance of it. Holding the little white baby in her arms brought it all back to her, and tears, just such tears as white mothers shed, ran down over her face.

The little baby was only three weeks old when the Inspector informed Mr. Parkman that he must leave within five days, and that is why he said nothing to his wife.

Mr. Parkman paid no attention to the order of the Inspector, and made no preparations to leave.

Around every agency there always congregate the very worst members of the tribe. Such men as we would call tramps, bummers or dead beats among us. They pick up a little English, do little jobs for the agent or trader, for which they are given small presents of tobacco, beads or scraps of food. Most of them would sell out the whole tribe for a pair of blankets. Their only aim seems to be to keep in the good graces of the agent. They always call him Major or Colonel, and adopt the same system of fawning and adulation which I have noticed in office-seekers at Washington, when they approach a Congressman, Senator or the head of a department. Nothing pleases these little monarchs of agents better than that sort of servile flattery. It is the height of all human glory to them. These villainous Indians do not hesitate to execute any order the agent gives. Many of them would do anything he would tell them to do, even if it were to roast a man alive. The trader generally has the same sort of a following.

When the five days' notice was up, Brown sent four of these Indians to Mr. Parkman's house, with orders to hitch his horses to the wagon, put his goods and family in, and drive him off the reservation.

The first thing Mr. Parkman knew of it, he looked out of the door and saw these Indians driving up to his house with his horses and wagon. He went out and asked them what they were doing with his team. They paid no attention at first, and then talked back to him in the Indian language, as if they did not understand a word he said. He knew very well that one of them could understand, and he went up to him and told him to stop, that that was his team, but the Indian only acted more insolent than ever.

He then went over to the Inspector's office, told him what was going on, and asked his protection.

"It comes with very poor grace from you," said Brown, "to be asking protection from me. If you are running this agency, you can protect yourself. If you are not, you had better obey orders. There ain't much security for anybody around here who disobeys my orders. I sent these boys after you. I know 'em. They are as true as steel. The first thing you know you'll get handled pretty rough."

"Mr. Brown, do you intend to force me off from this reservation?"

"I gave you an order to leave five days ago. My orders are generally enforced about this Agency."

"I came here to preach the gospel to these Indians, sent by the regularly-constituted authorities of my church. I have harmed no man. I have interfered with no orders of the government. I have violated no law. Aside from the authority of the church, I have the divine commission to go and preach the gospel to every creature. I have a right to point these poor, ignorant, dying men to the cross of Christ. There is no spot I know of in all the world where a missionary is denied the privilege of preaching the Gospel."

"Well, I know one spot where *you* can't preach. I've ordered you to go, and go you will, or ——— ——— you, or I'll know the reason why."

Brown was livid with rage and trembled from head to foot. Mr. Parkman said no more, but went back to his house. His bedding and furniture—it was very little the missionary had—was tumbled into the wagon. Mrs. Parkman and Jennie were standing in the middle of the denuded room. Jennie was holding the baby in her arms. Her face was calm and placid, and she seemed unmoved by the rudeness of the Indians or the uproar they created. A wonderful change had come over Jennie during the last year. She was ready to face death with a courage and calmness equal to Mrs. Parkman. The Indians motioned for them to get into the wagon. Mr. Parkman assisted the two ladies in, took the reins and drove away.

"The Secretary of the interior," said Mr. Parkman, "is more intolerant than the Sultan. We are exiles in our own country."

CHAPTER XXXV.

DAWSON'S DISCOVERY.

TO persons who have been accustomed to the usages of polite society, who endeavor always to avoid giving pain, and strive to make everybody with whom they come in contact comfortable and happy, the actions of Inspector Brown will appear inexplicable. Let such persons reflect that all history proves that cruelty and selfishness are the natural outgrowth of unlimited power. An Indian girl, who is now in a boarding-school in one of the Eastern States, said to me the other day, "I hate to study the history of the white people. It is nothing but murder, murder, murder, all the time. I read about the murder of two little princes in a tower yesterday. And then there is all that about burning people alive because they wanted to read the Bible. These things are so horrible that I dream about them at night."

All the cruelties recorded in history have grown out of the exercise of unlimited power by somebody. An Indian agent under our system is an absolute monarch. He can practice any cruelty and there is no appeal as long as he is in favor with the Secretary of the Interior. Absolute unquestioning obedience to his orders is the only safety for either white man or Indian in the limits of his dominions. There is no court and no jury. This breeds fawning sycophancy in those subject to his control. When he has become accustomed to that, then the slightest interference with his wishes throws him into a rage.

When Mr. Parkman left Inspector Brown that official's rage knew no bounds. The idea that a miserable missionary would dare to talk to him in that manner, was to him unbearable, and his only thought was how he could punish him. If Mr. Parkman had ever done anything that would have given him the slightest excuse to have imprisoned him, he would have ordered him put in the guard-house immediately. The deputy marshal whom he had incarcerated the day before had been released early that morning and marched off the reservation under guard.

The next day the trader came to his office.

"You are getting them pretty well cleaned out," said he.

"Yes," said Brown, "the last of them have gone, and I don't think they will trouble us soon. I guess they've got enough of it."

"There is one thing about that Parkman I ought to have told you before."

"What is it?"

"He's been writing letters for Red Iron and several other Indians to Badger's old band out on the Arickoree, without asking permission of anybody."*

"Why didn't you tell me that before?"

"Well, they didn't come exactly under the statute, with the exception of one. And then I thought at that time that Parkman was a pretty good fellow, and did not intend to meddle with our arrangements."

"He's been writing letters for the Indians, has he? Now, if I had known that, I needn't have gone this roundabout way to have got rid of him. He's gone off intending to make a row."

Brown fell into a brown study for a few minutes. Then he sent out for two Indians who were known at the agency by the names of Chisel and Dirty Face.

---

* I resolved that in writing this book I would not make one note, for if I commenced to write notes, citing proofs of the incidents recorded in this story, it would be a book of notes, and not a story at all. But, as Joe Jefferson says: "I won't count this time," and say that letter writing for Indians, under many circumstances, is made a felony by law. See *U. S. Revised Statutes* 1878, § 2111.

The names were given to them, one because he had been accused of stealing a chisel, and the other because he never washed his face. They had been employed to drive Mr. Parkman off, and had done the job so well, he could trust them with one still more important. He was determined to wreak vengeance on Mr. Parkman. He hated him with a sort of hatred which only dwells in the bosom of tyrants.

When these two Indians reported to him, he ordered them to take three of the agency horses and follow on after Mr. Parkman, overtake him before he crossed the line of the reservation, and bring him back to the Agency.

The reservation was a very large tract of country, and Mr. Parkman had driven seventy-five miles when the Indians overtook him. One rode in front, took the horses by the bits and stopped them, the other took hold of Mr. Parkman's arm, and jerked him out of the wagon.

Both Mrs. Parkman and Jennie thought the hour of death had come. Mrs. Parkman hugged her babe to her bosom and Jennie sat unmoved, closed her eyes and in a short prayer commended them all to God.

Dirty Face brought the extra horse, put a loaded revolver to Mr. Parkman's head and motioned him to mount. Then they turned their horses' heads toward the agency and rode away with Mr. Parkman.

It was one hundred and twenty-five miles to the nearest white settlement, and there these two women and little babe were left alone on the wide prairie.

Jennie kneeled down and poured out her soul in

prayer to Him who numbers the very hairs of our heads, and without whose notice not a sparrow falls to the ground. Then turning to Mrs. Parkman, she said :

"What shall we do?"

"I am too weak and sick," she replied, "to advise."

"There are but two things we can do. One is to go back to the Agency, and the other is to try and reach Council Bluffs, and ask for help."

"I think we had better try to get to Council Bluffs. Perhaps Mr. Wilmot or some other friends there can help us."

Jennie took up the lines and started the team. She had never undertaken to drive a pair of horses before. It took but little skill to drive, however, for the trail was broad, level and very plain, made so by the trains passing over it to the Agency. It was nine o'clock that night when they reached a camping place, where there was grass and water for the horses, and wood for a fire. It took Jennie a long time in the dark to get the harness off the horses, lead them down to the creek to drink, lariat them out, gather wood, make a fire and cook supper.

As soon as the first streak of red began to shoot up in the eastern sky Jennie arose from her couch in the wagon, made a fire and began to prepare breakfast. It took a long time for both her and Mrs. Parkman to harness the horses and hitch them to the wagon; but after many trials they succeeded. All day long over the silent prairie they pressed on, and just at night reached the river and were ferried over. It was after dark when they drove into Council Bluffs. They went to the house of a Methodist brother, and were welcomed joyfully.

Word was sent to Mr. Wilmot, and both he and Mr. Dawson called the next morning. The Deputy Marshal had returned the day before. The two lawyers got every fact and incident from the ladies, and then retired to Mr. Wilmot's office for consultation.

"What is to be done?" said Wilmot.

"That is what I am not prepared to say," said Dawson. "I've made up my mind on one point, and that is, that this Indian system is the most cunningly devised scheme for permitting robbery and tyranny that the mind of man ever devised. In the last few weeks I have read over the statutes under the title 'Indians,' at least fifty times. At first I saw nothing wrong; they looked as if they were for the protection and welfare of the Indians; but now I see villainy concealed in every line. Taken together, they create a system, and that system puts everybody, whites as well as Indians, entirely within the control of a ring of robbers, murderers and speculators. I am an older lawyer than you. I have practiced law for fifteen years, but I must confess that I never dreamed that there were in our statutes what I have discovered since I took your case. There seems to be a foreign country located out here, under a despotic government. It is not a government of Indians (I wish it was, for I had a hundred times rather deal with them than with white savages like Brown); but it is a government of a band of white thieves. In that country no process of our courts will reach. The only force that can be brought to bear on them is that of the army, and the action of the army is controlled by the head of the ring in Washington. Soldiers arrested Harkins; soldiers guarded you while you were imprisoned. Suppose that you and Harkins and Jack had arrested Brown. Would not the army have been ordered to release him? But when you were arrested there was no force which could be called upon to release you. You see there is a power behind these men which will crush any man to the earth who comes in contact with it."

"What do you propose to do?"

"There is nothing which can be done, except to commence at the foundations and overthrow the whole system; and that, I fancy, is too big a job for two country lawyers."

"I think Jack was about right concerning the process to be used with these men."

"What did he propose?"

"Put daylight through them."

"Who do you propose to commence on?"

"Loft."

Loft was the man whom Dawson caught eavesdropping, and afterward writing to the Secretary of the Interior.

"Is he watching you yet?"

"Yes; everywhere I go that thief is at my heels. I went down to St. Joe the other day. The next morning when I went into the office of the hotel, there was Loft."

"Do you think he is a detective?"

"I don't know what he is, but if he don't stop following me around, he'll get hurt."

Four or five days after this, Mr. Parkman came into Council Bluffs on foot. He said he was taken back to the agency, put in the guard-house and kept over night. The next morning he was set at liberty, and told to go."

CHAPTER XXXVI.

DOGGED BY DETECTIVES.

"HOW was Wilmot's plot discovered?"

When Parker reported the arrangement between him and Wilmot to Mr. Clark, that gentleman's suspicions were aroused. He sent for Perkins, but Perkins thought that it was all right, that likely he got Harkins to go out for two thousand five hundred dollars, and he would stay at home and pocket the five thousand himself.

"But no arrangement at all has been made with Harkins," said Clark. "Now I tell you, Perkins, that you have got us into an awful scrape. I can't be fooled in this way. I'm not going to run any risks. Things at that agency must be run straight, until Harkins makes some proposition or we can get rid of him."

In accordance with this, Parker was ordered to deal "straight" and keep a sharp look-out. The cipher letter was the first thing that looked "crooked." He sent it to Mr. Clark by special messenger. Mr. Clark took it to the Indian Commissioner.

This government has in its employment for its special work, the most skillful and expert scientists, engineers, engravers, accountants, mathematicians and detectives in the world. The heads of departments call upon them when their services are needed. The cipher letter was put into the hands of a detective skilled in those matters. He asked but one question about it. It was:

"What is it supposed to contain?"

"It is something about Indians, Indian agencies, supplies or appropriations."

The detective took it, went into a library and sat down."

"This," he said to himself, "is evidently a dictionary cipher."

Then he read it over very slowly, two or three times.

"There is likely to be in it something about appropriations."

Then he studied very carefully all the words which commenced with "a." He took down several dictionaries and counted the words backward or forward from the word "appropriation" to the word which he had selected, which commenced with "a," and tried each one as a key to the cipher, but none of them was the right word.

"It is evidently not appropriations," thought he. I'll try 'annuities.'

He then selected the word "annular." He found this word in the dictionary and then counted forward until he came to the word "annuities." After trying that for a key in five or six different dictionaries, he took up the American Pronouncing Dictionary, by Alexander H. Laidlaw, published in Philadelphia by Crissy & Markley, counting forward five words, from the word "annular," he came to the word "annuities." He tried this and found he had discovered the key. To read the cipher now, all he had to do was to find the word in Laidlaw's Dictionary, count five words backward and he had the translation. Within twenty-four hours after the cipher was given him, he handed the Commissioner of Indian Affairs (without ever imagining that he was using his skill to rob a tribe of poor Indians) the following paper:

"Dear Sir,—

"I have translated the cipher which was submitted to me. It reads as follows:

"'Forward by private messenger a correct and accurate account of all expenditures to date, with names of parties to whom money was paid, amount of annuities and rations so far received. State quality. Make careful inspection of sugar, coffee, flour, beef and pork. Report first indications of fraud.'

"I have the honor to be,
"Very truly yours,
"C. C. Axell."

The paper was soon in the hands of Clark and Perkins.

"There, what did I tell you?" said Clark.

"It's a bad job," replied Perkins.

"Well, what's to be done?"

"Indict him; that's the old way and it's as good as any."

"The grand jury don't meet until fall, and by the time you can get him indicted the whole year's appropriations will be gone."

"Arrest him on a warrant."

"Who'll swear out the warrant?"

"Hildreth, if you want him to."

"That won't do at all."

"Well, what do you propose?"

"I've a notion to give up that agency."

"You can't do it. What will you do with Parker? How will you keep him quiet?"

"Take him to your agency."

"You know very well that that can't be done. The places are all full, and I have Walker on my hands beside."

"Well, suppose we send Brown out there and let him inspect the agency."

"That's the very thing," said Perkins, "and you needn't give him any instructions either. Just tell him what you want done, and he'll find some way to do it."

A few days after this, Inspector Brown received the following letter from the Secretary of the Interior:

"You will proceed immediately to the reservation on the Baha Taha, and make a thorough inspection of the agency. You will summarily remove the agent or any employee, if found guilty of fraud, and take charge of the agency until you receive further orders."

It was in accordance with these instructions that Brown was acting. Besides this he had "verbal instructions." It is behind "verbal instructions" that Indian inspectors always find a safe refuge.

Brown's first report stated that things had a very "crooked" look, and asked for a detective to assist him in working up the case. In answer to this, Loft was sent on, and Brown assigned him to the task of watching Wilmot. Loft was a faithful worker, and earned his five dollars a day. He kept a perfect record of every movement of Wilmot. There was scarcely an hour in the day that Loft did not know where he was and what he was doing. He informed Brown of Wilmot's coming, and sent a messenger ahead of the marshal, so a reception could be prepared for him. He found out Wilmot's friendship for Mr. Parkman and reported that. He looked up Wilmot's past record and could have written an accurate biography of him.

His constant dogging of Wilmot's footsteps was intensely irritating—no one can tell how irritating, until he has himself felt that the eyes of a detective are ever on him.

One day Wilmot went into Dawson's office and said:

"You'll have another case on your hands before long, and this time it will be a murder case."

"Are you meditating murder?" asked Dawson.

"Yes," said Wilmot in a half serious tone.

"Who are you going to kill? Perkins or Brown?"

"Neither. I'm going to turn them over to Jack."

"Clark?"

"No."

"Who is it, then?"

"Loft."

"I don't see what you have against Loft. Let him watch. What harm will it do?"

"It's very easy for you to talk in that way, but if some fellow was constantly on your trail, you wouldn't find it so pleasant. There he is over on the other side of the street looking in at the window now."

"I'll tell you what to do. Get acquainted with him, invite him to dine, go on a fishing excursion, have a good time."

"I've a notion to try it."

Wilmot stood looking out of the window. All at once he exclaimed:

"Je-ru-sa-lem!"

"What's the matter?" said Dawson.

"There's Perkins himself."

CHAPTER XXXVII.

GONE TO THE ARICKOREE.

WILMOT had made frequent visits to Mr. Parkman's since their return. There had been several quiet evenings spent there. He went to church very regularly on Sunday nights. He always had a headache Sunday morning, but it always ceased in time for him to escort Jennie to church in the evening.

"Don't you believe in the Bible?" said Jennie to him one evening.

"Yes, of course I do. Our system of government and of law are both founded on the Bible."

"I wish you would join the church and become a missionary. I think you could preach much better than Mr. Parkman."

"What makes you think that?"

"Oh, I don't know. But people ask Mr. Parkman questions sometimes that he can't answer. Mr. Loft has been coming there pretty frequently lately. He doesn't believe in the Bible. The other day he asked Mr. Parkman what the text meant which said : 'He that believeth on me, the works that I do shall he do also, and greater works than these shall he do ;' and Mr. Parkman could make no satisfactory answer. Mr. Loft said that the Bible claimed that Christ raised the dead, and healed the sick by a touch of his hand, and here was a text which said that anybody who believed on him should do all this, and a great deal more. What answer would you have made?"

"I would have told him that men were doing a thousand times more wonderful things every day than Christ ever did. They take the lightning from the skies and send it with a message around the world in a second. What is stilling a storm on a little lake to a feat like that? Christ raised Lazarus from the dead. A physician walks into a great city. There is a pestilence. The dead are in every house. They are rotting on the pavements. Old and young lie together in putrid masses. The physician calls the living to him, makes a little incision in their arms, and the plague is feared no more. Is it not greater to save the lives of all the people of a great city than to raise one man from the dead? Christ was spirited away into a mountain in a night. Men now lie down to sleep in a palace in one city, and the next morning they find the palace in another, and they walk out in the streets, and buy and sell and get gain. Is that not greater than that night scene in the life of Christ? What nations of men do these things? The nations in which the truths which Christ taught form the basis of society. The nations who have believed on him. I would have said something like that to him."

"I do so like to hear you talk. It always makes me feel stronger and better. I wish you would join the church."

"Who ever heard of a lawyer belonging to the church?"

"Oh, I've read of real good lawyers."

"Did you ever see one?"

"Yes, one," said Jennie, timidly.

"I've read of young ladies who went out as missionaries. That was when I was a little boy and went to Sunday-school. I thought they were the noblest people who ever lived; but I did not know how really good and true and noble they were until I got acquainted with you."

"I have long wanted to tell you——"

"Mr. Wilmot!"

The voice came from behind. He turned and saw Mr. and Mrs. Parkman. They had overtaken them, and from there the two couple walked home together.

It was the next day that Wilmot saw Perkins on the street. He intended to call that night at Mr. Parkman's, but just as he was ready to start Loft came into his office.

"I came," said Loft, "to consult you about a very important case which is to come up at the next term of court. I am not personally interested in it myself, but a friend of mine has written me a letter, and asked me to call upon you. Here is the letter," and he handed it to Mr. Wilmot.

It proved to be a letter from Mr. Borden, requesting Loft to inquire into the character and trustworthiness of a firm of lawyers by the name of Bledsoe & Dosier, and if there was any doubts about them to put the case into the hands of Mr. Wilmot. The examination of the case occupied the whole evening.

The next night when Wilmot called at Mr. Parkmans, Jennie was not there. Mrs. Parkman said that Jennie's father had returned with Perkins, and he had taken her, and started at daylight that morning for the Agency on the Arickoree.

CHAPTER XXXVIII.

DEFEATED.

AFTER the banishment of Harkins, Jennie, Mr. and Mrs. Parkman, there was perfect quiet at Red Iron's agency. In a few days the new agent arrived. It was John Hildreth, the principal witness against Badger. Inspector Brown turned over everything to him and left, to go on his rounds to "straighten out" other agencies. He was complimented by the Secretary of the Interior for his efficient work. The letter was given to the Associated Press, and printed in all the dailies in the United States. It contained a statement of how he had discovered fraud at the agency, and had removed Agent Harkins, and prosecuted him in the courts. Then the editors all over the country complimented the Secretary of the Interior, for his energy in prosecuting thieves, and his efforts to break up the Indian Ring. When the Commissioner of Indian Affairs made his official annual report, he put into the permanent records of the country the statement that Harkins had been removed for fraud, and there it will stand to the end of time.

Wilmot made every preparation for a thorough defense of Harkins; but when the case was called the District Attorney entered a *nolle prosequi*, and that was the end of it.

When Wilmot's case for false imprisonment against

Brown was reached on the docket, a lawyer from Washington appeared for Brown. He was a lawyer of eminent ability, employed by the Department of Justice. He moved to dismiss the case for want of jurisdiction, and in the argument on that motion consumed a whole day. Dawson replied in a speech of an hour-and-a-half, his argument being based on broad constitutional grounds. The judge took the case under advisement and the next day rendered a decision refusing to dismiss the case.

Dawson was about to call his witnesses, when the Washington lawyer arose and said:

"May it please the Court: I will state that it will not be necessary to consume the time of the Court in examining witnesses to prove the fact of the arrest and imprisonment for four days, as charged in the papers. I will admit all that is set forth."

"What is the ground of your defense, then?" asked Dawson.

"The ground of the defense will be set forth in my argument, and if you will listen, I think I can fully satisfy you, and if not you, the Court, that Inspector Brown had legal authority for all that he did."

The argument, which lies before me, is too long for insertion here. It was based on the following sections of the Revised Statutes:

"Section 2,149. The Commissioner of Indian Affairs, is authorized *and required*, with the approval of the Secretary of the Interior, to remove from any tribal reservation any person being there without authority of law, or whose presence within the limits of the reservation may, *in the judgment of the Commissioner*, be detrimental to the peace and welfare of the Indians, and may employ for the purpose such force as may be necessary to enable the agent to effect the removal of such person.

"Section 2,150. The military forces of the United States may be employed in such manner and under such regulations as the President may direct.

"First. In the apprehension of any person found in the Indian country," etc.

The result of it all was, the Judge decided that there was "no cause of action," and assessed the costs against Wilmot.

In making the decision, the Judge remarked, that whether the exercise of such extensive discretionary power which the law vested in the Commissioner was wise and just, was not for him to decide. It was enough for him to know that the power legally existed, and while thus legally existing, the exercise of the power must be upheld by the courts.

Wilmot went to his office that night sad, disheartened and discouraged. The thieves had gained a complete triumph. He said to Dawson:

"There seems to be no recourse for an Indian who is wronged except he appeals to the rifle and the scalping-knife. Who can blame them, when every resource is exhausted, when they are starved and robbed and imprisoned on reservations, if, like brave men, they prefer to die fighting to being made beggars and paupers, and end a miserable existence by disease or starvation?"

"You undertook too big a job," said Dawson, "when you went into a contest with the Indian Ring. You see they have called to their aid three of the departments of the Government—the War Department, the Interior Department and the Department of Justice. All of them have been forced to do their bidding. No single individual has any chance in such a contest. Back of all that, they control all the avenues of information to the people at large, and thus control public opinion. The public look upon Brown as a very efficient and capable officer, and upon Harkins as a thief. Do you suppose that out of all the millions who read the Secretary's letter to Brown, which was published in the papers everywhere, that there will ever be five hundred who will know that they were forced, for want of evidence, to enter a *nolle pros.* in his case? I doubt if anybody outside of the court-room, when the record was made, will ever hear of it. Have you found out what the costs amount to?"

"Don't ask me," said Wilmot. "I wish I had taken your advice."

"Well, I suppose if I had been arrested, as you were, I would have done the same thing."

"I don't care for losing the case."

"Don't care for losing the case? What is troubling you so, then?"

"It's another matter altogether."

"I'll be glad to render you any service I can."

"I don't believe you can help me. I'll not talk about it. To drive all this annoyance out of mind I will tell you a story. Here, have a cigar."

The two men lit their cigars.

"Say, Dawson," said Wilmot, "just look out at the door and see if Loft is around anywhere listening."

"Oh, pshaw! Go on with your story."

"It happened about three hundred years ago. That's about the time of what they call the 'dark ages,' isn't it?"

"Yes, I guess so," said Dawson, puffing away at his cigar.

"Well, I don't know how long ago it was, but it was in the time of the 'dark ages.' I'm certain about the 'dark age' part of it."

"What happened? Why don't you tell your story?"

"I guess I won't tell it."

"Oh, go ahead."

"Well, a long time, ago in the 'dark ages'———"

"Confound your 'dark ages.' Go on with the story."

"A long time ago, in the dark ages, there was a beautiful young lady. She was riding along in a stage coach—no, a diligence. She hadn't seen her father for a long time, and she was going to meet him. The stage coach—no, the diligence—was met by a gang of robbers, and everybody in it was killed but her. The horses ran off into a river and she was rescued by a band of savages who lived in that neighborhood. They treated her very well for a while, but finally they went to war and tried to kill her. A young prince, who happened to find her just in time, took her on to his horse and fled away with her. His horse was large and swift-footed, and outran the horses the savages rode, so he got away in safety. Then another prince came, who was very bad and wicked, and it was said the young lady was to marry him. But she did not like him at all. So she went to church all the time, and at last went back to this very band of savages as a missionary.

"The young prince who had rescued her was afterward traveling through the country inhabited by this band of savages, and he was taken prisoner and confined in a loathsome dungeon. When the young lady heard that, she came to see him and planned a way for him to escape. There was another man chained to him in the prison, so he did not like to tell her how much he loved her, before him. After the prince escaped from that country she came away too, and he went to see her. One day, as he was walking along with her, he was just telling her how much he loved her, when her duenna came up and he could not finish the sentence. The next day, her father, who was a wicked old man, came and carried her off to another savage country farther away than where she was the first time. The government of that country was very despotic, and whoever went there was always put into a dungeon. So the young prince could not go there at all. This was all in the 'dark ages.'"

"Why don't you go on?" said Dawson.

"That's all there is of it."

"There's no point to that story."

"You are blinder than a bat," said Wilmot.

About a week afterward it flashed over Dawson all at once what that story meant.

CHAPTER XXXIX.

A COURT-MARTIAL.

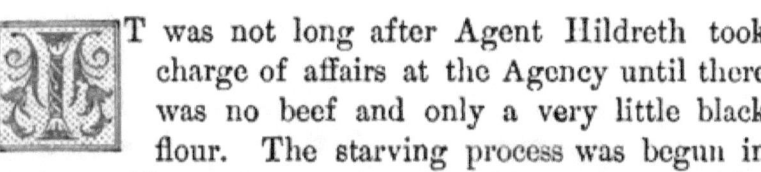IT was not long after Agent Hildreth took charge of affairs at the Agency until there was no beef and only a very little black flour. The starving process was begun in earnest. Haggard women, with skinny, bony babies on their backs, were hanging about the Agency, some of them with only an old, torn blanket for covering. When the chiefs called on Hildreth he told them that the contractors were not furnishing the supplies as they had agreed. It was not his fault. He had written to the Great Father, and done all he could. After about three weeks of starvation he called a general council. He told them that he had received a letter from the Great Father. The letter said he was very sorry for them. There was fifty thousand dollars due them, which was to be paid in cash. If they were hungry, the Great Father had ordered the trader to let them have all they wanted, and when the money came, they could pay the trader.

In answer to this Red Iron said he would consent to no such an arrangement. He understood that the treaty he had made with the Great Father provided for rations to be issued to them for thirty years, that they were to have schools, farming implements and a man to teach them how to farm. As yet, he had seen none of these things. A woman came and taught school for a little while, but the Inspector had sent her away.

Hildreth told them he could not help them. He had read the Great Father's letter to them. If any of them were hungry they could go to the trader's store and get provisions. It was there for them. The council then broke up.

After this, Red Iron got his people together and made a speech to them. He told them if they were starving to go to the trader's store, but to get just as little as possible, or when the money came from the Great Father they would get none, they would owe it all to the trader.

No pen can describe the suffering that was endured during the months that followed. The Indians got just as little as possible from the trader. No annuities or rations were issued to them at all by the agent. There were no troops at the Agency now. Lieutenant Blake and the detachment under his command had been ordered back to the fort on the Little Blue.

When Perkins reached the fort on his way to his agency he stopped for a few days. While there he was very intimate with Lieutenant Blake, and the Lieutenant was very glad to have some one to be intimate with, for he was in very bad order at the fort. Permanent quarters had been built, and a good many of the officers had their families there. He was not admitted to the social circles of the garrison. Blake complained to Perkins of the treatment he received, and especially of the commanding officer,

Colonel Greene. Perkins hated Colonel Greene as much as Lieutenant Blake did. One day Perkins said to him:

"Has a Colonel any right to communicate directly with the President?"

"No, certainly not. He could be court-martialed for it."

"I can tell you how you can get even with Colonel Greene. He wrote a letter directly to the President about affairs at this post."

"You must be mistaken; he never would do that."

"No, I'm not mistaken. I've got the letter."

"Are you sure it is his handwriting?"

"Would you know his writing if you saw it?"

"Of course I would."

"Well, then, I'll bring you the letter, and you can judge for yourself."

Perkins went to his trunk and got the letter which Colonel Greene had written to the President, at the earnest request of the head men of Badger's band.

When Lieutenant Blake saw the familiar handwriting his eyes gleamed in triumph.

"Let me have this letter," he said. "I'll settle him."

"What will you do?" asked Perkins.

"I will prefer charges against him, and have him court-martialed. That's what I'll do."

A court-martial was accordingly convened, and Colonel Greene found guilty. All he could do was to plead extenuating circumstances. He was sentenced to be suspended from the service for six months, and all pay and allowances stopped.

When Wilmot heard of this he remarked: "There's another man who has been made to feel the hand of power for meddling with the arrangements of the Indian Ring."

Colonel Coldcraft took command of the fort after Colonel Greene was removed. He was an entirely different officer from his predecessor. When it was said of him that he was a soldier, that was all that was to be said. Nothing would put a subaltern out of favor with him quicker than to intimate that he had opinions. Colonel Coldcraft held that no officer, no matter what his rank, had any right to opinions. War was a science. There was no place for opinions for anybody who had entered the army. He should understand his profession, and obey orders. As far as he was concerned, he knew every detail, from a linch-pin of a wagon to the exact amount of powder to be used in a siege-gun at two thousand yards to produce the greatest effect. His very religion consisted in obeying orders. For the result he had no concern whatever. Everything must be done in exact conformity with the orders and the regulations. He had no mercy on any one for the slightest variation from the letter of the orders.

About a week after he took command, an Indian, belonging to a small tribe located to the south of the fort, was one day standing near the post trader's store. There was a well there, and the Indian drew a bucket of water. As he was holding up the bucket trying to drink out of it, a clerk in the store came up and said he would hold it. As the Indian commenced to drink the clerk poured the cold water all over him. The Indian was a quick-tempered man, and, snatching an arrow out of his quiver, stabbed the man to the heart. It was done in a fit of passion, and before he thought. As soon as he saw what he had done he ran away.

Colonel Coldcraft made a report of the affair in due form. It was forwarded to Washington through the regular channels, and a copy was furnished the Secretary of the Interior. Shortly afterward Colonel Coldcraft received an order to demand the Indian of the tribe, and if he was not turned over to his custody in fifteen days to make war upon them. In conformity with this order he sent an officer to the tribe, who made the demand, and told them the consequence of a failure to deliver the culprit.

Consternation seized the Indians when this message was delivered. A council was called immediately. The tribe was a small one, and they very well understood that war meant extermination. The head chief's name was Wajapa. He was a man of about middle life, tall and dignified. He said to his people that every effort must be made to find this man. All their lives depended upon it. Every man must start out, and not cease to search. If he was not found in fourteen days, they must all return to camp, and another council would be held. He then went to the officer and told him that they would make every effort in their power to find the man, and deliver him, either dead or alive, in the time specified.

During the days which followed the Indians searched over the whole country, and visited every neighboring band and tribe, but the culprit could not be found. Wajapa went to Colonel Coldcraft and said:

"We have done all we can do. There are two days remaining yet, and we will search for this man. I pledge you if he is not found in that time we will continue to hunt for him. We will watch day and night, and if we ever find him we will bring you his body."

"My orders were," said the Colonel, "to demand this Indian of his tribe; and if he was not surrendered in fifteen days, to make war on the tribe."

"But we can't find him," said Wajapa. "We have hunted everywhere for him. He did not come back to his tribe after he committed this murder."

"You have heard what the orders were. That is all I have to say," replied the Colonel.

Wajapa went back to his camp. On the night of the fourteenth day all the Indians returned, and a council was held. After the chief told them the result of his visit to the fort, two or three went to one side, pulled their blankets over their heads, and began to sing their death-song.

There was silence in the council for some minutes, when an Indian by the name of Two Crow arose. He was a man of medium hight, rather slight, had an intelligent and mild countenance, and was respected and loved by the whole tribe. His family consisted of one wife and five little children, to whom he was very much attached. He spoke as follows:

"My friends: This is a sad day for us all. We have met perhaps in our last council. If the white officer makes war upon us he will kill us all. There are but very few of us. He has a great many warriors. It will not take him long to kill us. He will go out one day and come back the next. Our tents will be silent and our dead bodies will lie upon the ground. Now it is better for one to die than that all should be killed; all our women and the little children. Kill me. Take my dead body and lay it down at the feet of the white officer and save the lives of the women and children."

Two Crow folded his blanket around him and looked up toward heaven. Not an Indian said a word for a long time. Then the old medicine man of the tribe stood up. He made a long prayer to the Great Spirit. When he had finished, he took a rifle, placed the muzzle against Two Crow's head, and fired.

All night long the whole tribe, men, women and children, wailed for Two Crow. In the morning they wrapped the body in a blanket, placed it on a litter behind a pony and took it to the fort. The chiefs waited for the coming of Colonel Coldcraft, laid the body down at his feet, and walked away.

An hour afterward one of the interpreters, who had a grudge against the tribe, and hated them with all the malignity of an evil nature, came to Colonel Coldcraft and told him that that was not the body of the Indian who committed the crime. When the interpreter told him that, the Colonel came nearer having an opinion than he ever did in all his life before.

"Why did you tell me that?" said he.

"It's the truth. I can prove it by a dozen men."

Before taking any action Colonel Coldcraft made a full report of the whole transaction, and asked for orders. The report was forwarded to Washington and laid before the Secretary of the Interior.

A short time after this Colonel Coldcraft received orders to make war on this tribe, as it was the opinion of the Secretary of the Interior that the production of the dead body with a bullet wound in the head was only a ruse. They had committed another murder without any doubt, having killed some one of the friendly Indians who had a reservation near them. Colonel Coldcraft obeyed his orders. He made war upon this little band, if war it could be called, and so many of them were killed that they became extinct as a tribe, the few who escaped with their lives being adopted into other tribes.

When Wilmot heard of this he said:

"That's another specimen of our Indian policy. Make a whole community responsible for the act of one man, and shoot them down, men, women and children. If I were a member of that tribe, I would never cease to shoot and scalp, as long as I could hold a gun or handle a knife."

CHAPTER XL.

A SECRET COUNCIL.

AFFAIRS grew worse and worse at Red Iron's Agency. The young men became discontented, and blamed the chiefs for making such a treaty with the whites. They had always been accustomed to going on long hunts two or three times a year, which furnished them with excitement and occupation. Now, the chiefs told them they must stay on the reservation. An Indian is by nature of a nervous and active temperament. This confinement on a reservation was a good deal like imprisonment to them. They grew, as it is called in the official reports, "restless." Small parties, at different times, ran away and paid visits to other tribes. When they came back they always brought a lot of horses with them. Whenever Indians visit another tribe, it is their custom to give the visitors presents of horses, blankets, or anything they have. A great many of them get arms in some mysterious manner. Nobody has ever been able to find out how Indians get arms. A late Secretary of the Interior has "officially" informed the public that the statement that the traders furnished them was a slander, which originated with the officers of the army. As it would never do to intimate that an "official" statement of a Cabinet officer could, by any possibility, be incorrect, the question how Indians get arms, must remain unanswered. But that they do get them, and get the most approved patterns, too, is not denied by even the Secretary of the Interior.

Having got arms, and a pretty good supply of horses, the young men began to feel very independent. They did not exactly defy the authority of the chiefs, but they did a good deal of talking about what the chiefs ought to do, and a great deal more grumbling about what they had done They operated upon the jealousy existing among the chiefs. Little Wolf had never thoroughly recovered his standing since his defeat in the fight with Wilmot, and the young men turned to him for a leader. Several of the more venturesome even left their own bands and got adopted into his, so that Little Wolf had the largest band in the tribe. One day he had a council of his band, to listen to what the young men had to say.

When they got to speech-making, they had all sorts of grievances to relate. They blamed the chiefs for agreeing to stay on a reservation. They wanted the treaty altered so that they could go on a visit to another tribe just as often as they wished. They wanted the new treaty to state just how many beef cattle they were to have each week, just how many sacks of flour, bags of coffee, barrels of sugar and pork, and then they could count them themselves, and know whether they got what was due them or not. They were hungry all the time now, and the chiefs would not let them get enough to eat of the trader. The trader would not let them have things sometimes. His store was about empty, and they didn't believe he was going to get any more. What he let them have was not fit to eat. They did not get any fresh meat at all, nothing but salt pork, and that had a very bad taste. They didn't get any flour. He let them have some black stuff which he called flour, but they did not know what it was. It wasn't fit to eat. The Great Father had broken the treaty anyhow, and it was "no good" any more. They wanted a new one, the right kind of a one. They didn't believe the Great Father would ever send them any money. After this fashion they talked for three hours. Then Little Wolf made them a speech. He was a thorough politician. He commenced by complimenting them very highly.

"No chief," said he, "ever had such warriors around him as I see here to-day. It is said that young men do not know much, that they ought to listen and not to talk, and they should obey the counsel of the old men. In most tribes that is so. But when I listen to you to-day, I look to see if your hairs are gray. You have spoken what is true. You talk like old men. What I have heard are words of wisdom. The treaty is bad. I did not like it when it was made, and I was the last one to touch the pen. But the Great Father won't make a treaty with one band. It must be with the whole tribe. I want to go and see my friends, but I cannot go. I am, as it were, a prisoner. My wives and children are hungry, and I have nothing to give them to eat. Unless we make a new treaty we shall soon all be dead. I'm in favor of making a new treaty. What you ask is right. The chiefs ought to do it. I am but one chief. Some of the others must agree to it."

This speech was greeted with tremendous acclamations of approval. The young men declared that Little Wolf was the wisest and greatest chief who ever lived. When the council broke up and the young men from the other bands who were present went back to their tents, they were loud in their praise of Little Wolf. They said if they had him for head chief, instead of Red Iron, they would soon have every-thing just as they wanted it.

Day by day Little Wolf's influence increased, until he had with him a majority of the tribe. Then a general council was held among themselves. At the time this council was called, the whole tribe was in a terrible condition. The trader had furnished them but very little to eat for some weeks; many of them were so weak they could hardly walk. For days they had constantly been suffering from hunger. Skinny little children, crawled around the tents. Hollow-eyed and haggard mothers pressed starving babes to bosoms which furnished no nourishment for them. Many died from disease, engendered by want of sufficient food. When the formal council was convened, the young men kept silent, and the chiefs talked. Red Iron arose and made a long and fervent prayer to the Great-Holy-One. Some mysterious ceremonies were then gone through with by the medicine man, intended to appease the Great Spirit and secure his favor. After this, whatever the decision of this council might be, no man dare oppose it.

In ordinary councils, when comparatively trivial matters are under consideration, there is generally a great deal of speech-making, but in a weighty matter like this, where all their lives seem to be at stake, no one seemed to want to speak. The pipe was passed around a great many times, and a solemnity, like the feeling that some awful catastrophe was impending, pervaded every breast. At last, with a gravity that only such circumstances could produce, Red Iron arose.

"It seems," said he, "that I stood on the bank of a river, with my people around me, and little by little the bank was falling away, and now it had reached to our very feet. When I turn to flee away, there is a great army of white soldiers, with fixed bayonets and guns that shoot many times, behind me. They say, if you come this way we will kill you. If I stand still, I will fall in. Then I raise my voice to the Great Spirit, and say: Why have you forsaken me? But he answers not. When I turn to my young men, they say: Go back from the river's brink. Let us kill the soldiers. The soldiers stand there and laugh. There are many, many, many thousands of them. My young men are so few that I can call all their names at once. Darkness comes on. The river roars at my feet. The soldiers crowd up closer behind me. Then I look away through darkness, and I see a little path which goes down by the river's side. It is very narrow, and hard to walk in. It goes on and on for many days' journey. Toward the latter end it gets broader, and is smooth and easy to walk in. At the end there is a pleasant place to live. Through the ranks of the soldiers there comes one white man. He takes me by the hand, and says he is my friend. I ask him where the little path leads to, and if there are any soldiers who will stand across it and say: You cannot go by this path. My friend says that once his people stood by the bank of a river, and another nation came more powerful than they. They saw a path just like that. They walked in it for many, many years, and finally they came to the great country, where they all became rich. I say to-day to my young men: Let us go down by the river's side. Let us follow the little path, as the white men have done. But they say no. The Great Spirit made us Indians. He did not intend for us to live like white men. We will not walk in the little path.

"Then a powerful chief arises. He has a great many warriors, and they are very brave. They do not fear to die. He says the young men are right—that the old chief is childish. But the old chief remembers when he talked that way before. He went on the war-path with a great many brave warriors. When he came back they were not with him. The old chief has been on the war-path too. But when he came back his warriors came also. I want to make a new treaty, and when I do make one, I want an interpreter who won't lie. I want the Great Father to give us plows. Then we will raise from the ground what we want to eat. Many years ago, when our tribe lived near the great water, we had cornfields so large that you could not see the end of them. Then the Great Spirit was well pleased with us. We had no horses then. We always lived in one place. After the white men came, we got horses and commenced to roam around. The Great Spirit has been angry with us ever since, and we grow less and less every year. The path down by the river's side leads to big cornfields."

I am well aware that the beautiful imagery of Red Iron's speech is but poorly indicated in the above translation, the notes having been taken from a hurried interpretation, made years ago. It had a wonderful effect upon the assembled chiefs and warriors who stood in the mass behind them. It was expected by the young men that Little Wolf would make a spirited reply, but he had very little to say. For days Little Wolf had been cogitating over his speech, and he had prepared, in his own mind, what he considered to be the greatest speech of his life. He had supposed that Red Iron would oppose making a new treaty, but when that wise and wily old chieftain had finished, Little Wolf found that his set speech, if he delivered it, would only strengthen Red Iron's influence, so he kept silent. Red Iron had stolen his thunder.

The decision of the council was, that they would apply to the agent for permission to go to Washington and make a new treaty. When they came to Hildreth, he listened to what they had to say, told them he would write to the Great Father about it, and then went over and saw Parker. The two men had a good laugh over it, and that ended the matter.

CHAPTER XLI.

A REPORTER AND A PRIEST.

FEW days after this a correspondent of a great New York newspaper came to the Agency. As soon as it was known who he was, the greatest consideration was shown him. He had a letter from Commissioner Clark, introducing him to the agent, and said that he had been requested by Mr. Clark to come to the Agency if he possibly could, make an examination of the condition of the Indians, and write a full account of it for his paper. Hildreth got out his horses and carriage, and showed him all the places of interest in the neighborhood. After this he took him to his office and showed him a big bundle of papers, purporting to be vouchers for the money spent at the Agency. A summary of these he had on one sheet. These figures showed that the hundred thousand dollars appropriated had nearly all been consumed in removing the Indians and constructing the Agency buildings. There was nothing left to buy rations, and the Indians were actually starving.

Hildreth then praised the Indians for their patience, and said that no other people on earth would ever have endured what these Indians had. Yet they were so childlike and trusting, that they had hardly uttered a complaint, after he had told them that the Great

Father had so many red children to feed, that he had spent nearly all the money he had, but that pretty soon he would have some more and then he would send it. Ever since that they had been patiently waiting.

"Now," said Hildreth, "before you leave the reserve, I want you to go with me into some of their camps and see the suffering. It is almost enough to break a man's heart."

The article written by this correspondent was one of the most tender and pathetic stories I ever read. I have only room to insert one short paragraph.

"I went," said the reporter, "into one lodge, and saw two small, almost fleshless, children sitting on the ground. Their lips were thin and their cheeks hollow. In each of their little, bony hands they had a few grains of corn, which had just been given to them, and they were eating it ravenously. Lying on a blanket near them was a woman and by her side a little babe. It was very still. The mother laid her hand lovingly on its head. She, herself, was almost a skeleton. She did not seem to notice me. As I stood there, I saw the tears coursing one another down over her hollow cheeks. Her baby was dying. As I came out of the lodge I met a large, bronzed white man. He was dressed in a suit of buckskin. I said to him that these people were sick. 'No,' he replied, 'I wish it was sickness, but it is starvation.'"

No body of men ever received such a terrible upbraiding as Congress did at the hands of this writer for its niggardly policy in regard to these Indians.

The correspondent desired to get at the truth of matters, so he asked Hildreth for an interview with the head chief. The agent sent for Red Iron, and he came to the Agency.

It was explained to Red Iron that this man had a big newspaper (word carrier, the Indians call it), and that if he wished to say anything to the white people, this man would print it in his paper. Red Iron knew nothing about the man, and he was both suspicious and afraid of Hildreth, so he did not know exactly what to say. He told him that his people were very anxious to learn the ways of the white people; he wanted schools where the children could be taught, and he wanted a missionary to tell them what was in the Book which the Great Spirit had given to the white people. He thought he might say that much with safety, anyhow.

The reporter made this statement very prominent in his letter, and remarked that here was a heathen in our own country, holding out his hands, asking for the Bible and a missionary, and while the churches were sending hundreds to Africa and China, none of them heard his cry.

This article, which was widely copied and read by many thousands of people, happened to fall into the hands of a poor Catholic priest in the city of New York. The idea of that poor Indian begging to be taught so weighed upon his mind that he went to his Bishop and got permission to go out to him. When he arrived at the Missouri river, he went to the Catholic Bishop having jurisdiction in that part of the country, and obtained his sanction and blessing, and then went on to Red Iron's camp. The old chief did not live in a tent—he had built himself a rude house. When the priest arrived he was so delighted that he told him he would move out and let the priest live in the house and teach school, and he would live in a tent. But the priest said no, he would not do that. So Red Iron put up a tent for him beside his house.

The next day Hildreth appeared and ordered him to leave the reservation. The priest said he had come there to instruct the children and teach the Christian religion to the Indians.

"But this reservation has been assigned to another denomination by the Secretary of the Interior," said Hildreth. "I cannot allow you to reman. I give you orders to leave."

"There is no missionary of any kind here," said the priest, "and no school."

This was correct, for the man who was announced as a missionary when Mr. Parkman was expelled, only remained about a week. The agency pay-roll showed that there was a teacher receiving the salary. It was the wife of one of the employees who signed the pay-roll, and the salary was divided with Hildreth. She had not taught a day.

The priest went on to say that he should interfere with nobody, and that he should not leave. He would make no resistance, but he would not go off from the reservation unless he was carried off.

The next morning a light spring wagon was driven up, the priest was lifted up and put into it and driven off the reservation, a distance of about ninety miles, to the first station outside, and left there.

He got aboard of the first conveyance that was going to the reservation, and started back. Red Iron heard that he was coming. I don't know how he heard it; the swiftness with which news is spread among Indians always was a mystery to me; but in some way he heard it in time to go out and meet the priest, just outside of the reservation. He told the priest that it would never do for him to come there, it might make war; but to stop just over the line, and he would send some of the young men to help him build a house. After the house was finished he would send some of the children to him to be taught.

When the Bishop at the Missouri river was informed of what had happened, he started immediately to Washington. He went to the Secretary of the Interior, who received him in his most cordial manner. He wiped off his glasses, leaned back in his chair, and smiled his most fascinating smile. To everything the Bishop said, he replied, "Certainly, certainly." He was as "child-like and bland" as the Heathen Chinee. The Bishop was finally informed that while the grievance of which he spoke was a serious one, nothing could be done without action by Congress. Then the Bishop laid the matter before the Indian Committee of the House. They all agreed with him that it was a great outrage, and a Congressman drew up a bill to grant religious liberty to the Indians. The Bishop was informed that it would be passed immediately.

The bill lies in a pigeon-hole of the Indian Committee to this day.

CHAPTER XLII.

A "STRAIGHT" TRANSACTION.

THE newspaper correspondent's account of affairs at Red Iron's agency created considerable discussion and accomplished its purpose. It enabled Perkins' congressional friend to get through his bill for an additional appropriation of one hundred and fifty thousand dollars for the relief of the tribe. Neither the correspondent, the editor of the paper, nor the general public ever dreamed that they were being used as tools of the Indian Ring.

Finally, the paying agent of the department arrived at the Agency, and a council was called. All the Indians expected to be paid, and nearly the whole tribe assembled at the Agency. When the council was convened the paying agent of the department, Markam, and two commissioners who accompanied him, took their seats. Hildreth sat by Markam, and Parker, the trader, a little to one side. The latter had a huge bundle of papers on a table before him.

Markam made a long speech, telling them how the Great Father loved his red children. After about half an hour of such palaver, he came down to business, and told Red Iron that the tribe owed the trader one hundred and thirty-five thousand dollars, and he wanted him and the other chiefs to sign a receipt for that amount, and then he would pay them the fifteen thousand which was still due them.

Just as Markam finished his speech, two full companies of cavalry marched into the agency, ordered there at the request of the Secretary of the Interior. Major Hodson was in command.

As soon as Jack found that Major Hodson was there he went straight to him, told him what was going on and said that he feared there would be a general uprising of the Indians. It was a little more than human nature could stand. The Indians had been starving for months, patiently waiting for this money to come, and now they were told that the trader was to have it all.

"I don't see that I can do anything to help them," the Major replied. "My orders are to protect the agent, his employees and the commissioners. I have nothing to do with the settlement of their business. I can only obey my orders. I am practically under the control of Markam."

In the council-room there was intense excitement. It was not manifested in the way white men would have acted. To one unacquainted with Indian character, nothing to indicate that the Indians were excited would have been noticed; but Markam was an old hand at this business. The last twenty years of his life had been spent, half of it on Indian Commissions, and the other half in the East, lecturing "in behalf of the poor Indian," telling how badly they had been abused by the army, and how niggardly Congress had been in making appropriations for them. Once he had nearly lost his life at the hands of a chief, whose tribe he had swindled out of everything they had. He was desperately wounded, but as soon as he recovered he went back East, and told the people how he loved the poor Indian; and although he had been nearly killed, he did not blame them. They did not mean to kill him at all. They were shooting at some very bad army officers. Markam knew enough about Indians to know that there was serious trouble brewing. So when at last Red Iron arose to speak he was all attention.

Markam noticed that he did not come forward and shake hands, as is the invariable custom among them. He turned to the interpreter, and said in a stern, harsh voice:

"Tell that Indian, if he wants to make a speech, he must first come forward and shake hands with me."

Red Iron paid no attention to this when it was interpreted to him. He stood there with a dignity and consciousness of right about him that ought to have commanded the respect of any man.

At last he said:

"If the Commissioner desires to hear what we have to say, I will speak. If he does not, we will go back to our lodges."

"Tell him," said Markam, "to go to his lodge and stay there until he can learn not to be so impudent."

The Indians all left the council-room. Markam went immediately to Major Hodson and told him that Red Iron was in open rebellion, and ordered him to be arrested forthwith. When Red Iron saw the file of soldiers coming, and the remainder of the command up der arms, he knew in a moment what to expect. He said a few words to the head men who stood near him, and, folding his blanket around him, stood erect, and awaited their coming. They took him away to the guard-house, put irons on his wrists and ancles, and left him there.

Late that afternoon word was sent to Little Wolf and some of the young men to come to a council after dark. This was against their custom, as Markam very well knew. Red Iron heard of it, and sent out orders to kill any man on the spot who dared to go. Not an Indian responded to the call. The next morning another council was called, and when the chiefs began to assemble they found a guard of soldiers, who only permitted certain ones to pass through. All the leading men of the tribe were excluded, including Red Iron, who had been released from the guard-house that morning. Nothing was done worth noting at this council. The next day they were ordered to assemble again.

Another hand has recorded that day's proceedings and its results. I insert it here.

The council was crowded with Indians and white men when Red Iron was brought in, guarded by soldiers. He was tall and athletic, about six feet high in his moccasins, with a large, well-developed head, aquiline nose, thin, compressed lips and physiognomy beaming with intelligence and resolution. He was clad in the half-military costume of the chiefs of his tribe. He was seated in the council-room without greeting or salutation from any one. In a few moments, Markam, turning to the chief, in the midst of a breathless silence, by the aid of the interpreter, opened the council.

"What excuse have you," he asked, "for not coming to the council when I sent for you?"

Red Iron rose to his feet with native grace and dignity, his blanket falling from his shoulders, and, purposely dropping the pipe of peace, he stood erect, with his arms folded, and his right hand pressed on the sheath of his scalping knife. With a firm voice he replied :

"I started to come, but your braves drove me back. I have no other excuse to give."

"At the treaty," said Markam, "I thought you a good man, but since, you have acted badly. I am disposed to break you. I do break you."

(That is, he deposed him from his chieftainship, a thing that is very frequently done, when chiefs refuse to sign papers, after which some one is substituted who is mean enough, for a small bribe, to do anything. I know, personally, of five or six such instances.)

"You break me!" said Red Iron. "My people made me chief, and not you. My people love me. I will still be their chief."

"Why did you get your braves together and march around here for the purpose of intimidating other chiefs and prevent them coming to the council?"

"I did not get my braves together," replied Red Iron, "they got themselves together to prevent boys from going to the council to be made chiefs by you, to sign papers, and to prevent single chiefs going to council at night, to be bribed to sign papers for money we never got. I have heard how you have served other tribes; that by secret councils you get names on paper, and took away their money. We don't want to be served so. My braves wanted to come to council in the day time, when the sun shines. We want no councils in the dark. When we signed the treaty, the traders threw a blanket over our faces, and made us sign papers we did not understand. I want a new treaty, and I want the Great Father at Washington to know what has been done."

"Your Great Father has sent me to represent him, and what I say is what he says. He wants you to pay your old debts,—leave the money in my hands to pay your debts. If you refuse to do that I will take the money back with me."

"You can take the money back," said Red Iron. "We sold you our land and you promised so pay us for it. If you don't give us the money I will be glad and all my people will be glad, for we will have our land back if you do not pay us for it. I am told that that paper you want me to sign gives more than a hundred thousand dollars of our money to the trader. I don't think we owe him so much. If the Great Father will send three honest men here to examine the trader's accounts, whatever they say we owe the trader" (an offer of arbitration) "I will sign for. All our chiefs and all our people will agree to this."

All the Indians present responded "How! How!"

"That can't be done," said Markam. "You owe morenow than your money would pay, but I am willing to pay you the fifteen thousand dollars."

"I will receive the fifteen thousand dollars," Red Iron replied, "but I will sign no papers. We have been waiting a long time to get our money. We are poor; you have plenty. Your fires are warm. Your tepees keep out the cold. We have nothing to eat. A great many of our people are sick, for being hungry. We may die because you won't pay us. We have sold our hunting grounds and the graves of our fathers. We have sold our own graves, and you will not pay us the money for our lands."

The council broke up and Red Iron was again taken to the guard-house and loaded with chains. Between thirty and forty of Red Iron's warriors were present at the council. When he was led away, they departed in sullen silence, headed by Lean Bear, his Head Soldier, to a hill-top a quarter of a mile distant, where they uttered a succession of yells—the war-cry of the tribe. Ere the echoes had died away hundreds of Indians hurried toward them prepared for battle; Lean Bear was a resolute man, and had great influence in the tribe. He recounted the brave deeds of Red Iron, the long list of wrongs inflicted on them, and proposed that they should make a general attack on the whites.

It took all the weight of Jack's influence and all the power of his eloquence to persuade Lean Bear to give up his project. Late at night the Indians dispersed and went to their lodges.

Markam did not attempt anything further for three or four days. Then one night he got Little Wolf and several of the hangers-on about the agency together, the four scoundrels who drove Mr. Parkman away being among the number, and held a formal council, the proceedings being taken down in due form, and certified to by the agent, clerk and interpreter. The first thing they did was to depose Red Iron and install Little Wolf as head chief. Being duly declared head chief of the tribe, and the fact recorded in the minutes of the council, he then signed all the papers, by making his mark, which Markam presented. The next day the fifteen thousand dollars was paid over to the Indians, and the "paying agent" left.

I never knew how the proceeds of this transaction was divided. Hildreth shortly afterward invested about ten thousand dollars in a herd of cattle. But the papers were signed, the accounts were balanced, and the books of the Department of the Interior show, "officially," that the transaction was honest and "straight."

CHAPTER XLIII.

MEHA'S FATE.

A FEW days after Markam left, Major Hodson was ordered back to the fort on the Little Blue. Before he left, Jack had two or three long talks with him, after which he fell into a chronic melancholy. One day he came to Red Iron and told him that he was going away and would be gone several weeks, and that before he came

back he should visit Badger's old band on the Arickoree. He then saddled his horse, strapped on his blankets and started for the fort on the Little Blue. Arriving there, his first inquiry was made of Captain Belfor.

"Where is Lieutenant Blake?"

The Captain looked into Jack's eyes, and said:

"I wish you had come two weeks sooner. Then I think there would have been a pretty good prospect for him to have got his just deserts. But it's too late now. Colonel Coldcraft court-martialed him, and he was dishonorably dismissed from the service. I wish we could get rid of a few more just like him."

"Where is Meha?" asked Jack.

"She is staying with one of the laundresses who has taken her since she was abandoned. You will find her over on the north side, in the rear of the bake-house there."

When little Meha saw Jack she was delighted beyond measure. It was so good, she said, to talk to some one in her own language. It was two days before Jack could nerve himself to tell her that Lieutenant Blake had been dismissed from the army, and that he had abandoned her forever, and when he did she would not believe one word of it. She said that he had gone away on some expedition, like he had many times before. She said he had told her he would be gone a good while this time, but he was coming back again.

"Don't you want to see your mother and your little sister?" asked Jack.

"Oh! very much," she said.

"Well, a train is going to start for the Agency, and I am going there too. Will you go with us?"

"I want to see my mother and dear little sister very much, but Lieutenant Blake might come back while I was gone, and I don't know what he would think."

Jack tried every way he could think of to persuade her to go, but she would not consent. She had perfect faith that Lieutenant Blake would soon come back. At last he brought a paper, which he told her was an order from the Colonel, for her to join her tribe, and to remain there until Lieutenant Blake came back. If he ever came he would order him to come to her right away. She went back to her tribe, and years afterward I saw her. She was still patiently waiting him to come, who had long before forgotten her. She had refused offers of marriage from several of the young chiefs, and was still true to him.

"The Great Father," she said, "has sent him far away, perhaps beyond the great water, but some day he will come back to Meha."

CHAPTER XLIV.

JACK'S OPINION OF INJUNS.

JACK made inquiries of some Indians who came in with the train and were going back with it, about the place where Badger's band was located. Two of these Indians had their wives with them. He told them of his intended visit, but that he did not want the Agency people to know he was there. He learned that old Hairy Bear had been made chief of the band by the agent, after Badger had been hung by the whites. Hairy Bear was located on the Beaver, about fifteen miles from the Agency. It was very easy for Jack to find the place. He rode over to the Republican, crossed it, and went up the south side until he came to the Beaver, and followed that until he came to Hairy Bear's camp.

Things had been managed at Perkins's Agency in an entirely different way from the plan pursued with Red Iron's tribe.

Perkins commenced by proclaiming his absolute honesty, and to prove it he asked for a military officer to inspect his supplies before they were delivered to the Indians. An officer was accordingly sent. He inspected ten thousand sacks of flour, and some other articles. All of them were found to be fully up to the grade specified in the contracts. A few weeks afterward he asked for an officer to inspect supplies again. This time the officer found nine thousand sacks of flour of exactly the same grade as that of the previous lot.

The inspection of flour is made by thrusting an instrument, hollow on one side, into the sack, and when it is withdrawn the hollow is full of flour. As each sack is inspected, a brand is put upon it. The whole transaction was perfectly "straight," to all appearance, and the Indians were charged with nineteen thousand sacks of flour. The empty sacks, nineteen thousand in number, were piled up in the warehouse, each one having the United States Army Inspector's brand upon it.

When the Indians complained that they had only received half rations of flour, Perkins showed the sacks, to prove what liars they were. Notwithstanding all this, the contractors had only furnished, and the Indians had only received, ten thousand sacks of flour. The flour had been, what is called in the Indian Ring parlance "double sacked." The army officer had inspected ten thousand sacks and branded each one. When he went away, the outside sacks had been pulled off. When he came back, he inspected exactly the same lot over again, save the thousand sacks which had been issued in his absence. A plan very similar to this was successfully carried out in regard to the beef cattle. The contract specified that the cattle should average eight hundred and fifty pounds. A great herd of fine cattle were driven to the agency, and herded on a range near by. During the course of two or three months most of them had been driven away, and the number supplied with thin old cows, and oxen which had been broken down hauling freight, and turned out to die. The flesh of such cattle is black, and about the toughness of good sole leather. Notwithstanding all this, Perkins was a good agent, for he only stole half, while Parker and Hildreth stole about nine-tenths, and it was very wicked in these Indians to act the way they did.

When Jack arrived, he found that there was trouble brewing. Old Hairy Bear and his medicine man were holding orgies every two or three nights, in which the cruelties practiced upon them by the whites was told over and over. It was with difficulty Jack found out what was going on among the other bands and tribes belonging to this agency, for some of them spoke a different language. He soon learned, however, that they were plotting an extensive outbreak, as soon as they could conclude treaties with some tribes to the west, into whose territory they would have to go in case of a war. These negotiations would require some time, even if they were successful, of which there seemed to be some doubt. He also found that most of them had arms and horses. The Indians were still more enraged just when Jack arrived, for they said the beef was less in amount and blacker and tougher than ever before. Jack told them they were fools to talk about going to war. The Great Father would send an army of soldiers larger than the biggest herd of buffaloes they ever saw, but if they did go to war, the first man they were to kill was Perkins. If they didn't kill him, he would come down with some of Red Iron's warriors and scalp every one of them.

 Jack was accustomed to tough fare, but this beef was a little tougher than anything he had ever found before. He got a piece one morning and put it on the fire to boil. After he had kept the fire blazing hot for about six hours, he took it out, cut off a mouthful with his hunting-knife and chewed on it until his jaws gave out. The mouthful was still intact and about as elastic as a piece of caoutchouc. Then he put the beef back and boiled it until sundown. When he took it out of the camp-kettle, it was blacker and tougher than ever. An Indian woman who was watching his performance laughed at him, and said he ought to know how to cook the white people's beef, as he was a white man.

"I'll take pity on you," she said, " and give you something to eat."

She brought him some thick, black soup.

"What is this made of ?" said Jack.

"That's made of the white people's beef too, but I've learned how to do it."

"How do you fix it?"

"I cut the beef into thin slices, and roast it on the coals until it is cooked clear through. When it is dried, it is brittle. Then I pound it fine between two stones and make soup of it. That's all the way we can eat this black beef."

The next day the Indians went in to the Agency and drew a week's rations. When they came back to camp there was a general uproar. Threats were made by some of the young men, and they were not rebuked by the elder ones, of going to the Agency and killing everybody there. The cause of the trouble was, that in addition to black beef, they had received black flour. The ration thus made up was not fit for any human being to eat. Jack was fearful that they would break out into open war immediately, but after a day or two the excitement somewhat subsided, and as the next issue was a little better, they settled into their old way. The only action taken was to send another delegation to the tribes west of them, to hurry up the negotiations.

One day Jack concluded he would go into the Agency and see what Perkins would do about his presence on the reserve. He was well armed, and rather wanted Perkins to try to arrest him. He rode up to the trader's store, hitched his horse and walked in. Perkins was there, but he did not seem to recognize him. As Jack came out he met Jennie Walker face to face.

"Oh, Jack!" she said, and then, looking around, she spoke in a lower tone, "I want to talk to you so bad. How can I see you alone?"

"If you will walk down to that grove, yonder by the river," said Jack, "I will be there in about an hour." Then he turned and sauntered off in a different direction.

At the appointed time he met her there.

"How in the world did you ever get here?" said Jack.

"My father brought me."

"What does your father do here?"

"He helps the trader in his store."

"What made him come here?"

"Mr. Perkins owes him ever so much money, and he said if he would come out here he would soon pay him, but I don't believe he ever will."

"What do you do here?"

"I don't do anything. I wanted to teach school, but they wouldn't let me."

"How long is your father going to stay here?"

"I don't know."

"Would you like to get away from here?"

"I have no place to go to. If Mr. Perkins would pay father the money he owes him, I think he would go right away."

For a few moments there was silence. Then Jennie said.

"Jack, would you do one little thing for me?"

"Sartinly I would. Jest tell me what it is and it shall be done."

Jennie took a tiny little letter out of her pocket, and said:

"You won't tell any body, will you, Jack? I wrote a letter to Mr. Wilmot when I first came here, but I don't think Mr. Perkins let it go. I want you to take this letter and send it to him."

Jack took the letter and then looked at the fair-haired girl, as she stood there under the trees. She had taken off her hat. Little rays of sunlight played through her golden hair, as they found their way through leaves, stirred by the wind.

"Can you ride pretty well on a horse?" asked Jack.

"Yes," she replied. "I have ridden a good deal since I came out here. But why do you ask?"

"'Cause I thought that the best thing I could do was to take the letter and you both to Mr. Wilmot."

"Oh, Jack, I could not do that."

"Well, I didn't mean that. I meant I'd take the letter to Mr. Wilmot and you to Mr. Parkman's."

"Jack, you ought not to talk that way to me."

"I don't like to leave you here. There's no danger at present, and won't be for some time, but I'd feel a good deal better if you were at Council Bluffs."

"Oh, the Indians wouldn't hurt me. I know a good many of them."

"Injuns is Injuns," said Jack, dropping unconsciously into the frontier dialect; "and they has their ways. Some of 'em is mighty good ways, and some of 'em mighty bad. Now, thar's their religion. Part of it's jest like old Father Abraham's, and part of it is a sort of an improvement on it in the wrong direction. You see, when an Injun gits a religious fit on him he don't know what he's doing. When they git a notion the Great Spirit is calling on 'em to avenge their wrongs, they kill anything. Little babies, women and children is all the same to 'em then. It's mighty bad, but I've knowed 'em to do it. White people have done worse things, and thought they was serving God. I read when I was a boy about their breaking every bone in a woman's body, one at a time, one of their own race, too. I've knowed Injuns to do some mighty mean things, but nothing as bad as that. Now them Injuns is gitting up what you might call a revival. 'Tain't like one of Mr. Parkman's revivals. Them kind makes men better—this kind makes 'em worse. The fact is, these Injuns need some kind of improvement in their religion. I've been thinking of it considerable. If they'd quit holdin' these pow-wows, believing in them old medicine sticks, and the prophesyin's of them old frauds of medicine men, I think their religion 'ud be about right. If they didn't have faith in the old medicine man's charms against their enemies, they'd never go to war. There's lots of 'em that don't believe in 'em, but they pretend to, to control the others; 'cause you see they can hire the old medicine man to prophesy anything, or make a big medicine for them, for a blanket any time. Now, as I said, them Injuns is gitting up a revival. Among Injuns that means war; among white men it means peace. They are pow-wowing around in the tents every night, workin' themselves into a frenzy, tellin' over the crimes committed against 'em by the whites (and the Lord knows there's enough of 'em to keep 'em talking a year), prayin' to the Great Spirit, twistin' themselves into a thousand shapes, an' carryin' on worse than a nigger at a camp meetin', and some of these days, when they don't issue them any rations, they'll all git crazy mad at once, and cut up jack generally around here. Of course, if they issue them decent rations it'll spile the revival. These old Injun preachers allers have to have some present grievance to work on. Now, I've told you the whole thing, and why I thought you'd better go to Council Bluffs."

"Suppose you see father and tell him."

"I couldn't exactly do that. I'd be accused right away of workin' up a war, or something else. Everything is all safe for a month or two. Medicine sticks are mighty powerful things among Injuns, but they haven't quite faith enough in 'em to go to war, with the soldiers on one side and hostile tribes on the other."

"Suppose you tell Mr. Wilmot all about it," said Jennie."

"Of course I will; but he can't do anything."

Jennie had perfect faith in Mr. Wilmot's ability to do almost anything, and told Jack if he would only give him that letter, he would take such measures as would be best for them all.

"Let me see," said Jack. "It's three hundred miles from here to Council Bluffs. I can make it in six days. Wilmot shall have your letter in six days from to-morrow."

Jennie extended her hand and said "Good-bye."

Jack went back to Hairy Bear's camp and told them he must now go back to his tribe.

They made him a great many presents, and among other things two horses, and the next morning he departed.

CHAPTER XLV.

MRS. PARKMAN TRANSLATES A CIPHER LETTER.

JACK stopped at the fort on the Little Blue, on his way to Council Bluffs, and had an interview with Colonel Coldcraft, being introduced by Major Hodson. He told him the conditions of affairs at the Agency, the quality of the rations and the probability of an outbreak. The Colonel thanked him for the information, asked him where he could likely be found in the event of war, but made no other remark.

Coming away, Jack said to Major Hodson:

"This Colonel seems to be a mighty crusty sort of a fellow."

"Yes, he is a different man from Colonel Greene, but he is an excellent officer. Colonel Coldcraft never has any opinions to express to anybody."

"What do you suppose he will do?"

"He'll forward the information you gave him to the department commander, and await orders."

"What do you think of it?"

"The army can't interfere unless requested to do so by the Secretary of the Interior. He has absolute control of the Indians. His men out there are concocting a war. They don't care how many wars they get up. The more the better, as far as they are concerned. They know very well they don't have to fight them out. Now, if the Colonel had authority, he could send a battalion of cavalry out there, get after those contractors, make them furnish supplies as they have agreed and been paid for doing, and there would be no war. As it is, the Indians will first be half-starved and then we will be sent to kill them, because they are so impudent and rebellious that they won't stay there and die peaceably and without grumbling."

Jack did not delay longer than was necessary at the fort, but pressed on to Council Bluffs and delivered the tiny little letter. Mr. Wilmot opened it and read:

"DEAR MR. WILMOT,—

"I was so sorry I had to leave without seeing you. I did not know I had to go until nine o'clock the night before we started, and we left before six o'clock in the morning. When I arrived here I wrote you a letter, but I remembered that the other letter I wrote to you never reached you, and I thought you had never received it, so I write again. How is Mr. and Mrs. Parkman? I am very lonely here, but I hope Mr. Perkins will soon pay father and then we can come away. I don't like Mr. Perkins a bit. I wanted to teach school here and he would not let me.

"Very truly,
"JENNIE WALKER."

"Anything important?" said Jack.

"Yes," Wilmot replied, as he folded up the letter and put it in his pocket. "She says she wants me to come out there and marry her forthwith."

"I don't believe it," said Jack. "That 'ere girl would never write that way."

"Well, then, look at it and see," said Wilmot, handing him the letter.

"I knowed she never said any such thing," said Jack, after reading the letter.

"You can't read it, because it's written in cipher, and a cipher to which no Washington detective would ever find the key."

"I don't believe that thar's any cipher about it."

"You take it over to Mrs. Parkman and ask her if that is not what it means. She understands that kind of a cipher."

Wilmot had no idea of sending the letter to Mrs. Parkman, but Jack rose up and strode out of the office saying, "I'll do it. Hang me if I don't."

After giving Mrs. Parkman all the news, Jack took the letter out of his pocket and handed it to her, saying:

"Now, I want you to tell me honestly what that letter means. Wilmot says it means one thing. I say it don't."

Mrs. Parkman read the letter, and then said, in a somewhat excited manner:

"Mr. Wilmot ought to go right out there and see Jennie. I'll think he's real mean if he don't."

Jack took the letter and went back to Wilmot's office, saying to himself:

"Well, if that don't beat all creation. I didn't believe that was a cipher letter at all."

"What did she say?" asked Wilmot, as Jack came in.

"I give it up," said Jack. "I guess it is a cipher, but I wouldn't have believed it if it hadn't been for Mrs. Parkman. She says you ought to go right straight out there."

"That's a poser," he said, unfolding the letter and looking at it again. "Who'd ever thought of that innocent-looking letter meaning something else entirely from what it says. All the ciphers I ever saw didn't mean anything when you read them straight along. How did Mrs. Parkman learn to read it?"

"Oh! she learned that a long time ago; before she was married."

CHAPTER XLVI.

BEYOND CONTROL.

SEVERAL long conversations between Wilmot and Jack resulted in an agreement that they would both go out to the reservation on the Arickoree. Jack was to return to Red Iron's camp, Wilmot to go *via* the fort on the Little Blue, and the two to meet on a day specified at the forks of Turkey Creek.

Jack did not tell Wilmot why he desired to go first to Red Iron's camp, but simply said he must go there.

At the appointed time Wilmot rode up on a hill-top, overlooking the place of rendezvous, and was astonished to see a camp of about fifty Indians. He sat in his saddle hesitating about what he had better do, when some one in the camp mounted a horse and came galloping toward him. As he came near, Wilmot saw that it was Jack.

"What does this mean?" said Wilmot. "What are all those Indians doing here?"

"I kalkerlated there might be trouble over here, and in case there was, I wanted a few fellers along with me I could rely on. And then, if Jennie wanted to come back with us, it would be well to have some women along. As I couldn't git any white ones, I've got four or five Indian women. Two of 'em knew Jennie when she was in Red Iron's camp before the war, so I let 'em come with their husbands."

"I haven't any idea that Jennie will come back with us. I am going out there to see her, and have a talk with her father. I think he would come down as far as the fort on the Little Blue."

"Suppose Perkins tries to arrest you?"

"I don't think he'll do that. I'm out of the fight now."

"Well, I think if he does he'll have a warm time of it afore he gits through. I'm going to camp these Injuns right by the side of his house. These agents have a respect for a shooting-iron."

"I don't know but it is a pretty good plan," said Wilmot.

The next morning the party was on the move. It was understood where the camp was to be made that night, and the Indians scattered off each one to his own fancy. Some of them reached the camping-place by three o'clock in the afternoon, and some did not get in until after dark. They had killed, during the day, three antelopes and several jack rabbits. There was great good humor in the camp that night. They felt like they were free men once more, and they had plenty to eat.

About nine o'clock three of the young men came riding in. They were the last of the party to arrive. One of them came directly to Jack and handed him a piece of paper. He said, about ten miles above where they were camped, on the same stream, they had come upon the trail of two white men. They had stopped at the crossing but had made no fire. Their horses had been ridden very hard, and were very hungry. Their trail led over toward the Platte.

(I suppose that some persons will think it very strange that Indian could know that those horses had been ridden very hard and were hungry, but it was a very easy thing for him to tell that. The horses were lariated out, had laid down on the grass and rolled, and being covered with sweat had rubbed it off. The tracks showed how long they had been allowed to feed, and the grass that they had not wasted any time standing still.)

But the scrap of paper, that was the greatest mystery, and entirely beyond the reach of Indian lore. It was part of an envelope, and on it was written: "H. L. Perkins, Arickoree Agency." Was this Perkins and some one else? If not, who could it be? It made

Jack feel extremely uneasy. He broke camp early in the morning and gave orders to halt at the mouth of the Red Willow, a very hard day's march.

To understand what follows, it will be necessary to relate what had happened at Perkins's Agency since Jack was there. The delegations to the tribes to the west had returned with a favorable report. A treaty of friendship had been made, and a league formed to resist the encroachments of the whites. The principal chief at Perkins's Agency was a man named Little Warrior. He was a hereditary chief, and what is rather rare among that class, a man of great natural ability. He did not desire to go to war, if war could be avoided. Between starvation and fighting he would fight without any hesitation. He made this league so that in case of war he would not be perfectly helpless, with an army on one side and a hostile tribe on the other. When the result of the negotiations became known, there was great excitement among all the bands belonging to the agency, and old Hairy Bear was for war immediately. His medicine man prophesied all kinds of evil if they did not go to war, and great victories if they did. Just at this time the rations were worse than ever, and before Little Warrior was aware of the fact, his people were beyond his control.

The Indians around the agency, the hangers-on, the sycophants, became first sullen, and then insolent. The agent's power was broken, and they, as all such men of every race, forsook him for the favor of those who were to soon take control of things.

Perkins saw that there was trouble near at hand,

and held a consultation with Cox, his trader. That night, about midnight, without giving the least warning to any of the employees, they mounted two of the best horses and fled. In the morning, when the Indians found they were gone, they sacked the trader's store, broke open the warehouse, raided the employees' dwellings and took everything they could lay hands on.

The next day old Hairy Bear came dashing up to the Agency at the head of his warriors, all in their war-paint. The employees had all gone into the guard-house and prepared to defend themselves as best they could. The Indians, from an eminence near by, shot burning arrows into it and set it on fire. As the defenseless people were flying from it, they rode down on to them with their tomahawks to brain them as they ran.

At this juncture Jack and Wilmot, at the head of their band of Indians, dashed down on the Agency. As they came over the hill they began to shout their war-cry, and Hairy Bear and his band of warriors fled, carrying with them Jennie's father, Jennie, and two other women as prisoners. They fled down the bank of the river, with Jack, Wilmot and young Gray Cloud in hot pursuit. Hairy Bear, seeing they were hotly pursued, tomahawked Jennie's father as he rode by his side. As he fell from his horse, an Indian tried to scalp him, but he fell dead from a bullet from Jack's unerring rifle. They were so hotly pursued that, in dashing by the mouth of a ravine, Jennie was able to turn her horse behind the bank and up the ravine. One of the Indians who was riding beside her fired twice at her, but dared not stop his own horse for a second. Neither Jack nor Wilmot saw this, some bushes intervening just at that moment, which hid the Indians from their view. Gray Cloud, who was a little to one side, saw it, and when he came to the mouth of the ravine he turned up it and went after Jennie. The whole band of Jack's Indians soon swept by in hot pursuit.

Jack had gone up this stream when he went to the Agency, and he knew every turn in it. The Indians kept along the bank, and, there being a place where it made a sharp turn, Jack took fifteen or twenty men who were nearest, dashed across the point and came out ahead of Hairy Bear's band. Instead of capturing them between the two forces, as he expected, Hairy Bear forded the river, and he only captured the hindmost ones; but among them were the two white women. But Jennie! Where was she? Wilmot was nearly crazy, and wanted to press on. But Jack said:

"That's no sort of use. Their horses are fresh and ours worn out with two days of hard marching. We'll have to circumvent 'em some other way."

"They'll murder her or do worse. I am going on. How many men here will follow me?" cried Wilmot to the Indians, forgetting in his excitement that they could not understand one word that he said.

"Keep cool," said Jack. "It don't do no good to git excited. I'll——"

Just then they saw, coming down over the top of the hill, Gray Cloud and Jennie.

Wilmot leaped from his horse, ran to her and clasped her in his arms.

Jack looked on for a moment and then said:

"There; I've got you together agin. Now stick."

CHAPTER XLVII.

OH! FOR THE MILITARY.

THE first thing Jack did, was to get away from there as soon as possible, taking with him the five Indians he had captured. Gray Cloud and two or three others soon had them mounted, with their feet tied together under the ponies, and in that manner dashed away to the northeast. They traveled as fast as they could, until about sundown, when they halted on a little stream.

Jack tied the five prisoners to trees, and let them remain there until morning. Then he told them he was going to have a big scalp dance, and roast them all alive. He said:

"I'd adopt you into the tribe, but you are no warriors at all. You are cowards. I told you, when I was here, to kill the agent when you went to war. He is the man who has been stealing everything you have, but you were too big cowards to do anything until the agent was gone. When there was nobody left to fight, you got very brave. You are a set of cowards."

Not a muscle moved on one of their faces. They looked as imperturbable as if they had no concern about the matter at all. After a few minutes Jack came back again and said that they did not amount to enough to go to the trouble of scalping them. He could whip a thousand such warriors as they were, with the braves he had with him; and then he told one of the Indian women to give them something to eat, which was a sign that they were to be set at liberty; and, being set at liberty, the Indians of Jack's band were bound by their custom to make them presents, which they did. When they departed, Jack sent a message to Hairy Bear, that he intended to come down some day and scalp the whole band, because they had not killed Perkins. He took all their arms from them, for he did not want to run the risk of their following after him to revenge themselves, and recover their lost standing in their tribe, for being captured alive.

Jack resumed his march. Just before night, one of the Indians in advance returned and reported that a large body of troops was in their front. Upon the receipt of this news, Jack halted his band and camped. He then rode forward. When he came upon the soldiers he found that it was a force under the command of Colonel Greene, going to the Agency, to restore order.

Perkins had done as all his predecessors and all his successors have done, starved his Indians into rebellion, and then rushed to the military for a force to whip them into subjection. Colonel Greene went on to the Agency. There was not an Indian to be found on the whole reserve. As his orders left the settling of this matter largely to his discretion, he sent a messenger after Little Warrior, asking him to come in and hold a consultation, assuring him of a safe conduct back to his people. Little Warrior came. When the two men stood face to face, Colonel Greene said:

"Do you want to go to war, or do you want to have peace?"

"I want peace," said Little Warrior, "but I can't stay here on this reservation. My people are all starving. What the agent gave us was not fit to eat. I have brought some of it to show you."

Here the chief took from a pack a sample of the beef and the flour which Perkins had issued. The flour was what is known in the West as "shorts" or "middlings," such as is fed to horses and cows. The beef was black, and as tough as sole leather.

"The Great Father," said Little Warrior, "wants me to live here. I think it would be better for me to stay where I am. There I can make my own living. Why am I forced to live on the Government? If the Great Father intends always to feed all the Indians, I should think it would take all the money he has. I seem to be blind, I cannot understand these things. If the Great Father wants me to come back here, and will give us enough to eat, so we will not be hungry all the time, I will come."

Colonel Greene told him to come and he would issue rations to them for a while, anyhow. In a few days they were all back again. The Colonel summoned the contractors before him and forced them to deliver the supplies according to contract.

One day, Little Warrior appeared at his head-quarters

with old Hairy Bear as his prisoner. He said to Colonel Greene:

"This is the man who killed the white man at the Agency. I have brought him to you, to turn him over to the whites for punishment. I promised, in the treaty which I made with the Great Father, that if any of my people killed a white man, I would give up those who did it."

CHAPTER XLVIII.

THREE MILLION DOLLARS.

THE little party which we left on the open prairie returned, the Indians to their reservation, Captain Jack, Wilmot and Jennie to Council Bluffs. Mr. Borden had been waiting some days for Wilmot. The regular term of court was soon to convene, and the case which he had put in Wilmot's hands would come up for trial. He had also engaged Dawson. One afternoon the two lawyers explained to Mr. Borden the whole inside history of the transactions which resulted from the treaty that he and the other commissioners had made with Indians. Mr. Borden was stunned at the revelations they made, and the condition of the two Agencies at that time.

"Why," said Mr. Borden, "I saw the Annual Reports of Perkins and Hildreth, just before I started West, in the office of the Secretary of the Interior

They represent the Indians to be well contented and making great advancement toward civilization."

"I have in my office," said Dawson, "the reports of the Commissioners on Indian Affairs ever since they were published. I took the trouble to look up the representations of their agents, and according to their official reports, one tribe, whose present condition I happen to be acquainted with, has been making wonderful progress toward civilization every year for about a hundred years. General Wayne wrote a letter to the Secretary of War, describing the condition of these Indians nearly a hundred years ago (it was in August, 1794), in which he said they had 'highly cultivated fields and gardens' and 'I never have beheld such immense fields of corn in any part of America, from Canada to Florida.' Now, after nearly a century of Government civilizing and advancing, I know that these Indians are ten times worse off than they were when General Wayne described their condition. Indian agents have been advancing them, according to their official reports, toward self-support, ever since, and now I find them in utter poverty and destitution."

"What is to be done?" asked Mr. Borden.

"Give them civil rights. Extend over them the jurisdiction of our courts," said Wilmot.

"You would not extend over them our laws without their consent, would you?" asked Mr. Borden.

This question provoked Wilmot so much he lost his temper, and he arose hastily and walked out of the room, muttering to himself: "You're an old blockhead. I don't see how you can take care of yourself."

Mr. Dawson, who had not had so much to irritate him in regard to the present policy, replied as follows :

"The proposition you seem to reason from is, that we *have not* extended our laws over the Indians. That was done very many years ago. We have imposed upon them, by superior force, the most infamous code of laws ever enacted for the government of any people. Just get a copy of the Revised Statutes of the United States, and read the sections under the title, Indians. It is the enforcement of these laws which has caused all the cruelty and wrong which they have suffered. Had it not been for these statutes, Wilmot could have saved Badger and his companions. It is under cover of them that Clark, and Brown, and Hildreth have been able to rob Red Iron. They stand there, an impregnable fortification, behind which the thieves of the Indian Ring defend themselves, and any attack made upon them, until these, their defenses, are demolished, will end in total defeat. No wrong to Indians has ever been righted since they have been enacted, and none ever will be while they are in force."

"Do you suppose you could get Congress to repeal them?"

"No."

"What can be done, then?"

"If ever a case is taken to the Supreme Court of the United States, involving their constitutionality, they will be swept out of existence."

"I doubt that very much."

"Many of the best lawyers in this country have long held that opinion. This code of laws is perfectly infamous. At every term of the United States courts whose districts border on these reservations, there are Indians tried and convicted—for conviction almost invariably follows, as the Indians are taken hundreds of miles from their homes and the scenes of the alleged crimes, to be tried, where it is next to impossible to secure the presence of witnesses, or make a successful defense. You see the utter absurdity of talking about not extending our laws over them. What is needed is the total abolition of this infamous 'black code' of laws governing Indians, and the application to them of the same laws upon which white men rely for the protection of their lives, liberty and property. Give them an unincumbered title to their lands, perfect and absolute, and a chance to defend that title, as white men defend theirs."

"What about the annuities or money due them?"

"Let them be distributed through the quartermasters and paymasters of the army. They would get them then."

"I never could consent to that," said Mr. Borden, "and I think you and Mr. Wilmot are both very unjust to Mr. Clark."

"You do," said Wilmot, who had returned to the room. "Just read that," and he handed him the note which Parker had brought to him from Mr. Clark, authorizing him to make arrangements.

"I see nothing wrong in this note. How could Mr. Clark make anything out of this?"

"You know that he is one of the committee to supervise the purchase of Indian supplies."

"Yes, I am on that committee myself."

"You know that a bid was accepted from one Anthony Bluxhome, for a certain article which goes to all Indian reserves."

"Really, I don't remember it. In fact, I paid very little attention to the examination of the bids. Mr. Clark did that."

"Well, Mr. Clark awarded the contract for those supplies to himself, under the name of Anthony Bluxhome, and goods with the brand of his firm upon them can be found on every reservation east of the Rocky Mountains."

"I cannot believe that Mr. Clark would do anything dishonorable. He is known as an eminent philanthropist through all the East."

"I know that he is a scoundrel," said Wilmot, in a somewhat excited manner, "and rotten and corrupt from the crown of his head to the soles of his feet."

"We won't talk about the matter any more," said Mr. Borden.

"There's Perkins," said Wilmot, looking out of the window. "The last time he was here he thought he did a very smart thing in carrying Jennie Walker off to his Agency, and she was forced to submit. He didn't gain much by it. All his advances were repulsed and he was beaten for once. I wonder what he is after now?"

"He is after the remainder of his money. Haven't you noticed that Congress has passed a bill appropriating six hundred thousand dollars to re-imburse the State for expenses incurred in resisting an incursion of the Indians. Perkins raised a company, you know, and he will have a big slice of that."

"Dawson," said Wilmot, "how much do you suppose that gambling scrape of Perkins's down at Hickman's has cost the people of the United States."

"About three million dollars, as near as I can figure it up."

* * * * * *

The little Methodist church stood just under the brow of the bluff. It would not seat to exceed one hundred and twenty-five people. One evening about half that number gathered there. After they were seated Wilmot and Jennie walked up the only aisle, and Mr. Parkman arose, and in accordance with the ritual of his church, pronounced them man and wife.

On a little knoll, pushed out from the main hills into the bottom, covered with a beautiful grove of trees, was a cottage. Here Wilmot took his bride. Walking in, he stood in the center of the room and said:

"This is our home. Here is our place of refuge—our castle. Though the sun might shine in at a hundred crevices and the wind find ingress through countless apertures, the king cannot enter here without permission. Around it is thrown up a fortification for our protection, stronger than was ever made of stone and mortar. Armies cannot scale it. Time will not wear it away. Year by year it will grow stronger and higher."

"I see no fortifications," said Jennie.

"All the great forces of the Universe are invisible,

and while the parapets around our home cannot be seen by the eye, yet they are here, substantial, impassable. The best blood of a hundred generations has been poured out like water in the defense of their foundations. Armies have melted away before the fire of the enemy as they guarded the workers who laid them. Finished, impregnable, invisible, eternal, they stand around us to-night. All the gates open outward before him who approaches from within, but to the one coming from the outside they are locked, and the key to that lock is in our hands. Even God himself has forever relinquished control of that key. It is our volition."

"I do not understand," said Jennie. "What is it of which you speak?"

"I speak of the 'law.' May the time soon come when the Indian, long without its pale, shall find refuge and protection behind its defenses!"

The next morning Jack stood in the door of the little cottage. His revolvers were in his belt. He held in one hand the bridle rein of his horse, and extended the other with the words:

"Good-bye."

"Where are you going?" asked Jennie.

"Back to old Red Iron. I'm going to stand by him so long as there's a hair in his scalp-lock."

"Good-bye."

*   *   *   *   *

Ten years afterward I saw old Red Iron. He was sitting in the door of his tent. He had given up trying to live in a house. He had built two in that time, but soon after they were finished the government had changed his reservation, and he was forced to leave everything and go.

"What are you doing here?" I asked.

"Waiting for the Great Father to civilize me," he replied.

  * * * * *

The reader may say, "These things happened a long time ago. Nothing like it occurs now." A moment ago I took up a New York daily paper, and my eye fell upon this telegram:

"CINCINNATI, *May* 15, 1881.

"A special from Sante Fé, New Mexico, reports impending trouble with the Navajo Indians. A military force will be sent. The rations for the Navajos are exhausted. The younger Indians want war, while the older ones oppose it."

THE END.

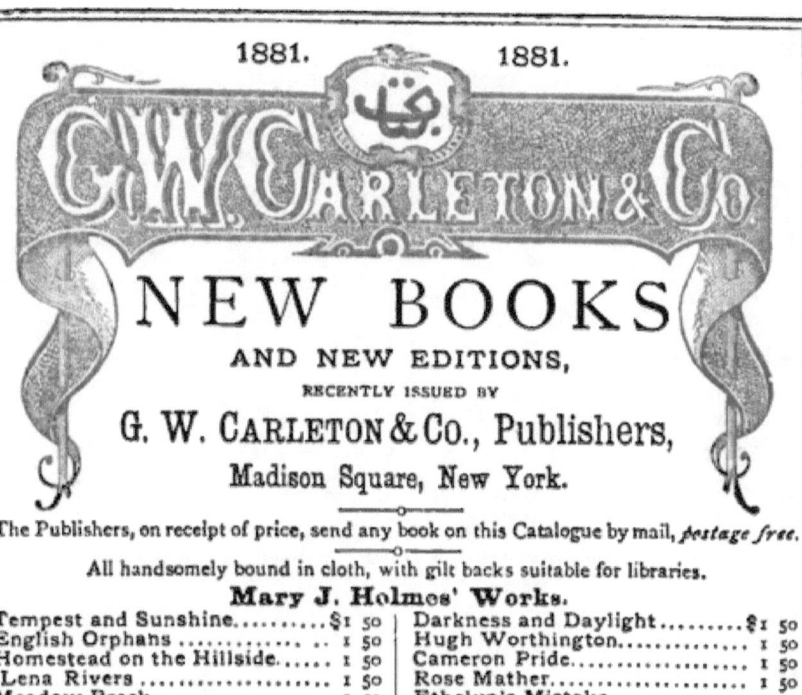

1881.

G. W. CARLETON & CO.

NEW BOOKS

AND NEW EDITIONS,

RECENTLY ISSUED BY

G. W. Carleton & Co., Publishers,

Madison Square, New York.

The Publishers, on receipt of price, send any book on this Catalogue by mail, *postage free*.

All handsomely bound in cloth, with gilt backs suitable for libraries.

Mary J. Holmes' Works.

Tempest and Sunshine	$1 50	Darkness and Daylight	$1 50
English Orphans	1 50	Hugh Worthington	1 50
Homestead on the Hillside	1 50	Cameron Pride	1 50
'Lena Rivers	1 50	Rose Mather	1 50
Meadow Brook	1 50	Ethelyn's Mistake	1 50
Dora Deane	1 50	Millbank	1 50
Cousin Maude	1 50	Edna Browning	1 50
Marian Grey	1 50	West Lawn	1 50
Edith Lyle	1 50	Mildred	1 50
Daisy Thornton	1 50	Forrest House....(New)	1 50
Chateau D'Or....(New)	1 50		

Marion Harland's Works.

Alone	$1 50	Sunnybank	$1 50
Hidden Path	1 50	Husbands and Homes	1 50
Moss Side	1 50	Ruby's Husband	1 50
Nemesis	1 50	Phemie's Temptation	1 50
Miriam	1 50	The Empty Heart	1 50
At Last	1 50	Jessamine	1 50
Helen Gardner	1 50	From My Youth Up	1 50
True as Steel....(New)	1 50	My Little Love	1 50

Charles Dickens—15 Vols.—"Carleton's Edition."

Pickwick, and Catalogue	$1 50	David Copperfield	$1 50
Dombey and Son	1 50	Nicholas Nickleby	1 50
Bleak House	1 50	Little Dorrit	1 50
Martin Chuzzlewit	1 50	Our Mutual Friend	1 50
Barnaby Rudge—Edwin Drood	1 50	Curiosity Shop—Miscellaneous	1 50
Child's England—Miscellaneous	1 50	Sketches by Boz—Hard Times	1 50
Christmas Books—Two Cities	1 50	Great Expectations—Italy	1 50
		Oliver Twist—Uncommercial	1 50

Sets of Dickens' Complete Works, in 15 vols.—[elegant half calf bindings]... 50 00

Augusta J. Evans' Novels.

Beulah	$1 75	St. Elmo	$2 00
Macaria	1 75	Vashti	2 00
Inez	1 75	Infelice......(New)	2 00

May Agnes Fleming's Novels.

Guy Earlscourt's Wife	$1 50	A Wonderful Woman	$1 50
A Terrible Secret	1 50	A Mad Marriage	1 50
Norine's Revenge	1 50	One Night's Mystery	1 50
Silent and True	1 50	Kate Danton	1 50
Heir of Charlton	1 50	Carried by Storm	1 50
Lost for a Woman—New	1 50	A Wife's Tragedy... (New)	1 50

The Game of Whist.

Pole on Whist—The English standard work. With the "Portland Rules." 75

Miriam Coles Harris.

Rutledge	$1 50	The Sutherlands	$1 50
Frank Warrington	1 50	St. Philips	1 50
Louie's Last Term, St. Mary's	1 50	Round Hearts for Children	1 50
A Perfect Adonis	1 50	Richard Vandermarck	1 50
Missy—New	1 50	Happy-Go-Lucky...(New)	1 50

Mrs. Hill's Cook Book.

Mrs. A. P. Hill's New Southern Cookery Book, and domestic receipts..... $2 00

Julie P. Smith's Novels.

Widow Goldsmith's Daughter	$1 50	The Widower	$1 50
Chris and Otho	1 50	The Married Belle	1 50
Ten Old Maids	1 50	Courting and Farming	1 50
His Young Wife	1 50	Kiss and be Friends	1 50
Lucy—New	1 50		

Victor Hugo.

Les Miserables—Translated from the French. The only complete edition..... $1 50

Captain Mayne Reid.

The Scalp Hunters	$1 50	The White Chief	$1 50
The Rifle Rangers	1 50	The Tiger Hunter	1 50
The War Trail	1 50	The Hunter's Feast	1 50
The Wood Rangers	1 50	Wild Life	1 50
The Wild Huntress	1 50	Osceola, the Seminole	1 50

A. S. Roe's Select Stories.

True to the Last	$1 50	A Long Look Ahead	$1 50
The Star and the Cloud	1 50	I've Been Thinking	1 50
How Could He Help it?	1 50	To Love and to be Loved	1 50

Charles Dickens.

Child's History of England—Carleton's New "*School Edition*," Illustrated.. $1 00

Hand-Books of Society.

The Habits of Good Society—The nice points of taste and good manners..... $1 00
The Art of Conversation—for those who wish to be agreeable talkers............ 1 00
The Arts of Writing, Reading and Speaking—For Self-Improvement.......... 1 00
New Diamond Edition—Elegantly bound, 3 volumes in a box................. 3 00

Carleton's Popular Quotations.

Carleton's New Hand-Book—Familiar Quotations, with their Authorship..... $1 50

Famous Books—Carleton's Edition.

Arabian Nights—Illustrations	$1 00	Don Quixote—Dore Illustrations	$1 00
Robinson Crusoe—Griset. do	1 00	Swiss Family Robinson. do	1 00

Josh Billings.

His Complete Writings—With Biography, Steel Portrait, and 100 Illustrations. $2 50
Old Probability—Ten Comic Alminax, 1870 to 1879. Bound in one volume..... 1 50

Allan Pinkerton.

Model Town and Detectives	$1 50	Spiritualists and Detectives	$1 50
Strikers, Communists, etc	1 50	Mollie Maguires and Detectives	1 50
Criminal Reminiscences, etc	1 50	Mississippi Outlaws, etc	1 50
Gypsies and Detectives	1 50	Bucholz and Detectives	1 50
A New Book	1 50		

Celia E. Gardner's Novels.

Stolen Waters. (In verse)	$1 50	Tested	$1 50
Broken Dreams. (In verse)	1 50	Rich Medway's Two Loves	1 50
Compensation. (In verse)	1 50	A Woman's Wiles	1 50
Terrace Roses	1 50		

G. W. CARLETON & CO.'S PUBLICATIONS. 3

"New York Weekly" Series.

Thrown on the World	$1 50	Nick Whiffles	$1 50
A Bitter Atonement	1 50	Lady Leonora	1 50
Love Works Wonders	1 50	The Grinder Papers	1 50
Evelyn's Folly	1 50	Faithful Margaret	1 50
Lady Damer's Secret	1 50	Curse of Everleigh	1 50
Peerless Cathleen	1 50	A Woman's Temptation	1 50
Brownie's Triumph	1 50		

Artemas Ward.
Complete Comic Writings—With Biography, Portrait and 50 illustrations.....$1 50

Charles Dickens.
Dickens' Parlor Table Album of Illustrations—with descriptive text........$2 50

M. M. Pomeroy ("Brick").

Sense. A serious book	$1 50	Nonsense. (A comic book)	$1 50
Gold Dust. Do	1 50	Brick-dust. Do	1 50
Our Saturday Nights	1 50	Home Harmonies	1 50

Magic Mother Goose.
Magic Transformation Pictures—Six books, 25 cents each. Bound in one...$1 50

Ernest Renan's French Works.

The Life of Jesus. Translated	$1 75	The Life of St. Paul. Translated	$1 75
Lives of the Apostles. Do	1 75	The Bible in India—By Jacolliot	2 00

G. W. Carleton.
Our Artist in Cuba, Peru, Spain, and Algiers—150 Caricatures of travel........$1 00

Miscellaneous Publications.

Hawk-eyes—a comic book by "The Burlington Hawkeye Man." Illustrated...$1 50
Among the Thorns—A new novel by Mrs. Mary Lowe Dickinson................ 1 50
College Tramps—Yale College students on a trip. By F. A. Stokes.......... 1 50
Our Daughters—A talk with mothers, by Marion Harland..................... 1 00
Redbirds Christmas Story—An illustrated Juvenile. By Mary J. Holmes.... 50
Carleton's Popular Readings—Edited by Mrs. Anna Randall-Diehl........... 1 50
The Culprit Fay—Joseph Rodman Drake's Poem. With 100 illustrations..... 2 00
L'Assommoir—English Translation from Zola's famous French novel......... 1 00
Parlor Amusements—Games, Tricks, and Home Amusements, by F. Bellew.. 1 00
Love [L'Amour]—Translation from Michelet's famous French work........... 1 50
Woman [La Femme]— Do Do Do 1 50
Verdant Green—A racy English college Story. With 200 comic illustrations.... 1 00
Laus Veneris, and other Poems—By Algernon Charles Swinburne............ 1 50
Birds of a Feather Flock Together—By Edward A. Sothern, the actor...... 1 00
Beatrice Cenci—from the Italian novel, with Guido's celebrated portrait........ 1 00
The Two Brides—A new novel by Rev. Bernard O'Reilly ; Laval............. 1 50
Morning Glories—A charming collection of Children's stories. By Louisa Alcott. 1 00
Some Women of To-Day—A novel by Mrs. Dr. Wm. H. White................ 1 50
Cashier's Scrap-Book—Anecdotes of Banks and Bankers. By H. C. Percy... 2 00
From New York to San Francisco—By Mrs. Frank Leslie. Illustrated...... 1 50
Why Wife and I Quarreled—A Poem by author "Betsey and I are out." ... 1 00
West India Pickles—A yacht Cruise in the Tropics. By W. P. Talboys...... 1 00
How to Make Money; and how to Keep it—By Thomas A Davies........... 1 50
Threading My Way—The Autobiography of Robert Dale Owen.............. 1 50
Debatable Land between this World and Next—Robert Dale Owen......... 2 00
Lights and Shadows of Spiritualism—By D. D. Home, the Medium......... 2 00
Yachtman's Primer—Instructions for Amateur Sailors. By T. R. Warren. 50
The Fall of Man—A Darwinian Satire, by author of "New Gospel of Peace.".. 50
The Chronicles of Gotham—A New York Satire. Do. Do. .. 25
Tales from the Operas—A collection of stories based upon the Opera plots.... 1 00
Ladies and Gentlemen's Etiquette Book, of the best Fashionable Society.. 1 00
Self Culture in Conversation, Letter-Writing, and Oratory.............. 1 00
Love and Marriage—A book for young people. By Frederick Saunders....... 1 00
Under the Rose—A Capital book, by the author of "East Lynne."............ 1 00
So Dear a Dream—A novel by Miss Grant, author of "The Sun Maid"....... 1 00
Give me thine Heart—A Capital new Love Story by Roe.................. 1 00
Progressive Petticoats—A Satirical tale, by Robert B. Roosevelt............. 1 00

4   G. W. CARLETON & CO.'S PUBLICATIONS.

Miscellaneous Works.

Dawn to Noon—By Violet Fane.. $1 50	Victor Hugo—Autobiography...... $1 50
Constance's Fate— Do. 1 50	Orpheus C. Kerr—4 vols. in one.. 2 00
H. M. S. Pinafore—The Play..... 10	Fanny Fern Memorials......... 2 00
A Steamer Book—W. T. Helmuth. 1 00	Parodies—C. H. Webb (John Paul). 1 50
Lion Jack—By P. T. Barnum..... 1 50	My Vacation. Do. Do. 1 50
Jack in the Jungle— Do ... 1 50	Sandwiches—Artemus Ward....... 25
Gospels in Poetry—E. H. Kimball. 1 50	Watchman of the Night......... 1 50
Southern Woman Story—Pember 75	Nonsense Rhymes—W. H. Beckett 1 00
Madame Le Vert's—Souvenirs.... 2 00	Sketches—John H. Kingsbury.... 1 50
Care of Children—Gardner...... 1 50	Lord Bateman—Cruikshank's Ill.. 25
Border War—T. B. Peacock...... 1 50	Northern Ballads—E. L. Anderson 1 00
Comic Primer—Frank Bellew..... 25	Beldazzle Bachelor Poems...... 1 00
He and I—Sarah B. Stebbins...... 50	Wood's Guide to N. Y. City.... 1 00
Annals of a Baby. Do 50	Only Caprice—Paper covers...... 75
Me—Mrs Spencer W. Coe 50	Was it Her Fault. Do. 75
Trump Kards—Josh Billings...... 10	Fashion and Passion. Do. 75
Little Guzzy—John Habberton.... 1 00	His Idol. Do. 75
Offenbach in America—.......... 1 50	About Lawyers—Jefferson... ... 1 50
Rural Architecture—M. Field..... 2 00	About Doctors. Do. 1 50
Coney Island and and the Jews. 10	Window Spriggins—Widow Bedott 1 50

Miscellaneous Novels.

Sub Rosa—Chas. T. Murray...... $1 50	All For Her—A tale of New York.. $1 00
Hilda and I—E. Bedell Benjamin.. 1 50	All For Him—By All For Her.... 1 00
Madame—Frank Lee Benedict.... 1 50	For Each Other— Do. 1 00
Hammer and Anvil— Do. 1 50	Janet—An English novel.......... 1 50
Her Friend Lawrence—Do. 1 50	Saint Leger—Richard B. Kimball. 1 75
Sorry Her Lot—Miss Grant...... 1 00	Was He Successful? Do. . 1 75
Two of Us—Calista Halsey....... 75	Undercurrents of Wall St. Do. . 1 75
Spell-Bound—Alexandre Dumas... 75	Romance of Student Life. Do. . 1 75
Wired Love—E. C. Thayer....... 75	To-Day. Do. . 1 75
Cupid on Crutches—A. B. Wood.. 75	Life in San Domingo. Do. . 1 75
Doctor Antonio—G. Ruffini...... 1 50	Henry Powers, Banker. Do. . 1 75
Parson Thorne—Buckingham..... 1 50	Baroness of N. Y.—Joaquin Miller. 1 50
Marston Hall—L. Ella Byrd...... 1 50	One Fair Woman— Do. Do. 1 50
Ange—Florence Marryatt.......... 1 00	Another Man's Wife—Mrs. Hartt.. 1 50
Errors—Ruth Carter............. 1 50	Purple and Fine Linen—Fawcett 1 50
Heart's Delight—Mrs. Alderdice.. 1 50	Pauline's Trial—L. D. Courtney.. 1 50
Unmistakable Flirtation—Garner 75	The Forgiging Kiss—M. Loth... 1 75
Wild Oats—Florence Marryatt ... 1 50	Flirtation—A West Point novel... 1 00
Widow Cherry—B. L. Farjeon... 25	Loyal into Death—............. 1 50
Solomon Isaacs— Do. ... 50	That Awful Boy—.............. 50
Led Astray—Octave Feuillet...... 1 50	That Bridget of Ours—......... 50
She Loved Him Madly—Borys.. 1 50	Bitterwood—By M. A. Green..... 1 50
Thick and Thin—Mery........... 1 50	Phemie Frost—Ann S. Stephens.. 1 50
So Fair yet False—Chavette..... 1 50	Charette—An American novel 1 50
A Fatal Passion C. Bernard..... 1 50	Fairfax—John Esten Cooke...... 1 50
Woman in the Case—B. Turner. 1 50	Hilt to Hilt. Do. 1 50
Marguerite's Journal—For Girls. 1 50	Out of the Foam. Do. 1 50
Milly Darrel—M. E. Braddon.... 1 00	Hammer and Rapier. Do. 1 50
Edith Murray—Joanna Mathews.. 1 00	Warwick—By M. T. Walworth ... 1 75
Doctor Mortimer—Fannie Bean.. 1 50	Lulu. Do. . 1 75
Outwitted at Last—S. A. Gardner 1 50	Hotspur. Do. . 1 75
Vesta Vane—L. King. R.......... 1 50	Stormcliff. Do. . 1 75
Louise and I—C. R. Dodge....... 1 50	Delaplaine. Do. . 1 75
My Queen—By Sandette.......... 1 50	Beverly. Do. . 1 75
Fallen among Thieves—Rayne... 1 50	Kenneth—Sallie A. Brock....... 1 75
San Miniato—Mrs. Hamilton..... 1 00	Heart Hungry—Westmoreland.... 1 50
Peccavi—Emma Wendler........ 1 50	Clifford Troupe. Do. 1 50
Conquered—By a New Author.... 1 50	Silcott Mill—Maria D. Deslonde. 1 50
Shiftless Folks—Fannie Smith.... 1 50	John Maribel. Do. 1 50
Drifted Together................. 75	Love's Vengeance............... 75

www.ingramcontent.com/pod-product-compliance
Lightning Source LLC
Chambersburg PA
CBHW020323240426
43673CB00039B/902